Starting To-day—TOPI

MODE

No. 49

EVERY

**BIGGLES GOES INTO ACTION—EXCITING MOMENT
FROM FLYING-OFFICER JOHNS' NEW THRILLER— WIN**

WHEN THE COMICS WENT TO WAR

WHEN THE COMICS WENT TO WAR

Comic Book War Heroes

Adam Riches

with Tim Parker and Robert Frankland

MAINSTREAM
PUBLISHING

Design: Tim Parker.
Concept and additional research: Robert Frankland.

First published in Great Britain in 2009 by
MAINSTREAM PUBLISHING COMPANY (EDINBURGH) LIMITED
7 Albany Street
Edinburgh EH1 3UG

ISBN 9781845965549

A catalogue record of this book is available from the British Library.

Printed by Butler Tanner and Dennis Ltd, Frome, Somerset

Note: The image on page 182 is from the Collector's Edition of the Hotspur Book for Boys 1966.
For further details contact ourcomicheroes@yahoo.co.uk

REFERENCES

The Battle of Dorking: Reminiscences of a Volunteer, George Chesney (Dodo Books)

Boys Will Be Boys, E.S. Turner (Penguin)

British Comics: An Appraisal, The Comics Campaign Council (1955)

The Best of Eagle, edited by Marcus Morris (Mermaid Books)

Cartoonists at War, Frank E. Huggett (Book Club Associates London)

Comics at War, Denis Gifford (Hawk Books)

Eagle Annual – The Best of the 1950s Comic (Orion Books)

Encyclopedia of Comic Characters, Denis Gifford (Longman)

First World War, Martin Gilbert (HarperCollins)

Great British Comics, Paul Gravett and Peter Stanbury (Aurum)

The History of The Beano (D.C. Thomson)

The History of England 1815-1927, Cyril Robinson (Methuen)

A Muse of War – Literature, Art and War, A.D. Harvey (The Hambledon Press)

Old Boys' Books: A Complete Catalogue, Bill Lofts and Derek Adley (private publication)

Over the Top: The Great War and Juvenile Literature in Britain, Michael Paris

Penny Dreadfuls and Comics, Kevin Carpenter (V&A, 1983)

The Riddle of the Sands, Erskine Childers (Penguin)

Take a Cold Tub, Sir!: The Story of the Boy's Own Paper, Jack Cox (The Lutterworth Press, 1982)

The Ultimate Book of British Comics, Graham Kibble-White (Allison & Busby, 2005)

The War Libraries, Steve Holland and David Roach (Book Palace Books)

The Imperial War Museum
The National Army Museum

Captain Hurricane's Best of Battle (http://bestofbattle.sevenpennynightmare.co.uk)
Comics UK (www.comicsuk.co.uk)

THIS BOOK IS DEDICATED TO:
Florence and Robin Riches
Sandra, Connor and Emily-Harriet Parker
and all the members of the extended Frankland family

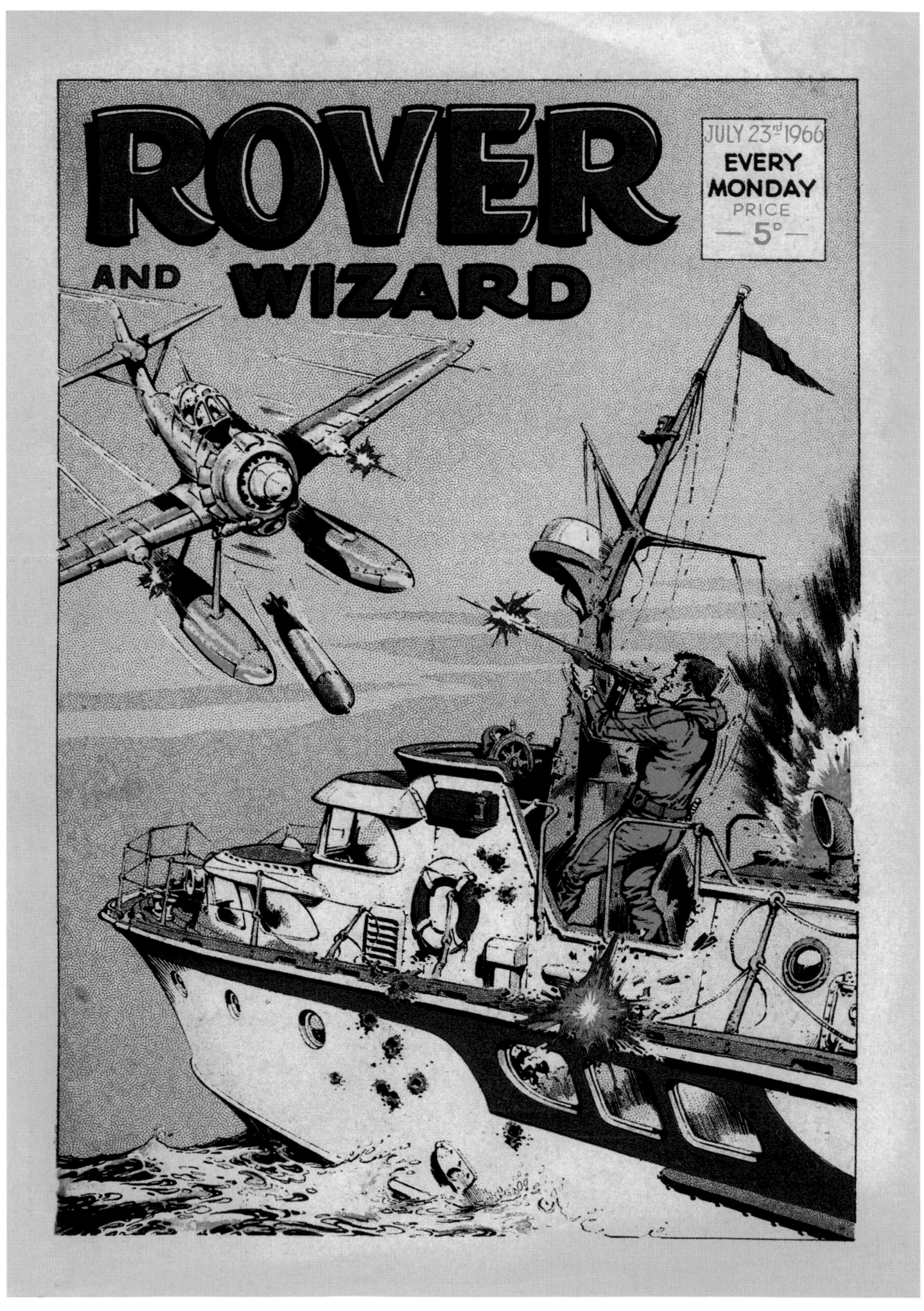
ROVER
AND WIZARD
JULY 23rd 1966
EVERY MONDAY
PRICE
5D

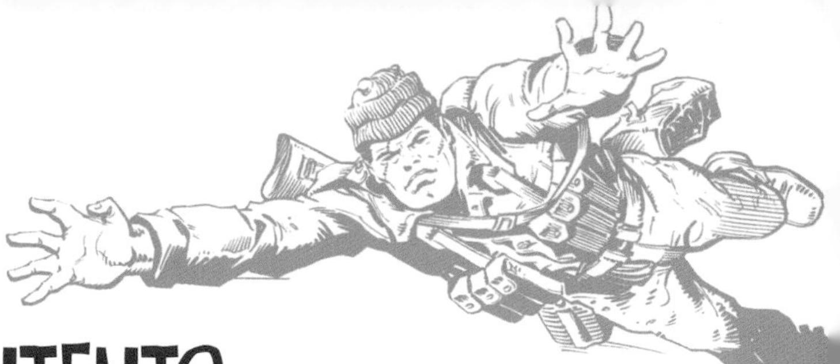

CONTENTS

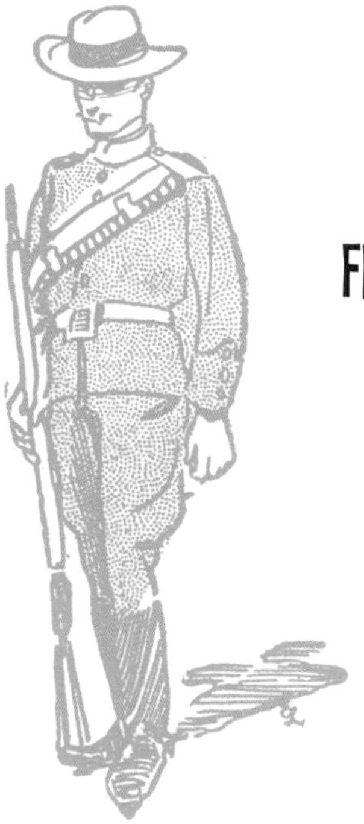

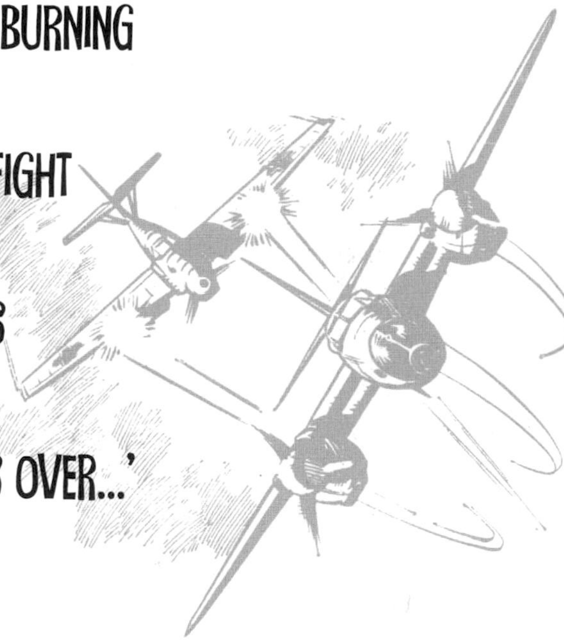

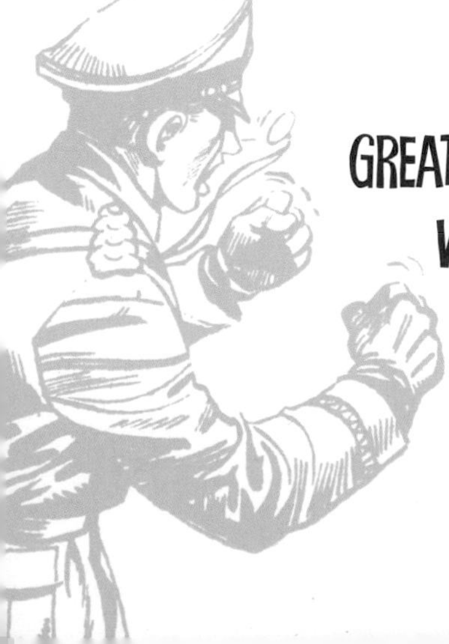

"THE MOST PERSISTENT SOUND WHICH REVERBERATES THROUGH MEN'S HISTORY IS THE BEATING OF WAR DRUMS"

Arthur Koestler (1905–1983)

INTRODUCTION

It is said that, at any point in time, in some foreign field, the British Army is fighting a war. The history of Britain has been shaped by feats on the battlefield, from the Lionheart's Crusades to Iraq and Afghanistan. Whether of glorious victory or ignominious defeat, these stories have echoed down the centuries; a rich source of inspiration for playwrights, poets, novelists and storytellers.

So it was only natural that, when the market for children's literature exploded into life in the latter half of the 19th century, publishers were quick to identify the appeal that war stories held for readers. Writers working for such titles as *The Boy's Own Paper* and the *Halfpenny Marvel* turned to the Napoleonic and Crimean wars for sources of inspiration. Interestingly, these tales focused more on battles at sea than on land, reflecting Britain's pride at ruling the waves.

While war stories were part of a mix that included tales of adventure, crime and, increasingly, sport, the emphasis changed at the end of the century, when the country became gripped by the wars in South Africa. At this point war stories started to dominate the comics and story-papers, reflecting the various campaigns against the Boer. These tapped into a deep well of patriotic fervour and the fictional tales were interspersed with true accounts of heroism in places etched on the national consciousness: Mafeking, Ladysmith and Kimberley. Titles including *Union Jack*, *Boys of the Empire*, *Young England* and *Dreadnought* prospered on a diet of war, sacrifice and heroism. These story-papers also functioned as recruiting tools, with boys and young men enamoured by the tales of derring-do encouraged to "do their bit".

By the early years of the 20th century comics and story-papers were enjoying a period of unprecedented growth, and the Great War saw a massive expansion in the number of war stories that appeared each week; again, true-life drama featured heavily alongside the fiction. The wartime government was quick to identify the comics as powerful weapons of propaganda; even when paper shortages became acute, the comics continued to be published. In the inter-war years there were significant new launches as the comics began to evolve in style. Titles including *Rover*, *Hotspur*, *Triumph*, *Wizard*, *Modern Boy* and *Champion* all included war stories as part of their staple diet. Many of these titles enjoyed a long and

He did it! He cartwheeled straight in! He's a better acrobat than he is a pilot!

illustrious history, overcoming the publishing restrictions in place during the Second World War. At their peak some were achieving weekly circulations well in excess of two million copies; it was the "golden age" of comics in Britain.

During the late 1950s and early 1960s, a new style of comic was introduced. These relied heavily on the comic-strip format, which gradually replaced the traditional text-heavy story-papers. Comics established during this period included *Valiant*, *Victor*, *Eagle*, *Lion* and *Tiger*, all of which included war stories. These comics soon enjoyed a significant and loyal following.

The final development was the establishment of the dedicated war publications, in the 1960s and 1970s, including *Commando*, *Air Ace*, *War at Sea* and *Action War Picture Library*. The launches of the much-loved *Warlord* and *Battle* comics was indicative of an insatiable desire for the genre. By the late 1980s, however, the war titles, along with the more established comics, were disappearing fast – although reprints of stories such as the estimable "Charley's War" show the genre is still very much appreciated today.

So welcome to the world at war, as portrayed by the comics and story-papers. Early in 2008, author Philip Pullman described the comic medium as "a wonderful way of telling stories, of imparting narrative". They are, he said, "vigorous, swift and immediate… they combine the immediacy and vigour of cinema with all the advantages of the book". I hope you enjoy reading about these warriors of fiction (and fact), and my sincere apologies if your favourite character is not here. A wealth of fascinating and fantastic material was considered for inclusion in this book; unfortunately, there was simply not space for all – or even one-tenth – of it. But I sincerely hope older readers enjoy catching up with their favourite comic characters, and enjoy meeting some

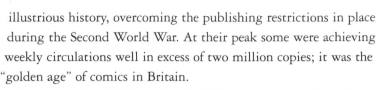

new ones, too. And to younger readers, welcome to the magical world of the British comic that so entertained your fathers – and grandfathers, too!

Adam Riches, March 2009

Postscript: As this book was being prepared for the printers, I was saddened to hear of the deaths of Henry Allingham and Harry Patch. Unfortunately, there are now no more British veterans of the Great War still living, and so a link with the past is broken. Their deaths underline the need to keep alive the stories of heroism and courage that took place on too many battlefields down the ages.

A.R., July 2009

HERE'S ALL THE BEST FOR CHRISTMAS!

VALIANT

AND *LION* **5p**

EVERY MONDAY   28TH DECEMBER, 1974

THE RIVALS
ENGLISH *versus* GERMANS
CHRISTMAS 1914

IT WAS CHRISTMAS EVE, 1914, AND THE FIRST WORLD WAR WAS ALMOST FIVE MONTHS OLD. THE TITANIC BATTLES OF MONS, THE MARNE AND LE CATEAU HAD ALREADY CLAIMED THE LIVES OF THOUSANDS OF MEN IN THE OCEANS OF MUD AND TANGLED WIRE CALLED "NO-MAN'S" LAND!

BUT ON THE EVENING OF 24th DECEMBER, A BRITISH SENTRY NOTICED THE GERMANS HAD PUT UP CHRISTMAS TREES ALONG THE TOP OF THEIR TRENCHES. MEN CAUTIOUSLY PEERED OUT TO CATCH A GLIMPSE... AND WHEN NO SHOTS WHISTLED AROUND THEIR HEADS, THEY CLIMBED OUT OF THEIR TRENCHES AND MOVED TOWARDS THE GERMANS. THEY MET AT THE BARBED WIRE... WHERE GIFTS WERE EXCHANGED AND CAROLS WERE SUNG. ON CHRISTMAS DAY THE FORMER BITTER RIVALS OF WAR TOOK PART IN A FOOTBALL MATCH... SURELY THE STRANGEST INTERNATIONAL EVER. THEN, ALMOST AS SOON AS IT HAD BEGUN, THE TRUCE ENDED. MIDNIGHT THE NEXT DAY CAME..., AND THE GUNS OPENED FIRE AGAIN!

"A SOLDIER WILL FIGHT LONG AND HARD
FOR A BIT OF COLOURED RIBBON"

Napoleon Bonaparte (1769–1821)

CHAPTER ONE
THE VICTORIANS MARCH ON

"I AM PREPARED TO GO ANYWHERE, provided it be forward." So said David Livingstone, world-renowned explorer and one of the most popular men of his age. His famous quote could be the clarion call for Victorian Britain, a period defined by radical social, technological, cultural and political change, as epitomised by Livingstone himself. He embodied the spirit of the age; he was a Scottish Protestant missionary yet a man of science, an advocate of Empire while also an enemy of slavery. Furthermore, his was a classic "rags-to-riches" story.

When Livingstone "discovered" the Victoria Falls in 1855, Britain was enjoying a period of relative peace, particularly domestically. While her European neighbours endured unrest and revolt, Britain's political stability at home enabled business and industry to expand unencumbered. The Empire was expanding, with exploitation of its raw materials bringing unprecedented wealth, while the British Navy ruled the seven seas.

While characterised by many as a deeply conservative age, in fact the Victorian era was a radical one. Much of this radicalism was driven by social campaigners; they included factory and child protection reformer Anthony Ashley-Cooper, the 7th Earl of Shaftesbury, prison and social reformer Elizabeth Fry, educationist Joseph Rowntree, and political philosophers Marx and Engels. But the enterprise culture was alive and kicking, too, and this was certainly true in the publishing sector, where, by the mid-19th century, a number of entrepreneurs were focusing on the

Facing page *The Union Jack* gloried in battles past, including this story of the Indian Mutiny of 1857

THE UNION JACK

ONE PENNY WEEKLY.
SIXPENCE MONTHLY.

Vol. I.—No. 33.]   Edited by G. A. HENTY.   [August 12, 1880.

IN TIMES OF PERIL.

A TALE OF THE INDIAN MUTINY.

BY THE EDITOR. (*Continued from p. 500.*)

UP to the 20th the palace still held out. This was a fortress in itself, mounting many cannon on its walls, and surrounded by an open park-like space. On that morning the engineers began to run a trench, to enable a battery to be erected to play upon the Lahore gate of the palace. Before, however, they had been long at work, a party of men of the 61st, with some Sikhs and Ghoorkas, ran boldly forward, and taking shelter under a low wall close to the gate, opened fire at the embrasures and loopholes. The answering fire was so weak that Colonel Jones, who was in command of the troops in this quarter—convinced that the report that the king with his wives and family, and the greater part of the garrison of the palace, had already left, was true—determined upon blowing in the gate at once. Lieutenant Home, was appointed to lead the party told off for the

THE SHOOTING OF THE PRINCES OF DELHI.

Facing page The Boy's Own Paper's depiction of "Saving the Colours" during the Zulu Wars. On 22 January 1879 at Isandlana, British forces suffered a catastrophic defeat. Some 1,200 troops were wiped out by an army of 12,000 Zulu warriors, armed mainly with spears

Below A typical "penny dreadful" cover, a tale of "Spring-Heeled Jack", published in 1890

increasingly lucrative boys' fiction market. They were greatly aided when William Gladstone, then Chancellor of the Exchequer, abolished duty on paper, a move that ushered in the era of mass-market publishing. With literacy rates rising, there was a rapidly growing demand for cheap fiction from poorer boys who could not afford to buy novels (when *Alice's Adventures in Wonderland* was published in 1865 it cost six shillings, equivalent to a third of an industrial worker's average weekly wage). In *Penny Dreadfuls and Comics*, Kevin Carpenter writes: "Many working boys could, however, afford a penny a week, or contributed their farthing towards 'clubs' which bought their favourite paper, or were given a ragged read-to-death copy of the previous week's issue. It is reckoned that on average these publications were shared by around nine readers – meaning leading publications such as *The Boys of England*, with a peak circulation of 250,000 copies (in 1871), was actually read by more than two million children per week."

Foremost among this breed of thrusting paper-story entrepreneurs was Edwin Brett, who fed this appetite for salacious storytelling with his "penny dreadfuls", published by his Newsagents' Publishing Company. But Brett was also responsible for, among other titles, the rather more genteel story-paper *The Boys of England*, which was first issued on 24 November 1866 and appeared every week until 30 June 1899. Brett was quick to realise that there was a market for more wholesome literature, inspired no doubt by the success of rival Samuel O. Beeton's *Boys' Own Magazine*, first published in 1855. Many cite *Boys' Own Magazine* as the first reputable publication that focused on amusement rather than education – and a far cry from the "bloods", as some critics had dubbed the penny dreadfuls. Frequently sold in weekly parts, the

SPRING-HEELED JACK,
THE TERROR OF LONDON.
By the Author of "TURNPIKE DICK, the Star of the Road."

Issue Nº 1   SPRING-HEELED JACK FINDS THE MURDERED BODY OF HERBERT LEIGH.   PRICE 1d

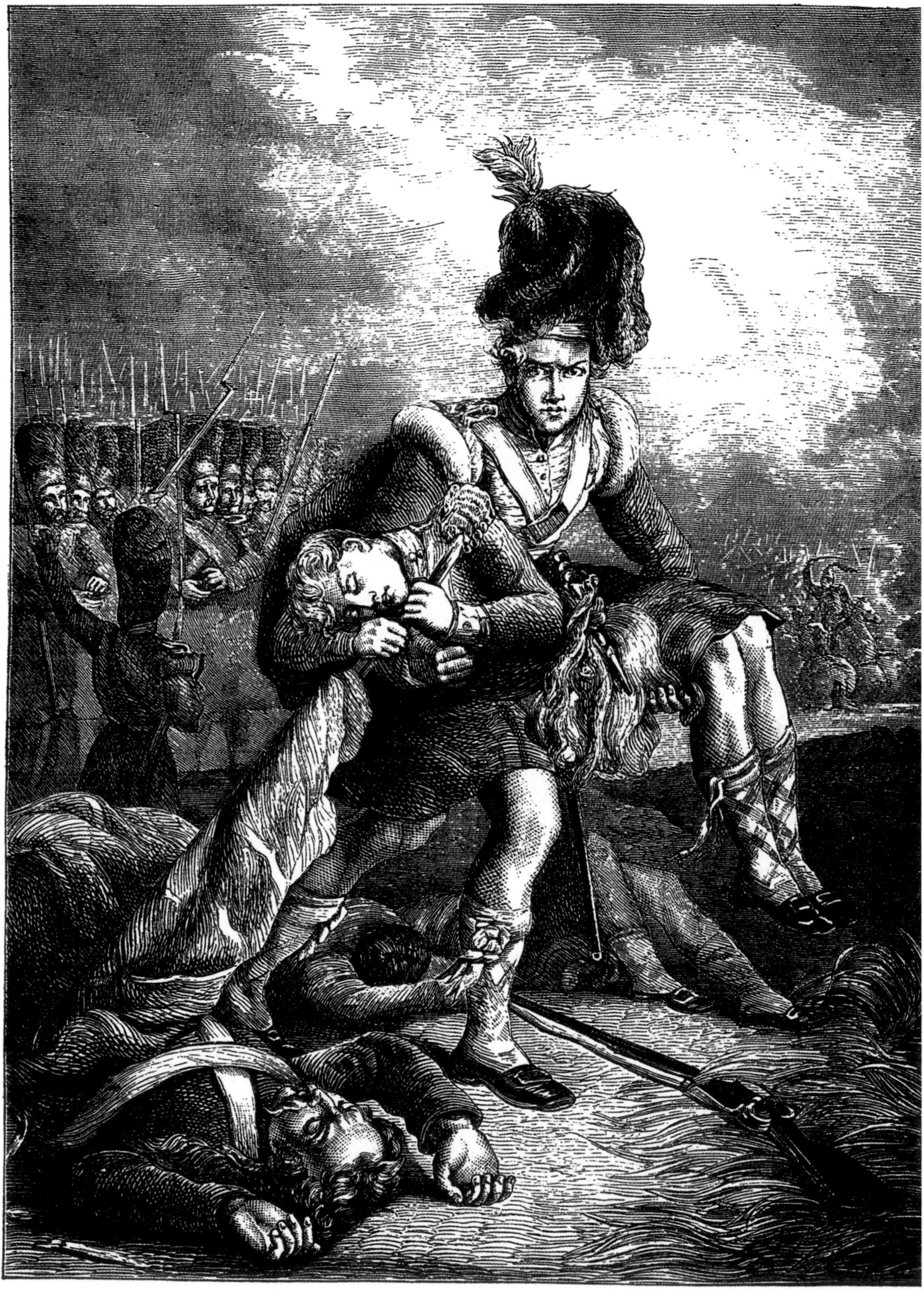

Above A copy of Sir Edwin Landseer's painting "War", reproduced by *The Boy's Own Paper* in 1880. The scene is from the Napoleonic Wars

Facing page A typical war story of the era, in the story-paper *Golden Hours*, dated 30 May 1896

penny dreadfuls were, in effect, part-work novels. Their subjects encompassed crime, murder, street violence and other lurid subject matter, presented in sensational form with graphic illustrations to match. Particularly notorious was Brett's ***The Wild Boys of London*** series (sub-titled "The Children of Night"), which featured the escapades of a group of juvenile street criminals in the capital and was published in 1866. War was not a subject matter for the penny dreadfuls; Britain's city streets were chock-full of incidents that provided subject matter with which to entertain and terrorise British boys.

In the mid-1850s, the penny dreadful market was hotly fought over. Brett's rival publishers churned out many (largely inferior) titles, typically more extreme in their shocking and brutal depictions of violence and crime.

But times were changing; and part of the reason for that was a backlash against the penny dreadfuls, for they deeply offended middle-class sensibilities.

According to Lord Shaftesbury, speaking in 1878, the malign influence of the

PRIZE PUZZLE COMPETITION.

SEE PAGE 7.

PUZZLE COUPON No. 5.

GOLDEN HOURS

Vol II.—No. 62.   Week ending MAY 30, 1896.   PRICE ONE PENNY.

"CHARGE!"

A BRAVE YOUNG SOLDIER FROM DRUMMER BOY TO GENERAL

COLONEL McMICHAEL PATTED THE PROUD BOY'S SHOULDER AND SAID: "MY BOY, YOUR NAME WILL GO TO THE PRESIDENT AS THAT OF ONE WHO WAS BRAVE BEYOND HIS FELLOWS."

A BRAVE YOUNG SOLDIER;

OR,

From Drummer Boy to General.

BY JOHN DE MORGAN.

CHAPTER I.

A SPARTAN MOTHER.

"MOTHER, dear, such news!" exclaimed Harry Winter as he rushed excitedly into the room where his mother sat sewing.

"News, Harry?" she said, looking up.

"Yes; but, mother, I am afraid——" and the boy paused, not knowing how to utter the words which he knew would almost break that fond mother's heart.

Mrs. Percy Winter looked at her light-hearted, joyous, sixteen-year-old boy, and as she did so, her eyes were dimmed with tears,

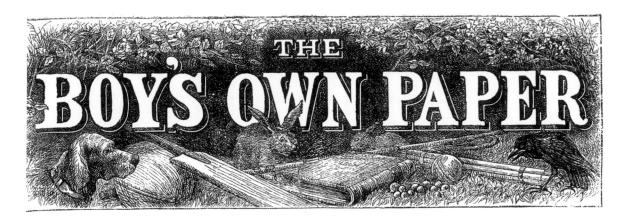

THE BOY'S OWN PAPER

No. 4.—Vol. I.   SATURDAY, FEBRUARY 8, 1879.   Price One Penny.
[ALL RIGHTS RESERVED.]

FROM POWDER MONKEY TO ADMIRAL:

r, the Stirring Days of the British Navy.

By W. H. G. KINGSTON,

Author of "Peter the Whaler," "True Blue," etc.

CHAPTER IV.—THE FRIGATE BLOWN UP.

HE Americans had been joined by a number of the Frenchmen, and some w of the worst characters of the English ew; the jail-birds chiefly, who had been on over with the idea that they would il away to some beautiful island, of which ey might take possession, and live in dependence, or else rove over the ocean ith freedom from all discipline.

A Critical Moment.

"bloods" was "creeping not only into the houses of the poor, neglected and untaught, but into the largest mansions; penetrating into religious families and astounding careful parents with its frightful issues".

Unlike his rivals, Brett was quick to clean up his act, and *The Boys of England*'s launch in 1866 was a nod to the forces of moral conservatism. He had noted the prevalent mood of displeasure, echoed later in Lord Shaftesbury's speech, and was determined not to get caught up in a moral backlash. The aim of *The Boys of England*, according to "The Editor's Address" in the launch issue, was to "enthral" its readers and also to "sooth and enliven care-tired thoughts".

It was for boys who wanted to make something of their lives. According to Kevin Carpenter: "*The Boys of England* contained advice about various occupations open to working-class youth, and snippets from Samuel Smiles' [book] *Self-Help*. Another significant element of the new paper was its patriotic tone, intended to display the strengths of English national character, particularly 'that true manliness, which is the cause of England's moral as well as physical supremacy over the other nations of the earth'."

Sir James Outram.   Sir Colin Campbell.   Sir Henry Havelock.

Above The lives of the war heroes and their exploits proved a rich seam for *The Boy's Own Paper* to mine. These profiles appeared in 1880

Facing page "From Powder Monkey to Admiral" was one of *The Boy's Own Paper*'s most popular stories

Brett's publishing empire was soon to face a major challenger, surfing the wave of moral indignation that surrounded the penny dreadfuls. Lord Shaftesbury's apocalyptic speech about the dangers of "gallow's literature" (as some called it) had been made to the Religious Tract Society. In 1879, the society launched what was to become one of the most enduring and popular of all the boys' story-papers – *The Boy's Own Paper*. The Religious Tract Society's Annual Report of 1879 outlined the problem as they saw it: "Juvenile crime was being largely stimulated by the pernicious literature circulated among our lads. Judges, magistrates, school masters, prison chaplains, and others were deploring the existence of the evil..."

The first issue of **The Boy's Own Paper** (dated 18 January 1879) proved an instant success, selling out within three days. This was largely due to editor G.A. Hutchison's insistence that it contain a strong emphasis on fiction; the Religious Tract Society wanted a more pious publication. Hutchison argued that this would deter boys from buying it, and that "admirable behaviour, and values of honesty, industry and perseverance could be skilfully embedded in fiction in such a way as to be palatable for children". That initial issue contained sports and adventure stories, features on hobbies, nature and health – and also turned to warfare for its subject matter. "From Powder Monkey to Admiral", sub-titled "The Stirring days of the British Navy", plotted the career progression of one young lad during the Napoleonic Wars.

W.H.G. Kingston wrote the story in 1870, shortly after the story-paper started. It related the tale of how it might be possible for an ordinary boy joining

the Navy in the lowest rating – "powder monkey" –and ascend to the very highest rank, admiral. While this might sound unlikely, history in fact proves otherwise. Admiral Edward Hopson (1671-1728) was just one example of a lad of humble stock who rose through the ranks. In "From Powder Monkey to Admiral" three boys – Jack, Tom and Bill – join up at the same time. They share many adventures, but only Bill makes it to the rank of midshipman. This was the hardest promotion for any low-ranking sailor to make, but it was Bill's bravery, honesty and good manners that won the day.

T he story was later published in book form, with the introduction written by Dr James MacCaulay, founder and Supervising Editor of *The Boy's Own Paper*. He wrote: "Talking the matter over, it was objected that such a story

THE YOUNG FRANC-TIREURS.
BY THE EDITOR.

Above From *Union Jack*, "The Young Franc-Tireurs", which appeared throughout 1882, was set in the Franco-Prussian War of 1870-1871. Franc-Tireurs were soldiers who fought unconventional warfare, the guerillas of their day

might offend peaceable folk, because it must deal too much with blood and gunpowder. Mr Kingston, although famed as a narrator of sea-fights, was a lover of peace, and he said that his story would not encourage the war spirit... he chose the period of great war for his story, because it was a time of stirring events and adventures." He added: "Throughout the tale, not 'glory' but 'duty' is the object set before the youthful reader."

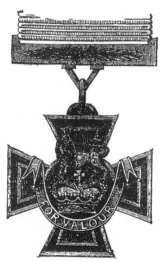

From the start, *The Boy's Own Paper* featured war stories as part of its staple diet. In general these tales harked back to the Crimean War (1853-1856), the Napoleonic Wars and others against the French (1793-1815), the Indian Mutiny (1857) and even the imperial campaigns in India that took place the previous century. While "From Powder Monkey to Admiral" was a nautical yarn, others were Army-rather than Navy-based. "A Narrow Escape", subtitled "By An Old Soldier", (a two-parter starting 17 April 1880) is centred on the Indian Mutiny and, as the subtitle suggests, is the reminiscence of an old man – one Private George Parsons.

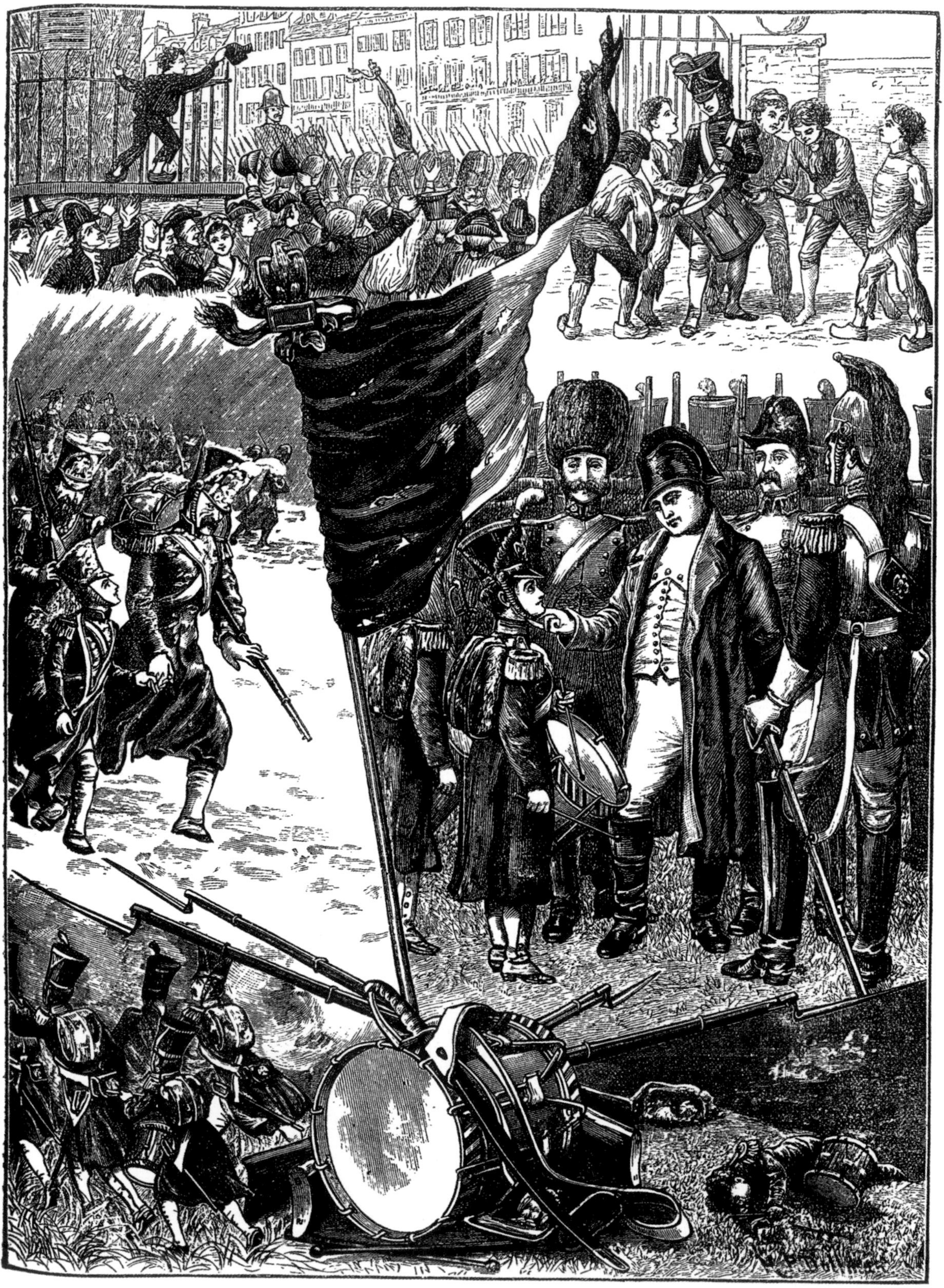

Interestingly, *The Boy's Own Paper*'s war stories, shot through with patriotism and national pride, did not always see things from a British perspective. Readers were treated to the story of "Jacques Faubert, the Drummer Boy" (issue dated 18 June 1881), in which the eponymous hero is conscripted to the French army for Napoleon's ill-fated campaign in Russia, in 1812.

Above Action scenes from the "Battle of Pinkie", as seen in the pages of *The Boy's Own Paper*, October 1880

Facing page "The Drummer Boy" signs up to fight with Napoleon in Russia, from *The Boy's Own Paper*, June 1881

As well as fictional adventures, *The Boy's Own Paper* also carried a regular feature called "Some Famous British Battles". The issue dated 9 October 1880 features the Battle of Pinkie, where the English, led by Edward Seymour, Duke of Somerset, defeated the Scots in 1547. In the issue dated 30 October 1880, "The Glorious First of June" was remembered – it was the first and largest naval battle between Great Britain and the First French Republic during the French Revolutionary Wars, in 1794.

Undoubtedly, *The Boy's Own Paper* was the most high profile of the new breed of story-papers; no other title could match its star roster of writers that included, at various times, Sir Arthur Conan Doyle, Jules Verne, R.M. Ballantyne, cricketer W.G. Grace and Robert Baden Powell, founder of the Scouts and hero of the Boer War.

But it did not have the field to itself. *Union Jack* launched on 1 January 1880, describing itself as "A Magazine of Healthy, Stirring tales of Adventure by

Vol. I.—No. 6.]   Edited by W. H. G. KINGSTON.   [Feb. 5, 1880.
[All rights reserved.]

THE CAPTURE OF THE ENVOY.

TIMES OF PERIL.—A TALE OF INDIA.—BY G. A. HENTY.—(Continued from p. 89.)

Land and Sea for Boys". It was "Every Boy's Paper", costing one penny for the weekly issue and sixpence for a monthly bound edition, which included a free print ("The Early Days of Our Popular Sport" was one). The main story in the launch issue was "Paddy Finn, or the Adventures of an Irish Midshipman, afloat and ashore". Inside was "With Fire and Sword", a tale of the Russo-Turkish war, a bloody encounter that had taken place just a couple of years earlier. *Union Jack* covered familiar territory with stories such as "Times of Peril – a Tale of India" (5 February 1880), which continued with a subtle name change as "In Times of Peril – A Tale of the Indian Mutiny". It was written by editor G.A. Henty (who later wrote for *The Boy's Own Paper*), as was "Jack Archer: A Tale of the Crimea", which ran throughout 1883. A blood-and-thunder escapade, it vividly brought to life the fear and mayhem of the battlefield. "Desperately, the men bent to their oars, and the heavy boat surged through the water. Around them swept a storm of musket balls, and although the darkness and

Above Fighting the Russians in the story "Jack Archer: A Tale of the Crimea", *The Boy's Own Paper*, 1883

Facing page More action in India from the pages of *Union Jack*

their haste rendered the fire of the Russians wild and uncertain, many of the shots took effect. With a sigh, Mr Pascoe fell against Jack, who was sitting next to him, just at the moment when Jack himself experienced a sensation as if a hot iron had passed across his arm. Several of the men dropped their oars and fell back, but the boats still held rapidly on their way, and in two or three minutes, were safe from anything but random shot. At this moment, however, three field pieces opened with grape, and the iron hail tore up the water near them. Fortunately they were now almost out of sight, and although the forts threw up rockets to light the bay, and joined their fire to that of the field guns, the bats escaped untouched. 'Thank God we are out of that!' Mr Hethcote said, as the fire ceased and the boats headed for a light hung up to direct them."

While most of *Union Jack*'s stories harked back to previous wars (Napoleonic, Crimean), the story-paper did, occasionally, touch on campaigns that were ongoing. In the issue dated 24 October 1882, an article entitled "Peace After

War" reflected on the Battle of Kassassin, which took place during the Sudan Campaign. Egyptian forces attacked the British on 28 August 1882 and again on 9 September 1882. Both attacks were repulsed, and the Household Cavalry counter-attacked in an action that came to be known in popular lore as the "Midnight Charge". In a sermonising editorial the **Union Jack** instructed its readers about how they should live their lives, drawing parallels between life's battles and Kassassin: "The strife of arms has ceased, and swords are being sheathed and guns are left unloaded; for the war is done. Brief, if bitter, it has been; and now that victory has crowned our hopes, peace comes again. So may it be with all of you. So may the story of your lives be as has been the story of that war. Nor flinch, nor yield an inch, nor stand aside from your set purpose, until victory is fairly yours... Let there be no nonsense about an easy life being a pleasant life. It is nothing of the kind. Just pull yourselves together. Aim for a prize! and fight until you get it; and then see if your days have not been happier than his who has let his life slip easily, objectless away... Strive to be true. Strive to be pure. Strive to leave the world better than you found it. Have some object in your life; some prize, and strive until it is yours...never be discouraged. Let your trust be in God; and in the right fight on – fight ever – and, if needful, fighting die."

But to the disappointment of its readers **Union Jack** was not to last – after just 129 issues the story-paper ceased to be.

But there was certainly no shortage of reading material for British boys, with titles launched (and closing) with great frequency. **New Boys' Paper** launched

Right The cavalry charge at Kassassin, from *Union Jack*, 24 April 1882

READY IN A FEW DAYS—ORDER AT ONCE.

MOST LAUGHABLE STORY OF MILITARY LIFE EVER WRITTEN ! ! !

OUR BOYS IN THE ARMY.

NO. 2 GIVEN AWAY WITH NO. 1,

IN BEAUTIFULLY COLOURED WRAPPER.—ALSO A SUPERB COLOURED PLATE, GRATIS.

TO THE RESCUE! TO THE RESCUE!

This Splendid Tale is a Sequel to

THE SCHOOL OF THE REGIMENT.

Above Publishers were keen to promote their other publications. Here the *British Boys' Paper* advertises a new launch, *Our Boys in the Army*, which first appeared in June 1888

WAR.

BLACK darkness reigns o'er the tented field,
Save the flickering light that the watch-fires
    yield,
Then a few stars sail into heaven's deep dome,
And the soldiers are dreaming of loved ones at
    home.

The sentinel silently paces his round,
In the sleeping camp there is never a sound ;
But the crack of a rifle rends the air,
And the bugle rings out an angry blare.

Then all in the darkness they rapidly form,
They charge at the foe with a rush like a storm,
The fight is soon over, but, wounded and slain,
Many gallant young fellows lie stretched on the
    plain.

And many a mother will weep for her son
As she kneels on the bed when the day is done ;
And many a maiden will sorrow in vain,
For the lover she never will welcome again.

PAUL BLAKE.

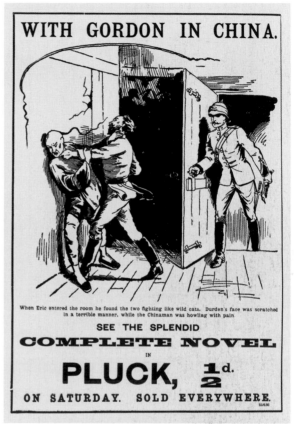

on 2 October 1886, carrying the story "Cruise of the Phantom – A Mystery of the Sea", centring on the centuries-old conflict with France. Issue two brought readers "How I Became a Soldier", a fictionalised account that was described thus: "This highly Exciting and Interesting Story graphically describes the Life of a Young Recruit, as well as giving a stirring description of Adventures and Hair breadth escapes."

Facing page The tragedy of war... tugging at the heartstrings in *The Boy's Own Paper*, September 1881

Above Two plates from *The Halfpenny Marvel* advertising sister publications: the one on the left is from 1896, the other is from 1895

This was followed up in issue three with "How I Became a Sailor"; it also carried "The School of the Regiment, or Our Boys in the Army", which was "The Most Laughable story of Garrison Academy Life ever written".

New Boys' Paper ran for 74 issues before morphing into the ***British Boys' Paper*** in 1888. That title ran for 86 issues, until October 1889. The highly volatile nature of the story-paper publishing market is encapsulated in what happened to ***New Boys' Paper*** and its subsequent incarnations. Typically, rather than closing titles, publishers preferred to amalgamate them with others. So when ***British Boys' Paper*** ran out of steam it was incorporated into Guy Rayner's ***Boys' Own Journal***. In 1890, this was incorporated into ***Boyhood***, which after only 13 issues was incorporated into ***Boys' Graphic***, in 1890. And so on.

Above In a spot of bother... to find out how our hero escapes you need *Pluck!* From The *Halfpenny Marvel*, July 1895

Our old friend Edwin Brett was continually trying to innovate, and he notched up another first by publishing the first boys' weekly printed in full colour. This was *Boys of the Empire* (1888), but because of the high cost of colour printing it reverted to monochrome after 51 issues. The title was struggling due to its penny-ha'penny price tag (which was later reduced to a ha'penny), and was eventually closed by Brett in 1893, after 277 issues. Yet the title was to make a comeback in bizarre circumstances seven years later, when a rival publisher, Melrose, was about to launch its own *Boys of the Empire title*. Immediately, Brett rushed a *Boys of the Empire* (New Series) on to the bookstalls, beating Melrose to market by two weeks – his first issue being dated 9 October 1900. So for a time young readers had the choice of two *Boys of the Empire* titles. Eventually, Melrose gave way and changed the name of its paper to *Boys of Our Empire* (launched 29 June 1901). As an indication of the level of activity in the market, Brett's company published 28 different titles in the latter years of the 19th century.

Of the many new publications that flooded the market, the most important was *The Halfpenny Marvel*, launched by publishing magnate Alfred Harmsworth. He controlled a massive empire that included *The Times* newspaper and the popular *Comic Cuts*; he was later to launch the *Daily Mail* and the *Daily Mirror*. He also rescued the ailing *Daily News*, turning it into a "tabloid"-style publication – a move that proved hugely popular. Sales nudged 800,000 in 1896, which Harmsworth claimed was a world-record sale for a newspaper.

The Halfpenny Marvel was launched on 11 November 1893 with the publisher on a mission: "to counteract the pernicious influence of the Penny Dreadfuls". For Harmsworth, this moral crusade was designed to appeal more to parents than young readers. It was a continuation of a campaign he had started in

Comic Cuts, where he once wrote that he would "throw downstairs" any penny dreadful authors who submitted unsolicited contributions. He certainly pulled no punches – a statement in issue one of **The Halfpenny Marvel** read: "No more penny dreadfuls! These healthy stories of mystery, adventure, etc., will kill them. Boys who become inflamed by reading 'penny dreadfuls', were robbing their employers, buying revolvers with the proceeds and setting themselves up in the back streets as highwaymen. This and many other evils the penny dreadful is responsible for. It makes thieves of the coming generation and so helps to fill our jails. If we can rid the world of even one of these vile publications our efforts will not have been in vain."

Above *Chums* ran a feature in the issue dated 13 February 1895 on troops around the world – here are the Italians

Below From *The Halfpenny Marvel*, 5 November 1895

He continued to hammer away; virtually every issue carried a message of support from a "pillar-of-the-establishment"-type figure. Issue 121 (24 February 1896) carried on its cover a "Letter from a Schoolmaster", imploring "Parents should read this". It was from a W. Lloyd Summers of Newchurch, Manchester, and read: "As a schoolmaster of many years' standing I have taken great interest in your adventure. I must confess that, when I read your first editorial, by which I saw that you hoped to push the cheap and nasty boys' stories off the market, my admiration for your sanguine temperament was only equalled by my pessimistic doubts as to your success." He continued: "A

By S. CLARKE HOOK, Author of "By Nelson's Side." "The Wreckers," &c., &c., &c.

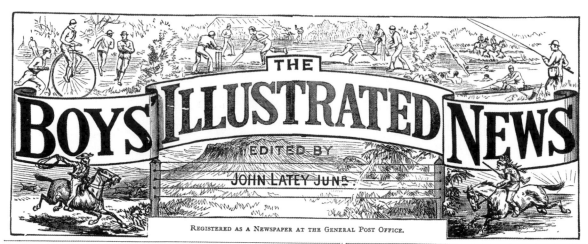

THE BOYS' ILLUSTRATED NEWS

EDITED BY JOHN LATEY JUNR.

REGISTERED AS A NEWSPAPER AT THE GENERAL POST OFFICE.

No. 34.—Vol. I. WEDNESDAY, { ISSUED BY THE PROPRIETORS OF "THE ILLUSTRATED LONDON NEWS." } NOVEMBER 23, 1881. ONE PENNY.

A Fight in a Flood;
OR,
KIN AGAINST KIN.
A Romance of the Forest of Dean.
BY
CAPTAIN MAYNE REID.

CHAPTER XXVII.
FIENNES SHOWS THE WHITE FEATHER.

ALLER'S stay in Bristol was of the shortest — only long enough to rest his wearied men and their jaded horses. The "Night Owl!" was not the bird to relish being engaged in a besieged city, and this he anticipated Bristol would soon be. The field, not the fortress, was his congenial sphere of action; and, though sadly downcast, his army scattered to the four winds, he had not yet himself surrendered to despair. He would raise another, if it cost him his whole fortune. So "To horse!" and off again, Hesselrig along with him.

London was their destination, and to reach it, with such feeble escort, a dangerous enterprise. For it was but continuing retreat through a country swarming with their triumphant foemen. But with a skill worthy of Cyrus himself, Waller made it good; going round by Gloucester, Warwick, and Newport Pagnell, at length to arrive safe in the metropolis.

But how of Bristol, and its defenders left behind? If these were despondent on seeing the shattered cuirassiers re-enter their gates, they were soon to witness another spectacle causing them dismay.

Even on the very next day it appeared, in fulfilment of their worst forebodings. Another body of horse it was, also approaching the place; not the skeleton of a regiment in retreat, but the vanguard of a victorious army —the same that had won the day at Roundway Down. And as the defeated one had suffered utter annihilation, there was now nothing to stay the victors.

So, when the citizens of

Bristol beheld the Light Horse of Wilmot and Byron scouring the country outside, and up to their very gates, they had little doubt of these being the precursors of a larger force—the whole Royalist army.

Soon it appeared in formidable array, making *leaguer* all around. For there was more than one force there to enfilade them. First came the conquering hosts of Hertford and Prince Maurice, fresh from the field of Lansdown. Then, on the Oxford side, appeared Rupert with his Cavaliers, a full *corps d'armée*, fire-handed from the burning of Birmingham, and red-handed from the slaughter at Chalgrove; where, by the treachery of the infamous Urrey, they had let out the life-blood of England's purest patriot—the noble Hampden.

In a very revel of delight they drew around the doomed city, as eagles preparing to stoop at prey. For they knew it had neither strength of fortification, nor defending force,

"A FIGHT IN A FLOOD": EUSTACE TREVOR ANGERED.

sufficient to resist them. Waller going west had almost stripped it of its garrison, numbers of whom were now lying dead on the downs of Wiltshire. So there was no question as between siege and storm, the fiery Rupert, soon as arrived on the ground, determining on assault.

And assault it was, commenced the next morning at earliest hour. Successful on the Gloucester side, where the bold Rupert himself attacked, and the timid Fiennes defended. After all his boasting, the lawyer-soldier let the enemy in, almost without striking a blow! Nor did they pass over his dead body either.

Very different was the defence on the southern side, for of different stuff were the defenders. There Colonel Walwyn with his Foresters, and Birch with his Bridgemen, held the ramparts against Hertford and Maurice, not only foiling their attack, but beating them off. In that quarter were blows enough, and blood flowing in rivers.

The Cornish men were cut down by scores, among them some of their best leaders, as Slanning and Trevannion. But all in vain. Alike bootless proved the gallantry of the soldier - knight and the courage of the merchant-soldier. Unavailable their deeds of valour; for while they were fighting the foe in front—in the act of putting him to rout—behind they heard a trumpet sounding signals for a parley! And turning, beheld a white flag, waving from a staff, *within* the city's walls! Saw and heard all this with amazement. On their side the assailants were repulsed, and Bristol safe. Why, then, the display of peaceful signals? Were they for an armistice? Surely it could not be for capitulation?

While Colonel Walwyn and his victorious comrades were still in doubt about the purport of these unlooked-for signs, they saw a mounted *aide-de-camp* coming towards them in a gallop. He was the same who had brought the despatch to Montserrat House at the breaking up of the ball. It was a verbal message he bore now, delivered in loud voice as he drew up.

"His Excellency's orders to cease fighting."

"And why?" demanded the astonished knight, other voices asking the same, all in anger and amazement. "For what reason should we cease fighting? We're on the eve of victory."

"I know not the reason, Colonel Walwyn," responded the *aide-de-camp*, evidently ashamed of the part he was constrained to play; "only that they've beaten us on the Gloucester side, and got into the works. Colonel Langrish advised the Governor to ask for an armistice; which Prince Rupert has granted."

"Oh! you've got Langrish round there? That

wise man is never ashamed to confess his mistakes, and I hasten to lay claim to the title by at once allowing that you were right and I was wrong. I have nothing but congratulations to offer on the very decided success your books have had. In conversation with some Manchester news agents, I have elicited the fact that in the city the sale of the Halfpenny Marvel has had the desired effect of greatly reducing the demand for trash. May your circulation ever increase!"

There is no doubting that Harmsworth's titles, along with *The Boys' Own Paper*, ate into the circulation of the penny dreadfuls. The fact that *The Halfpenny Marvel* cost, as suggested, half-pence, meant it was 50 per cent cheaper than its rivals. He also used his newspapers and other magazines to advertise the boys' story-papers. As Kevin Carpenter wrote: "The price of Harmsworth's story-papers was, however, not the only factor in their success. His publications were emphatically up-to-date, reflecting hectic life in a hectic decade, whereas his main rival E.J. Brett's papers had changed little over thirty years. Above all, it was attitudes to the Empire which separated the old from the new. For Brett, the Empire had never been more than a colourful backcloth to the wild and wonderful fiction his hacks produced. Harmsworth's *Pluck*, with its emphasis on the deeds and bravery of the men who had laid the foundations of the Empire, and those who were still busy expanding its borders, and with its plea for a course of Empire-related studies and cadet training for all boys, was an efficient mouthpiece for the jingoism of the age."

The same could be said for *The Halfpenny Marvel*. The story "Under Nelson's Flag, or The Wooden Walls of Old England", concerns the adventures of one Alec Turner – "Nelson's Favourite Little Powder Monkey" (the expression "the wooden walls of old England" was a term of respect for the British Navy).

The story's blood-and-thunder narrative revolves around Alec fighting for Britain in the Napoleonic Wars, illustrated by his encounters with a brutal French officer, La Combe, and Meredy, "a noted duellist and scoundrel". In the episode dated 24 September 1895, Alec blows up a French fort, and while making his escape is blown into the water with a French soldier. Our

Facing page A story of the English Civil War from *The Boys' Illustrated News*, November 1881

Below Empire-building in "The White Lion-King", a story from *The Halfpenny Marvel*, November 1895

THIS NUMBER COMMENCES A NEW VOLUME.

½ THE WHITE LION-KING.

The beast crept slowly towards the white hero, his head low, his eyes seeming to emit a lurid glow under his shaggy brows. . . . The interest of the spectators became breathless, absorbing, intense. It was only relieved when the lion sprang. (See page 9.)

THE "HALFPENNY MARVEL"

NO. 105 21, WHITEFRIARS STREET, LONDON, E.C.

This Journal was founded to counteract the pernicious influences of the Penny and Half-penny Dreadfuls.

NEW BOOK, CONTAINING COMPLETE STORY, EVERY WEDNESDAY.

DOGS ON THE BATTLEFIELD.

No. 106.—Vol. III.] SEPTEMBER 19, 1894.

"THE FIGURE BEFORE THEM SWAYED AND FELL FORWARD—DEAD." (See page 50.)

hero decides to swim to his ship, the *Vanguard*: "Directly, he got under cover of the cliff, the soldiers opened fire on him; but a yell of terror caused them to stop. The Frenchman had risen close to him, and he stood as much chance of being hit as Alec did. The man could swim, though only indifferently; and now it occurred to Alec that, were he to seize him and swim out to sea by his side, the enemy would be able to fire. This thought no sooner struck him than he put it into execution. A couple of strokes took him up to the Frenchman, whom he gripped by the back of the neck, and, taking no heed of his shouts, swam with him out to sea." Thus shielded from French bullets our hero swims back to the *Vanguard*, on the way depositing the by-now exhausted Frenchman on a convenient buoy, from where he can be rescued by his comrades. Alec is brave, resourceful and strong – a fine specimen of British manhood. He wreaks revenge on the murderous La Combe, who at one point captures and tortures our hero, but whose spirit he can never break.

Facing page A firing squad goes about its deadly business in "For His Brother's Sake", a story of the Franco-Prussian War. It appeared in *Chums* throughout 1894

Empire-building and exploration in Africa was another rich source of material for *The Halfpenny Marvel*. Issue 105 (5 November 1895) carried the story "The White Lion-King", in which three adventurers entered the "heart of darkness". George Gough, Frank Hawtree and Albert Lyall were warned that "Somaliland is a dangerous place for white men, when they go beyond the coast". Issue 119 (11 February 1896) contained the story "The King's Oath, or the Romance of the Dark Contintent", featuring Lieutenant Albert MacGregor, "a finely built handsome young fellow". His regiment is occupying Elmina, a town on the Atlantic coast of Ghana, lying west of Cape Coast. In the late nineteenth century, Elmina was an important strategic location. The port was Portugal's West African headquarters for trade, and eventually became a hub for the export of thousands of slaves. The Dutch West India Company captured it in 1637, and it remained in Dutch hands until 1872, when it was sold to the English. Our fictional story concerns an uprising of the 'Ashantee' (usually spelled Ashanti) during the third in a series of real Anglo-Ashanti Wars during the 19th century. The Third Anglo-Ashanti War lasted from 1873 to 1874. General Wolseley, with

2,500 British troops and several thousand West Indian and African troops, was sent to defeat the Ashanti, who believed Elmina was their territory. Correspondents covering the fighting included G.A. Henty – a prolific writer of tales for the boys' story-papers and editor of ***Union Jack***. While Albert MacGregor was a fictional character, the "King's Oath" is based on actual events. It starts with a blood-curdling warning to the British from Koffee Calcalli, who was king of the Ashanti during the Third Anglo-Ashanti War: "These British have marched into Elmina; their red coats are on the heights of Cape Coast Castle. That is our territory. Now I will slay every white man in my country!" Our hero is taken prisoner during the fighting, and is tortured. He eventually escapes in time to help the British to victory. The war ended with the Treaty of Fomena, signed in July 1874.

The issue of ***The Halfpenny Marvel*** dated 26 November 1895 also contains a story based in Africa called "The Diamond of Doom". The unfortunate Eric Scott is seeking diamonds and his fortune when he is captured by the Masai. His punishment is to be staked out in the burning sun, and smeared with honey – for Eric was "doomed to be eaten alive by red ants". In vivid prose his demise is depicted: "The red pests fell to work upon their horrible repast of living human flesh, while their victim writhed in agony indescribable… In vain did Eric call upon death to come to him. Hour after hour went by, and came it not. At last they ceased, and his tortured limbs quivered with pain no more. The work of the Masai fiends was finished."

Scary stuff to fertile young minds – a passage that could have come straight from the pages of the much-despised penny dreadfuls. Indeed, many thought ***The Halfpenny***

D.H.PARRY.

PRICE ONE PENNY.] **TWO SERIALS AND THREE COMPLETE STORIES.**

No. 126.—Vol. III.] FEBRUARY 6, 1895. [ALL RIGHTS RESERVED.

"'HE FELL AT THAT MOMENT, LITERALLY RIDDLED WITH BULLETS.'" (*See page* 370.)

Marvel to be not-too-distantly related to the "bloods" – as A.A. Milne famously said: "Harmsworth killed the penny dreadful by the simple process of producing the ha'penny dreadfuller."

The Halfpenny Marvel ceased publication on 22 April 1922, when it was superseded by *Sport and Adventure*.

Along with *The Halfpenny Marvel* and *Pluck*, a third new launch in the 1890s was also to break new ground. *Chums* was launched on 12 September 1892, published by Cassell. At one penny for 16 pages, *Chums'* selling points were its highly stylised front cover illustrations and its varied and topical content. Unlike many of its rivals, which often featured one extended story per issue (which could be as long as 25,000 words), *Chums* contained a number of short stories, plus other features. Its tales focused on the traditional adventure and exploration genres, but increasingly added war stories to its roster. Many of these short stories were complete, one-off tales; it also carried a serialised story, of which Robert Louis Stevenson's *Treasure Island* was one. (Interestingly, the story-paper *Young Folks* also ran a serialised

version of the tale, between 1881-82, under the title "The Sea Cook, or Treasure Island".) But *Chums* had much more than fiction; it carried sports features, primarily focusing on cricket; competitions with excellent prizes; puzzles, cartoons and jokes. It also had interviews with high-profile figures of the day – and these were no minor celebrities. Sir John Millais, Hiram Maxim, inventor of the machine gun, and Major General Sir Francis Grenfell were among the early interviewees.

Like many of its rivals, the war stories in *Chums* looked

back to previous encounters; but unlike many of them, it also focused on contemporary wars, including those in South Africa, the Sudan and Afghanistan. In the issue dated 29 August 1894 is the short story "Why Afzul Missed his Mark – An Episode in the Afghan War". Afzul is a crack marksman with the British Army, and the tale relates how during a raid on an Afghan hill village his famed shooting skills desert him. He is ordered to shoot a village elder who is organising the defence but, despite three clear sightings of his target, Afzul "misses his mark". Legend has it that a divine power protects a father from being shot by his son; and, sure enough, we discover the village elder was indeed Afzul's father.

I n "Nearly Forty Years Ago – A Reminiscence of a Waterloo Veteran" an old man is recounting tales of the Napoleonic War to a young boy, the story's narrator. The old man also reflects on the Crimean War, in which his son is involved, and the Sepoy Mutiny in India (issue dated 6 June 1985). A poignant tale, it's almost a potted history of Britain's 19th-century military campaigns. The old man, John Locke, was "tall, thin, white-haired and always dressed in knee-breeches and long stockings, he was an antique and martial figure", who kept his Waterloo campaign medal under his shirt. The narrator takes up the tale: "It must have been in late 1854 or early 1855 that I first saw the medal. Going home from school on a bright winter afternoon I met old John walking very erect... A dull white spot was clasped to the left breast of his coat. 'Mr Locke,' I said, staring with admiration, 'is that your glorious Waterloo medal?' 'You're a good little lad!' he stooped to let me see the noble 'pewter'. 'War's declared against Rooshia,' went on the old man, 'and now it's right to show it. The old

Below Seeing the funny side of war...the story-papers often printed lighthearted cartoons. This one appeared in *Chums* on 5 May 1895

He Didn't Count.

AMBULANCE CORPORAL (reporting): "Nothing in the last case, sorr; man was only in a fit. Brought him to with ammonia, and came back, sorr."
SURGEON CAPTAIN: "But you've got a case in the waggon there!"
AMBULANCE CORPORAL (carelessly): "Oh! yes, sorr. That's a fellow we ran over coming back."

Above The story "Captured by Dervishes" was described as "an incident of the Soudan War". This picture was in the issue of *Chums* dated 16 January 1895

Below In the story "Old Fire and Sword's Nephew", Corporal Cuthbert Delancey had a very strange experience. While in action he fell through a hole on the battlefield and found himself wandering through a dark underground cavern, fearing the worst. Eventually he spotted daylight, and emerged through another hole – straight into the middle of a fierce fight. Such was the enemy's surprise Corporal Delancey was able to save the day! The story appeared in *Chums* on 3 January 1895

regiment's sailed, and my only son is with the colours.' Then he took me by the hand and led me into the village post-office, where the post-master read aloud the news from the paper the veteran gave him. In those days there was no railway station within fifty miles of us. It had chanced that some fisherman brought old John a later paper than any previously received in the village. 'Ay, but the old Duke of Wellington is gone,' said he, shaking his white head; 'and it's curious to be fighting on the same side as another Boney.'

"All that winter and the next, all the long summer between, old John displayed his medal. When the report of Alma came, his remarks on the French failure to get into the fight were severe. 'What was they ever without Boney?' he would inquire. But a letter from his son after Inkerman changed all that. 'Half of us was killed, the rest of us clean tired with fighting,' wrote Corporal Locke. 'What with a bullet through the flesh of my right leg, and the fatigue of using the bayonet so long, I was like to drop. The Russians were coming on again as if there was no end to them, when strange drums came sounding in the mist behind us. With that we closed up, and faced half-round, thinking they had outflanked us and the day was gone, so there was nothing more to do but to die hard, like the sons of Waterloo men. You would be pleased to see the looks of what was left of the old regiment, father. Then all of a sudden a French column came up the rise out of the mist, roaring "Vive l'Empereur!" their drums beating the charge. We gave them room, for we were too dead tired to go first. On they went mad at the Russians, so that was the end of a hard morning's work. I was down, fainted with loss of blood, but I shall be fit for duty again. When I came to myself there was a Frenchman pouring brandy down my throat and talking his gibberish as kind as any Christian. Never a word will I say agin them red-legged French again.' 'Show me that man that would,' growled old John. 'It was never in them French to act cowardly. Didn't they beat all the world, except only us and the duke?'"

The story ends on a sad note, with old John's son killed in India. "There was a long silence in the post-office till old John spoke once more. 'Heaven be thanked for all its dealings with us. My son, Sergeant Locke, died well for England and duty.' Nervously fingering the treasure on his breast, the old soldier wheeled about and marched proudly straight down the middle of the village street to his lonely cabin. The villagers never saw him in life again. Next day he did not appear. All refrained from intruding on his mourning. But in the evening, when the minister heard of his parishioner's loss, he walked to old John's home. There, stretched upon his straw bed, he lay in his antique regimentals, stiffer than at attention, all his medals fastened below that of Waterloo above his quiet heart."

The wars in Africa were also a great source of material for the editor of *Chums*. "Captured by Dervishes" was "An Incident of the Soudan War" in which Troopers Anderson and Beaumont are sent out into the bush on a reconnaissance mission (issue dated 16 January 1895). "Only the night before there had been a desperate struggle between our brave lads in red and swarms of black, swarthy dervishes..." and the British were keen to wreak revenge. But the heroes are captured and believe they will "die like rats in the hand of these fanatics". But they make their escape and return to destroy the enemy camp – and earn VCs in the process.

Interestingly, while *Chums* held a very pro-Empire and patriotic stance, not all the stories involved the British. The story "For His Brother's Sake" (issue dated 19 September 1894) takes place against the backdrop of the Franco-Prussian War. While the story is prosaic in terms of action and plot (one brother is executed in place of his twin by the Prussians; revenge is sought and gained), it is notable in other ways. A Prussian victory in France in 1871 had led to the unification of Germany and a new European superpower was born.

For the first time, Germany was coming to be seen as the new foe, replacing Spain and France (the old enemy). As the turn of the century approached, more and more of the story-papers turned their attention to this new perceived threat. Editors started to look to the future for sources of material, and also at the present, rather than the past.

The Boer War and heightened tension across Europe were to change the nature of the boys' story-papers, providing them with an endless source of contemporary material for readers.

Above Competitons proved very popular with readers. This one was published in *The Boys' Friend* on 24 September 1895. Readers had to find the name of two British battles in the jumble of letters – can you?

"IN TIME OF WAR THE LOUDEST PATRIOTS
ARE THE GREATEST PROFITEERS"

August Bebel (1840-1913)

CHAPTER TWO

FROM THE BOER WAR TO THE BRINK

WHILE THE BOYS' STORY-PAPERS INCREASINGLY turned to military matters during the 1890s, the Boer War proved to be a watershed for Britain's publishers. Whereas the Napoleonic, Crimean and Indian wars had been rich sources for the story-writers, the Second Boer War (1899–1902) offered them a momentous and contemporary event with which they could enthral their readers.

The progress of the Boer War gripped the nation; details of the unfolding events in Southern Africa were pored over by anxious British patriots up and down the land. This interest was reflected in and fuelled by blanket coverage in the press; Alfred Harmsworth's *Daily Mail* saw its daily sales rise from half-a-million in 1899 to one million by the end of the Boer War. Harmsworth's publication appealed to the patriotic nature of his readers: he declared that the *Daily Mail* stood "for the power, the supremacy and the greatness of the British Empire".

Harmsworth's editors and writers followed their boss's lead, devoting huge amounts of space to stories of the heroism of British soldiers in the face of the enemy. **The Boys' Friend** is typical. Its story "When Britons Face the Foe", subtitled "Pat Murphy of the Dublins", which ran throughout 1899, is the tale of Pat Murphy and Larry O'Brien, both "Mounted Infantrymen of the Dublin Fusiliers". Their fictional adventures are played out

In the Battle of Tamai, Lieutenant Marling, of the 60th King's Royal Rifles, gallantly galloped back in the face of hundreds of the fierce enemy, and succeeded in safely moving to the lines a wounded soldier. For this he was deservedly awarded a V.C

POWERFUL NEW WAR STORY.   START IT NOW!

WHEN BRITONS FACE THE FOE;
OR,
PAT MURPHY OF THE DUBLINS.

Left *The Boys' Friend* featured many Boer War stories, including "When Britons Face The Foe". The image above the headline tells the story of Lieutenant Marling of The King's Royal Rifle Corps. On 13 March 1884, at Tamai in the Sudan, Marling risked his life to save a private of The Royal Sussex Regiment who had been shot. During the rescue the injured private fell off Marling's horse, so Marling carried the wounded man, under heavy fire, to safety, for which action he was awarded the Victoria Cross

Facing page *Pluck's* "Grand Double Number" of 9 December 1899

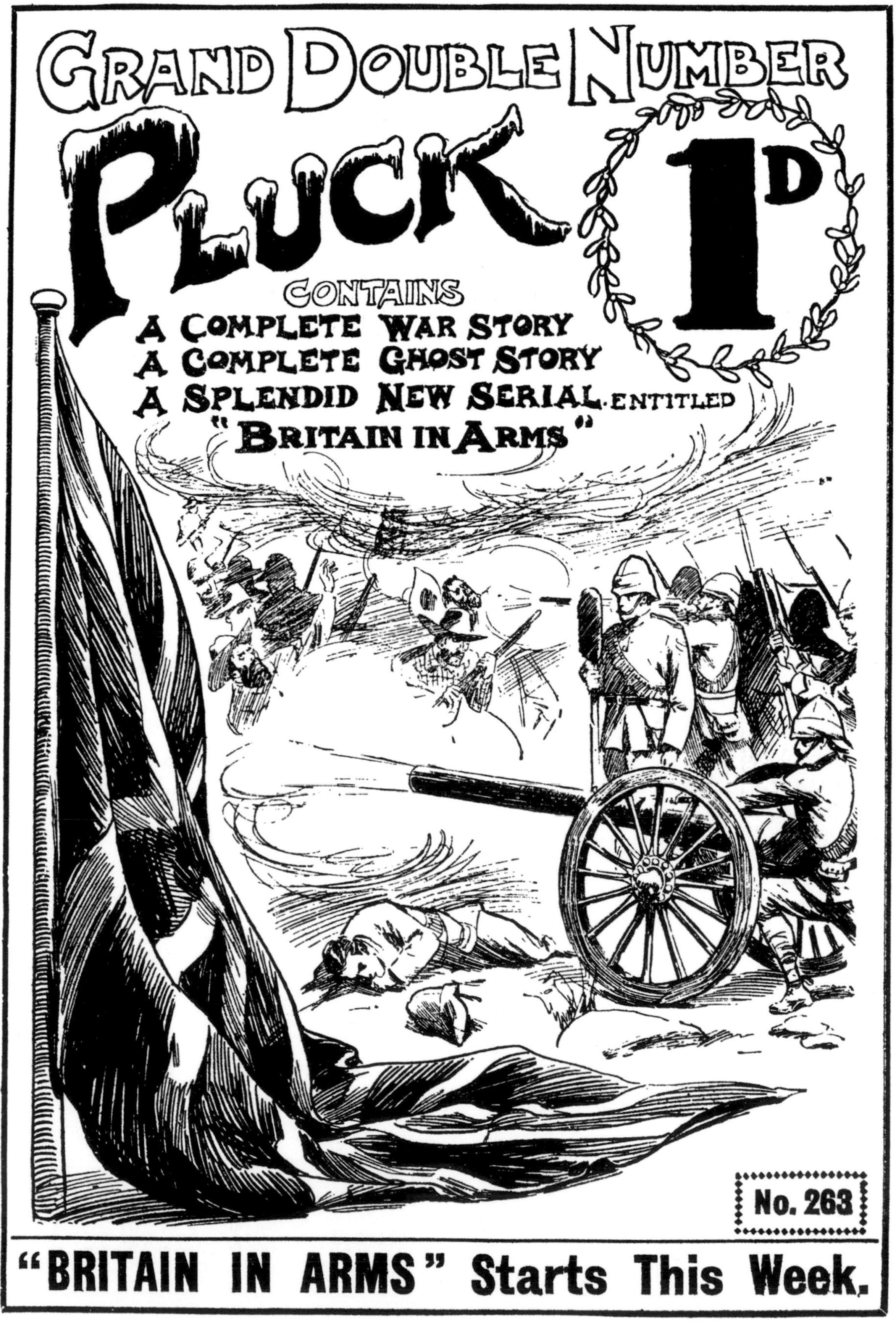
GRAND DOUBLE NUMBER
PLUCK
1d
CONTAINS
A COMPLETE WAR STORY
A COMPLETE GHOST STORY
A SPLENDID NEW SERIAL ENTITLED
"BRITAIN IN ARMS"
No. 263
"BRITAIN IN ARMS" Starts This Week.

against a backdrop of real events, giving them a relevance seldom seen in the story-papers previously. So we see the pals in action at the Battle of Glencoe, which took place on 20 October 1899. It was the first major engagement of the war, and preceded the retreat to Ladysmith by the British forces, and subsequent siege of that city by the Boers. A serialised story, each new episode opened with a summary of events so far "For the new reader". So by Chapter 21 we know that Pat "escapes this fierce contest almost unscathed, and is ordered to ride to Ladysmith with despatches for Sir George White". White, an Irishman and British military hero, achieved distinction in the Afghan War of 1878–80, where he was awarded the Victoria Cross for his bravery. White's reputation was sealed when he defended Ladysmith against a 118-day siege by the Boers (1899–1900). On his (fictional) journey to Ladysmith, Pat Murphy is taken prisoner but "escapes to take part in the memorable British victory at the Battle of Elandslaagte" (21 October 1899); he is, however, captured again and taken to General Joubert's tent (General Piet Joubert was Commandant-General of the South African Republic, from 1880 to 1900). Here Pat is astounded to see "Captain Theodore Loop from his own regiment basely betraying his own country, and giving information about the British forces". Pat vows to keep tabs on the trecherous Loop, and expose him.

Below left an all-action cover from *The Marvel*, dated 26 May 1900

Below right A *Pluck* story of the Boer War, dated 6 January 1900

Facing page *Boys of our Empire* often featured military heroes on its front page in its "Champion of the Week" feature

No. 46.—Vol. I.   SATURDAY, SEPTEMBER 7, 1901.   PRICE ONE PENNY.
[All Rights Reserved.]

Our Champion of the Week.

At Work.

MAJOR DRISCOLL,

"King of Scouts."

EVERY boy knows the dashing work done in war by scouts—how they make the most daring surveys of the enemy's outposts, how they venture up to the limits of an encampment, how they ride for dear life and their country's cause.

In the South African war we have had valiant service performed at the risk of their lives by the scouts under the command of gallant Major Driscoll, whose life is a romance in its deeds of courageous enterprise. If you get the chance you should read the book entitled "Driscoll, King of Scouts," in which Mr. A. G. Hales, the brilliant war correspondent, tells of some of the most remarkable episodes in the life of his hero, depicting them under the slight glamour of fiction. Major Driscoll is Irish by birth, but in his youth he went out to India, where he obtained plenty of experience in perfecting his natural gift for scouting. He has fine eyes, of that blue which always reminds me of the blue light you see when you look down some deep hole in a glacier. They will espy at a long distance objects on the horizon which would pass unnoticed by you or me.

A fine, tall man, the Major has a grand face, stern when he is "on business," but relaxing into a gentler expression when he is in social life. You can see at a glance that here is one who would stand no trifling, and also one who carries a kind heart. He is a man who is happiest when he is out of doors, roving on some dangerous adventure requiring constant care and insight. Like all scouts, he has a natural gift of remembering topography, so that he can lead the corps which is proud to be known as "Driscoll's Scouts" by the shortest and safest routes after very little acquintance with any neighbourhood. The Boers owe most of their success in the war to their extraordinary knowledge of the country.

Major Driscoll attaches great importance to this faculty of observation—a faculty which one of our greatest writers has called "one of our lasting pleasures." He trains his scouts to be accurate in estimating distance by sound as well as sight, and he expects them to learn all that can be learnt about their whereabouts in the shortest possible time. So brilliant a career as that of Major Driscoll will not end with the attainment of the D.S.O., which he gained some time ago as a recognition of his achievements. We shall hear of him reaching still higher honours—and he deserves to reach them.

Again he escapes, this time by pretending to be sympathetic to the Boer cause and agreeing to act as a spy for them. The story is, in effect, a contemporary account of the events of the war, and no punches are pulled when describing the action: "As they stood waiting for the truce party to advance, about thirty streaks of flame burst from the kopje, thirty puffs of white smoke, and then the deadly crack of rifle fire. Phut! phut! phut!. 'By Heaven they're firing on us!' gasped Loop. R-r-r-r-r! Phut! phut! phut! A perfect hail of bullets! 'By gad, I'm done for!' Down went a man next to Pat, and then another, and yet another. They were falling on all sides. 'Go on! For Heaven's sake, stop it!' yelled a man in mortal agony, as he plunged on his face with a bullet in his stomach – a dum-dum, which killed him before it got to his spine. Lucky it was for them that a great many of the shots went too high, and did nothing more than whistle over their heads. It was frightful! It was sheer murder! Seventeen men went down in as many seconds. Captain Loop's horse reared and plunged on his head with a bullet in its skull, and a moment afterwards Loop himself threw up his arms in agony and fell."

The Boys' Friend continued to produce Boer War stories for the duration of the conflict, interspersed with bulletins containing facts about the various battles, often accompanied by an illustration. Issue number 250 (dated 11 November 1899) announced a "Startling and Patriotic Development!" The Editor went on to announce: "At great cost and an immensity of trouble and anxiety, I have produced a great issue of **The Boys' Friend**. It is full of stirring tales and special information about the war sent straight from South Africa by our Special Correspondent at the front. It will be on yellow paper and cost 1d. Look out for next week's DOUBLE WAR NUMBER." In that issue it introduced a new story, "Briton v Boer",

Facing page *Boys of the Empire* pulled no punches when it came to describing the life – and death – of Tom, a troop horse. This appeared in the issue dated 16 March 1901

Below This story from *The Boys' Friend*, dated 5 March 1898, was called "The Russian Foe" and concerned an imaginary war in the Crimea in 1900. The scene here is of an aerial battle between our hero Jack Hinton and the Russian spy Subon – a fight Subon loses, along with his life

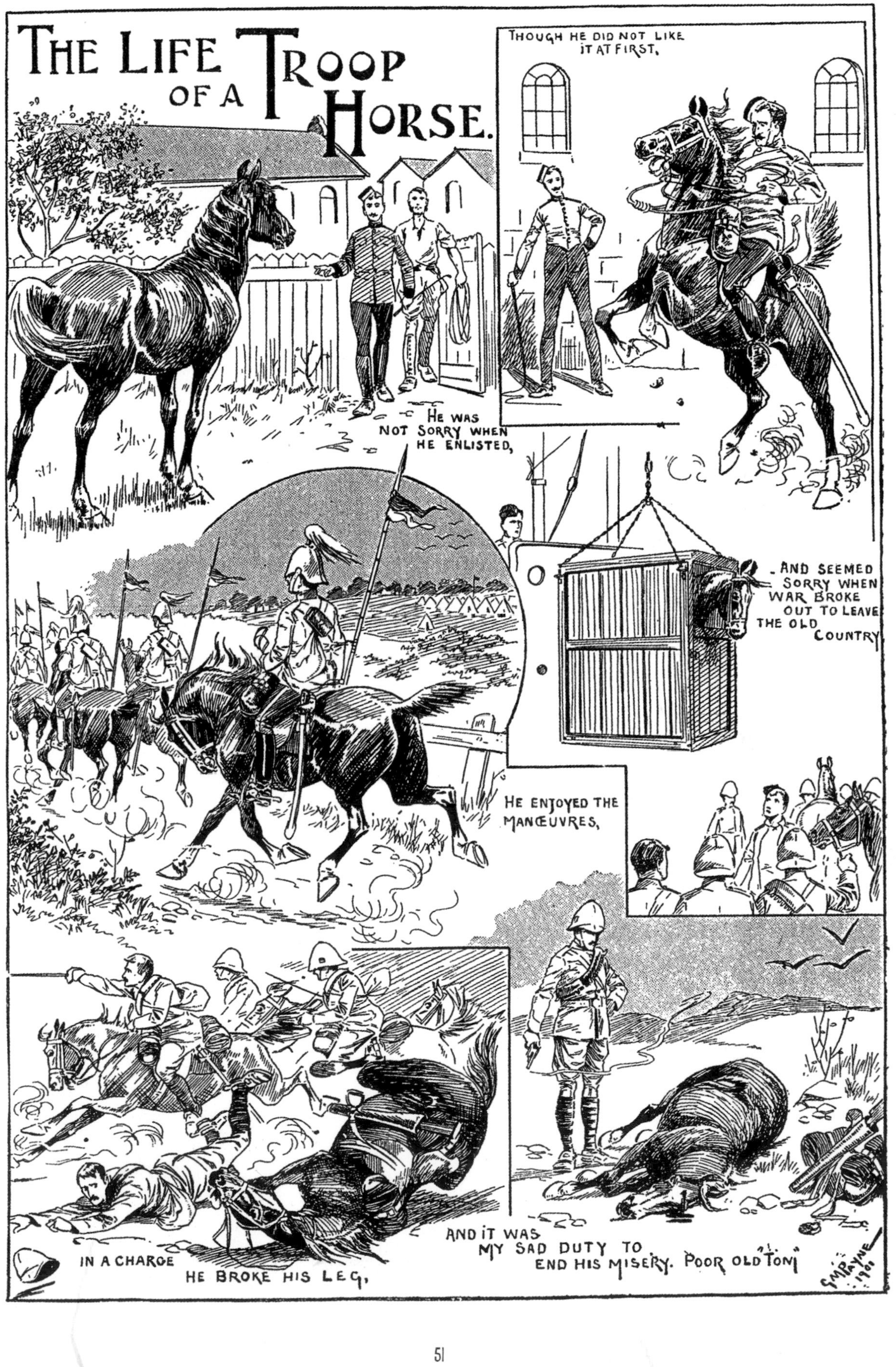
THE LIFE OF A TROOP HORSE.
THOUGH HE DID NOT LIKE IT AT FIRST,
HE WAS NOT SORRY WHEN HE ENLISTED,
...AND SEEMED SORRY WHEN WAR BROKE OUT TO LEAVE THE OLD COUNTRY
HE ENJOYED THE MANŒUVRES,
IN A CHARGE
HE BROKE HIS LEG,
AND IT WAS MY SAD DUTY TO END HIS MISERY. POOR OLD "TOM"
G.M. PAYNE 1901

a serialisation featuring more tales of action from the Boer War.

However, in truth, the early days of the war were disastrous for the British, with the prose of the boys' story-paper writers at odds with the dispatches from the war correspondents on the front line. In his 1902 book *The Great Boer War*, Arthur Conan Doyle, a regular contributor to **The Boy's Own Paper**, reflected on the Siege of Ladysmith: "Monday, October 30th, 1899, is not a date which can be looked back to with satisfaction by any Briton. In a scrambling and ill-managed action we had lost our detached left wing almost to a man, while our right had been hustled with no great loss but with some ignominy into Ladysmith. Our guns had been outshot, our infantry checked, and our cavalry paralysed. Eight hundred prisoners may seem no great loss when compared with a Sedan, or even with an Ulm; but such matters are comparative, and the force which laid down its arms at Nicholson's Nek is the largest British force which has surrendered since the days of our great grandfathers, when the egregious Duke of York commanded in Flanders."

P*luck*, also owned by Harmsworth's Amalgamated Press, followed a similar formula to **The Boys' Friend**. It too mixed fact and fiction, using real engagements from the Boer War as the settings for the adventures of its fictional heroes. Issue number 262 (dated 2 December 1899) was flagged a "Special War Number", with the main story being "With White

Above The Dublins storm a Boer position in the story "When Britons Face The Foe", from *The Boys' Friend*, dated 11 November 1899

Right A "Special War Number" of *Pluck*, dated 2 December 1899, on the death of British hero Colonel John James Scott-Chisholm. A cavalry officer, he died on 21 October 1899, leading a charge at the Battle of Elandslaagte

Facing page *Boys of the Empire*'s potted biography of Major General Hector Macdonald, a hero of the Afghan and Boer wars. This appeared in the issue dated 11 May 1901

Up they went, with grim, set faces, some with blood streaming down from wounds they did not notice.
"On, Dublins, on!" yelled the colonel, who was with the fighting line. "A commission for the man who's at the top first!"

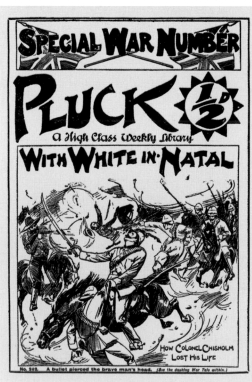

SPECIAL WAR NUMBER

PLUCK ½
A High Class Weekly Library
WITH WHITE IN NATAL

HOW COLONEL CHISHOLM LOST HIS LIFE

No. 262. A bullet pierced the brave man's head. (See the dashing War Tale within.)

FROM·PRIVATE·TO·GENERAL.

THE LIFE OF MAJOR GENERAL HECTOR MACDONALD.

P.B.E.L.

WHEN HIS MARTIAL SPIRIT FIRST ROSE.

FINDING THE DRAPERY RATHER DULL, HE'

LISTED IN THE GORDONS IN 1870.

SERGEANT MACDONALD   AFGHAN WAR 1880

LEUT MACDONALD FOUGHT WITH HIS FISTS AT MAJUBA HILL, 1881, & WAS TAKEN PRISONER.

LT. COL. MACDONALD ENTERING OMDURMAN AT THE HEAD OF HIS SOUDANESE BRIGADE, 1898.

MAJOR GEN. MACDONALD SOUTH AFRICA 1900.

G.M. PAYNE

in Natal". The "White" in question was Sir George White, the commander of forces in Natal referred to in "When Britons Faced the Foe" in *The Boys' Friend*. "With White in Natal" concerns the adventures of two young British bank clerks, Jack Dare and Phil Lawrence. The story assumes a huge amount of knowledge on the part of the reader, mentioning, without explanation, real-life incidents and characters such as the Jameson Raid (an ineffective attempt to overthrow President Paul Kruger of the Transvaal Republic in December 1895), John James Scott-Chisholme (who died leading a cavalry charge at the Battle of Elandslaagte) and Paul Kruger himself. Our heroes Jack and Phil make an enemy of an Afrikaaner farmer called Piet Vanjue. Says Jack: "He's one of those ungrateful beasts who, whilst partaking of British hospitality, and working and making money under the British flag, is scheming all the time to undermine the Queen's sovereignty. A typical Dutchman in every respect, he accepts everything but will give nothing away." The pair stumble upon some British boys being attacked. "Several great, hulking fellows, dressed in the typical costume of the Dutch, were ill-treating a number of English boys, whose ages could not have been more than fifteen or sixteen. Two of the youngsters were even tied to a tree close by, whilst a cowardly ruffian was flinging a horrible looking

Below A Boer War scene, in *Pluck*, dated 13 January 1900. The boys' story-papers at this time were heavily illustrated with similar pictures of British troops in action

Specially drawn for " Pluck "]   **GORDONS CHARGING A BOER POSITION.**   [*By Warwick Watts.*

sjambok [whip] around their little bodies. The other boys were undergoing various other cruel punishments at the hands of the Dutchmen." Our heroes rescue the smaller boys, despite being outnumbered by the Boers and, at that moment, vow to fight for Queen and country.

Pluck also carried a regular feature called "War Echoes – Interesting Items supplied Straight from the Seat of War". Snippets for the issue dated 9 December 1898 included: "The 5th Lancers crowned their success at Dundee Hill by taking a Transvaal flag, and another with an Orange emblem of the United South Africa that was to be under Dutch domination"; and "The hill which the British infantry stormed at Glencoe is 1,000ft high. The scaling of it by the Dublin Fusiliers and the King's Royal Rifles, in the face of the deadly

HOW OUR TOMMY FIGHTS.

Here is a stirring picture by our clever artist which graphically illustrates the dash, vivacity, and absolute fearlessness with which our Tommies go into action. They don't seem to fear it, but yell and even swear most lustily as they rush up to their enemy.

fire they encountered, may safely be put down as one of the most brilliant deeds in the records of the British Army". And more bizarrely: "Philip Kock, nephew of General Joubert, has said that the Boers suffered most from 'the soldiers in little clothes, half men, half women' – meaning the Gordon Highlanders – in the charge by the 5th Lancers."

So voracious was the appetite for Boer War literature that one publisher chanced his arm by producing a paper dedicated to the South African conflict. *The Boy's War News* ("Price One Halfpenny") was launched on Saturday, 2 December 1899, with a full-page illustration with the question: "How the bugler boy of the gallant Gordons won the victory at Elands Laagte. Will he get the Victoria Cross?"

Above Jack Hinton in action again, in the story "Britain in Arms", from *The Boys' Friend*

Below Publishers frequently used one story-paper to advertise another; here, *The Halfpenny Marvel*, dated 3 October 1903, promotes a forthcoming issue of re-vamped stable-mate, *The Union Jack*

The paper focused on the courageous deeds of the boys and young men serving in South Africa, eschewing fictional stories and concentrating on actual events. Its debut front cover was explained in an article headlined "British bugler boy saves the situation – and gains the Glorious victory of Elands Laagte". It read: "The Boer ruse of blowing the British 'Cease fire' on a bugle, mentioned by the '*Times*' correspondent was denied success, it seems,

A : WONDERFUL : NEW : DEPARTURE!

THE UNION JACK

OCTOBER 16TH. — PRICE **1**D.

NELSON said: "England expects that every man this day will do his duty."

The obvious duty of every British boy is to buy No. 1 of the great new story paper, published on FRIDAY, OCTOBER 16th.

A 3/6 BOYS' STORY BOOK FOR ONE PENNY!

The following unique list contains only a few of the contributors to the new "Union Jack": HERBERT MAXWELL, ALLAN BLAIR, HENRY ST. JOHN, MAXWELL SCOTT, PAUL HERRING, SIDNEY DREW, ALEC G. PEARSON, C. E. PEARCE, CECIL HAYTER, A. S. HARDY, T. C. BRIDGES, REGINALD WRAY, JOHN STANTON, and CLARKE HOOK.

32 pages, enclosed in a handsome plate-paper cover, price 1d. Order Early.

mainly through the audacity of a British boy-bugler. Mr Pearse, the veteran war correspondent writes in the *Daily News*: 'The Devons had gained the crest on its steepest side and the Gordons, with Manchesters and Light Horse, were sweeping over its nearer ridge, when, to our astonishment, we heard the 'Cease fire' and 'Retire' sounded by buglers. It was difficult to account for them, but not so now, when we know that the Boers had learned our bugle calls. In obedience to that sound the Gordons were beginning to fall back when their Boy-bugler, saying, 'Retire be hanged!' rushed forward and blew a hasty charge. Whereupon ranks closed up, and the victory of Elands Laagte was won. Boys, take your hats off to this hero. Three cheers for him."

A nother article, headlined "Gallant captured war correspondent", read: "Mr Churchill, one of the *Morning Post* correspondents in Natal, is not the first correspondent captured during this war. A correspondent of the *Standard* was taken prisoner at the Battle of Elandslaagte, but subsequently rescued. Mr Dunn, the representative of the *Central News*, was made captive when Dundee was occupied and set at liberty by the Boer commander. Mr Churchill, however, enjoys the distinction of being the first newspaperman to reach Pretoria since war was declared, though it is in the capacity of a prisoner." Winston Churchill, aged just 25, was not a captive for long – he escaped within two months. Churchill's daring made him a hero in Britain, and he rejoined General Buller's army on its march to relieve the British at the Siege of Ladysmith. While continuing as a war correspondent, he also gained a commission in the South African Light Horse regiment, and was among the first British troops into Ladysmith.

Issue number two (9 December 1899) carried more stories and snippets from the war, and also introduced the "Transvaal War Game", in which readers had to guess the positions of British divisions the following week and plot them on a map provided. The winner was to receive "an income of two shillings and sixpence per

Above A paean to the fallen British heroes, in *Boys of Our Empire*, 14 December 1901

Above A scene from the *Boys of Our Empire* story "The Drummer Boy" – a tale of fighting the Dervishes in Sudan, issue dated 14 December 1901

Facing page While most story-papers focused on the events of the Boer War, *The Boy's Own Paper* ran this tale of Empire-building in India

Below Hand-to-hand combat in the Boer War, as seen in *Pluck*, 13 January 1900

week for 13 weeks". Unfortunately, there was to be no winner – ***The Boys' War News*** ceased publication after just two issues.

While editors and writers were exploiting the public's insatiable appetite for the Boer War, at ***The Boy's Own Paper*** war stories tended to look to the past rather than the present. Its issue dated 11 November 1899 – a month after the start of the Siege of Kimberley – had a cover story called "A Bold Climber, or For an Empire".

It concerned British and French rivalry for possession of Fort St David, which was located near the town of Cuddalore, south of Madras, on the Coromandel Coast of India. Robert Clive served as the governor there, but in 1758 the French captured it. In 1785 it finally passed back into British possession.

"A Bold Climber" centred on a guerrilla attack on the fort, and described the tension and agonies of the conflict: "…for the Eastern warfare of that age knew no mercy, and, if the attack failed, a few hours more might see their last refuge on fire over their heads, and themselves butchered or dragged away to be sold as slaves, or to rot in foul or stifling dungeons, as was the fate of many an English captive…"

Ensign Clive led his troops to success, a true British hero: "But before the young leader's indomitable spirit all obstacles appeared to melt away. Foremost in that weary struggle, from first to last – encouraging, helping, cheering, commanding – he seemed to pour all the fire of his own unquenchable energy into every man who followed him. ''E's the sort 'o chap for my money, 'e is,' whispered one of the men to his mate. 'Take 'e's share of the rough work, 'e does.'"

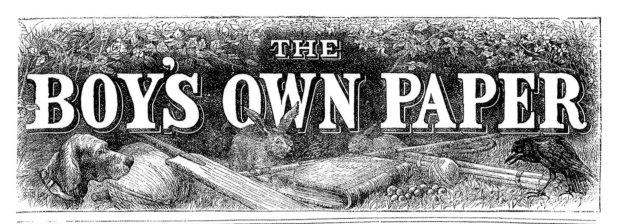

THE BOY'S OWN PAPER

No. 1087.—Vol. XXII.
[NO. 6 OF NEW VOL.]

SATURDAY, NOVEMBER 11, 1899.

Price One Penny.
[ALL RIGHTS RESERVED.]

A BOLD CLIMBER;

OR,

FOR AN EMPIRE.

BY DAVID KER,

Author of "Hunted Through the Frozen Ocean," "The Finder of the White Elephant," etc.

(Illustrated by ALFRED PEARSE.)

Clive coming to the Rescue of the English.

All stirring stuff, but strangely outdated – after all, the action had taken place more than a century earlier. *The Boy's Own Paper*'s other war stories also harked back to previous wars – Napoleonic, Sudan, and even the English Civil War.

With a roar like an avalanche, the flame sped through the giant balloon from end to end. Blazing fires leaped a hundred feet into the sky. The Scourge's mighty bulk withered at their breath, and the car fled downwards amid the shrieks of its panic-stricken crew.

Above Action from the story "The Scourge of the Skies", in *The Boys' Herald* issue dated 6 February 1909

Facing page Britain beware! More adventures of the "Death-or-Glory Boys" in the pages of *Pluck*, in the issue dated 9 December 1899

But while *The Boy's Own Paper* tended to look backwards, a new phenomenon was emerging within the pages of the boys' story-papers. It had its roots in a late 19th-century fiction genre, popularly called "invasion literature". The genre was kick-started by George Chesney's serialised story "The Battle of Dorking: Reminiscences of a Volunteer". Published in 1871, the year Germany was unified after Prussia's victory against the French and its annexation of Alsace-Lorraine, the story concerned an imaginary invasion of Britain by the new Teutonic superpower in Europe. The Prussian army had battered the French into submission in 1870–71, reaching Paris, and suddenly, in the mind of the British patriot, matters were confused. The old enemy – the French – were supplanted by the new threat, Germany, and the "Battle of Dorking" tapped into the groundswell of public paranoia. The story, which first appeared in *Blackwoods Magazine*, was wildly popular and spawned a host of imitators (H.G. Wells is said to have been influenced by it when he penned *The War of the Worlds* in 1898).

Another hugely influential novel of the genre was *The Great War in England in 1897*, written by William Le Queux and published in 1894. It depicts the invasion of Britain by the French with Russians, with the invading forces reaching London. Unlike in "The Battle of Dorking", where the British are defeated, in Le Queux's story the British are victorious – aided by Germany. Interestingly, the alliances the book predicted were the reverse of those of the actual First World War. But in 1894 the scenario of a British alliance with Germany was not so far-fetched – in reality Britain and France were hostile to one another, especially concerning territories in East Africa. This was brought to a head with the "Fashoda Incident". Both France and Britain laid claim to the strategically important town of Fashoda, in Egyptian Sudan; both countries felt their standing within the African continent was at stake. In the event, France backed down, but for a time in September 1898 the two great powers were on the brink of war.

Britain in Arms!

A GRAND MILITARY ROMANCE.

By HAMILTON EDWARDS.

The story of how Great Britain fought the world in 1902, showing what Britons can do for their Queen and country in the hour of need. A tale of loyalty and devotion to the Old Flag.

How the Frenchman and the Russian Declared War against Britain, and how we took the News—How Jack Hinton and Bob FitzGerald, of the "Death-or-Glory" Boys, got their Orders to March.

War !

"Jack, d'ye see this ? It's come at last !" cried Bob FitzGerald, an Irish trooper in the 17th Lancers, to his chum, Jack Hinton.

"This" was a copy of the London "Daily Mail," which had just arrived in Aldershot by an early train that morning. Bob FitzGerald pointed to a great staring column in the paper :

WAR !
THE DREAD BLOW HAS FALLEN !
FRANCE AND RUSSIA HAVE DECLARED WAR AGAINST GREAT BRITAIN.

LATEST TELEGRAMS.

Paris, June 17.—The Russian Ambassador had a long consultation with the French War Minister this evening, at which the German Ambassador was present. There is reason to believe that the topic was one in which Great Britain was keenly interested, being no less than that of a declaration of war.

LATER.

The British Ambassador has left Paris. War has been declared.

And then followed a number of telegrams from the paper's various correspondents in Berlin, St. Petersburg, and Vienna.

Jack Hinton was busy perusing the details of the account of how the Russians were to join the French, and how a huge army of 150,000 French and Russian troops was to be landed on the shores of England, somewhere between Dover and Brighton ; whilst another army, composed of Russian troops, was to land and seize Edinburgh.

Around Bob and Jack were grouped a hundred stalwart troopers, all listening in silence to the report as Jack Hinton read aloud the dread news. On their faces, as they realised the fearful nature of the information, came a stern, set look, which suggested a bad time for their foes when they met the Death-or-Glory Boys.

"Hark ! D'ye hear it, boys ? It's the 'Assembly'—tumble out sharp !" cried Bob FitzGerald, as the clear notes of a bugle called the men to parade.

In a few minutes the barrack square was filled with nearly four hundred men of the regiment standing at attention, awaiting the coming of the officers. Presently a group, headed by Major Fortescue, stood before the expectant men. It was a solemn moment. The voice of the major rang out clearly in the summer air ; every eye was fixed on him, every man listened intently.

"Men of the 17th Lancers, I have bad news to tell you. You have doubtless heard something of what I am about to speak. France and Russia have declared war against Great Britain. But this is not all. At this very moment the French and Russian forces are steaming towards our shores ; before night we may be fighting for our homes—nay, for our lives.

"My men, in this, the hour of her trial, your country relies upon you. Now has the time arrived for Britain's defenders to prove that they still can fight and win for the honour of their country, for the love of their Queen (God bless her !), for their sisters and wives, for the safety of their homes. The evil hour has come ; will you risk the result ?

"It will be no child's play, my men, for the enemy are at our doors. Long have they been preparing for this dastard stroke ; but, thank Heaven, Great Britain, too, has not been asleep ! Slowly, but surely, without unnecessary noise, has she been laying her plans for this unwelcome hour ; and now that it has come, officers and men, citizen soldiers and civilians, all are ready—ready, ay, and eager—to fight for their own ! And fight we will, my men. Under the grand old Flag we'll show these foreigners that the British lion still has teeth, and that Britons either conquer or die !

"Remember you are Britons ! Remember that you are fighting for your Queen, for your homes, for the old country, and for the grand old Flag of freedom ! Stick to the traditions of the regiment, boys, and fight until we die !

"Now, three cheers for her Majesty, and a fourth for the Death-or-Glory Boys !"

"Hip, hip, hurrah !"

Again and again, and yet once more, the lusty shouts resounded, and—happy, inspiriting sound !—from every quarter came round upon round of hearty cheering.

Surely Britain would do well if her men entered on the campaign under such emotions as these !

The excitement was subdued ; the men were busily preparing for the field. The 17th had received orders to prepare for active service, and await conveyance by train from Aldershot to Lewes, where the men would form part of the Army of Defence and encamp.

"She's rammed her, Jack ! Look at the Frenchman sinking !" cried the Irishman.

ANOTHER LONG instalment of the above strikingly new Serial in next week's number. Price ½d.

The editors and writers of the boys' story-papers were far too switched-on to miss the opportunity to jump on to the "invasion literature" bandwagon, and tackled the genre with aplomb.

The Boy's Friend story "The Russian Foe, or Jack Hinton's Adventures in the Crimean War of 1900" started on 20 November 1897 and concluded on 30 July 1898. Written by Hamilton Edwards, it concerned the eponymous hero's adventures with the 17th Lancers, the "Death or Glory Boys", with his pal Bob Fitzgerald. Jack's nemesis is the Russian Gortchoff, and their personal battles are set against a British invasion of Russia. Gortchoff eventually comes to a sticky end, while Jack gets promoted to major, winning the Victoria Cross in the process. The tale ends with the Russians' surrender – and the victors claiming £1 billion in reparations!

P*luck* was also among the first of the story-papers to feature 'invasion' stories. In the 1899 serial "Britain in Arms", a joint Russian/French force invades Britain, in 1902. Like *The Boy's Friend* story "The Russian Foe", it was also written by Hamilton Edwards. The invaders are repelled – thanks to the efforts of our old friends, the indefatigable Jack Hinton and Bob Fitzgerald – and Britain launches a counter-invasion of French soil. In the issue dated 9 December 1899, the defeated French lay down their arms and we discover "How the Russians were beaten at Edinburgh". This was in no small measure

This striking picture illustrates three scenes from the

GREAT WAR STORY

commencing in the issue of

"THE BOYS' FRIEND"

NOW ON SALE.

Get a copy and begin reading it now !

The Peril to Come!

SPLENDID NEW WAR SERIAL STARTS THIS WEEK!

The Dreadnought 1^D

Vol. 2. No. 24   WEEK ENDING NOVEMBER 9, 1912.   ONE PENNY.

THE WAR IN THE CLOUDS.

PREPARING FOR THE STRUGGLE!

The Heights of Hampstead were covered with struggling teams; guns were dragged upwards, their noses pointing skywards in preparation for the approach of the enemy.

(See the Great Aerial Invasion Story which starts this Week.)

due to the efforts of the "British Flying Squadron" – some 19 years before the formation of the Royal Air Force, which happened in 1918 with the amalgamation of the Royal Flying Corps and the Royal Naval Air Service.

In the story, readers learned how: "The British Flying Squadron were successful in reaching Edinburgh before the Russian fleet appeared in sight, and lay calm watchful for the appearance of the enemy. Nor had they long to wait. But a few hours passed, though they were of horrible suspense to the inhabitants of the great Scottish

THE MESSAGE ON THE WINDOW.

Dick Halliday scarcely heard the German General's ominous farewell, for though apparently looking immediately in front of him, his eyes were fixed upon a shot-splintered window in a house oppo ite, in the broken panes of which was quivering almost imperceptible rays of light in the long and short flashes of the Morse code.

Above Britain's ill-preparedness for a war to come was a major theme in the boys' story-papers, echoed here in the story "While Britain Slept", which appeared in *The Boys' Herald* throughout 1911

Facing page The French are coming! *The Boys' Friend* of 31 March 1900 carried the story "Britain Invaded!"

Below Speculation in *The Boy's War News*, December 1899

town, when the enemy hove in sight – a magnificent fleet of some twelve warships, and about a dozen troopships. Directly they came within gun range, the British fleet moved out to meet them, and a fierce and bloodthirsty encounter ensued. The carnage was frightful, and once again British pluck repeated the victory of the great battle of Newhaven, and the enemy were put to utter rout, and driven back to the sea in wild confusion. The British loss was heavy – indeed, in proportion, far heavier than the damage inflicted in the South; and many a British home was left to mourn the loss of husbands and brothers, who gave up their lives fighting in defence of their country. The frenzied delight with which this news was received throughout the country was overwhelming. Huge celebrations were held everywhere. Bonfires were lighted,

Will the Kaiser be King of England

SPECIAL NUMBER! War Picture Puzzles.

£26 FOR SOLVING 24 WAR PICTURE PUZZLES.

THE BOYS' FRIEND

1^{D.}

½

No. 270. Vol. VII.]　　ONE HALFPENNY.　　[EVERY WEDNESDAY.

Bombardment of London. The French at our doors.

Indeed, then would come our great hour of woe, when French shot and shell fell in a horrible rain along the fair streets of the Empire's City. One shell, for instance, would strike the Clock Tower of the Houses of Parliament, flinging it down in a hall of destruction. (See "Britain Invaded.")

THE INVASION THAT FAILED.

The Story of Germany's Invasion of Great Britain in 1910.

By AMBROSE EARLE.

Above Don Spriggs, aged 16, was the saviour of the nation in the story "The Invasion That Failed", which appeared in *The Boys' Herald* on 1 May 1909. The story was set just one year in the future

Below *The Boy's War News* is less than polite about Britain's Teutonic neighbours, December 1899

and thanksgiving services were held in all the churches throughout the realm. Britain was indeed proud of her sailor defenders. The brave bluejackets had proved that the spirits of the men who fought under Nelson still lived in the bluejackets of today. Thus had a crushing defeat been inflicted upon the combined enemies, and Britain was still empress of the seas. Although her fleet was badly battered she had still the powerful Mediterranean Squadron at her call with ships in all other parts of the world. And now began the serious preparations for the invasion of France. It was proposed to send an army of one hundred thousand men to France, divided into two sections. One army of forty thousand men were to land in Antwerp, which by private treaty had become a British port... while the second army, under Lord Roberts, was to land at Havre and march on Paris."

The ubiquitous Jack Hinton and Bob Fitzgerald appear in another Hamilton Edwards story in **The Boy's Friend**, "The Invasion of England" (31 March 1900). The author sets the scene under the heading "Invasion No Wild Dream": "It is no wild dream of the imaginative novelist, the threat of an invasion of our beloved shore. It is stolidly discussed in French and Russian – ay, and German – newspapers... The Frenchman and the educated Russian talk of such a thing as coolly as we talk about sending out a punitive expedition to the Soudan or up into the hills of North-Western India." Edwards cranks up the rhetoric: "In the secret offices of the French and Russian Armies there lie piles of papers, plans, maps, and much reliable intelligence concerning the state of the military and naval defences of these islands. Every weak point in our defence is marked and specially emphasised; every strong point is debated, and the best

> ... not satisfy
> to inquire again, which
> officer did, recording, "Apr...
> still dead."
>
> **Rats.**
>
> LIKE many other nasty things, rats come from Germany. The queer part of it is they came with the first of our Hanoverian Georges — about 180 years ago.
>
> Not content with conquering Britain, the big brown rat of Hanover crossed the Atlantic, and is at present hard at work clearing the United States of its native rats. It has got down into the West Indies as well, and causes no end of trouble by climbing into the cocoanut trees and eating the nuts.—*Answers.*

way of destroying it carefully indicated." In the pages of **The Halfpenny Marvel**, a similar tale was unfolding. In the story "London in Danger!" (26 May 1900), Londoners are panic stricken as the Chinese invade – in a fleet of air balloons!

During the rest of the decade there was no let up in the public's appetite for "invasion literature" – in fact, the genre grew in popularity, boosted by Erskine Childers' seminal novel, *The Riddle of the Sands*. Hugely popular right across the empire, the story centres on the discovery of a huge German fleet of warships, hidden off the coast of Heligoland in the Fresian Islands, for Germany is preparing to invade England. It was written in 1903, and the level of paranoia was cranked up in William Le Queux's *The Invasion of 1910* (written 1906),

Below Unlike many of the boys' story-papers, *The Boys' Friend* has no doubts about the supremacy of British sea power, 10 February 1900

JACK TAR'S DOUBLE NUMBER

NEXT WEEK'S "BOYS' FRIEND WILL BE EIGHT PAGES, GREEN PAPER. ½d. ½d.

THE BOYS' FRIEND 1D.

No. 263. Vol. VII.]   ONE PENNY.   [EVERY WEDNESDAY.

WHAT WILL HAPPEN IN THE NEXT GREAT NAVAL WAR.

Here is seen the sinking of a French man-o'-war, battered by the guns of the British Navy. There can be no question that our Navy is more than the equal of any two of the great European Powers. Long may it be so!

which heightened British fears with its anti-German sentiment. While considered an invasion fantasy, Childers' novel did, in fact, reflect what was happening in Germany. In his *A History of England*, written just after the end of the Great War, Cyril Robinson concluded that, pre-1914: "Germany, beyond a doubt, was strong for war. Her army since its celebrated triumph over France was the finest in the world; and it did not stand alone. For side by side with it the Kaiser had built up a formidable fleet... it was clear the growing German Navy was a challenge to our own." Robinson added: "Heligoland, which we had captured in the Napoleonic wars, but restored to its natural owners by Lord Salisbury in 1890, was rapidly converted into a fort of monstrous strength."

As ever, the story-papers were quick to catch the zeitgeist. *The Boys' Herald* story "The Scourge of the Skies" (2 January 1909) had a similar plot to *The Riddle of the Sands*, except the perceived threat was from German zeppelins rather than warships. *The Boys' Herald* quickly followed up with "The Invasion That Failed' (issue dated 1 May 1909), a story in which the Germans launch their attack on East Anglia by air and sea. The hero of the tale is 16-year-old Don Spriggs, a farmer's son who inadvertently stumbles across the enemy's forward landings on a trip to the beach with his brother Harry, 13. We are told that "they were neither of them bad boys, nor were they in any way different from the great majority of hardy British lads. Daring and high-spirited may be, but frank and fearless." Their father warns of the danger, saying: "There's been a power of strangers about these parts lately", to which Harry asks his brother: "Does he mean those foreign looking chaps, who dodge away as soon as they catch sight of you?" Don replies: "Early

A DESPERATE CHARGE BY
THE 16th LANCERS!

The SCOURGE of the SKIES.

By Andrew Gray.

A THRILLING WAR STORY,

last year, everybody was talking about the possible invasion of Great Britain. There were stories in the papers. There was even a play about it in a big London theatre."

Above The Boys' Herald, issue dated 2 January 1909

The Germans catch the boys spying on them, beat them and tie them up. They manage to escape as the invasion begins, and it is a race against time to warn their community as the German march begins. The story pulls no punches. The Germans arrive at the boys' farm, and as the lads escape to raise the alarm, the invaders shoot their father and imprison their sister and mother. Don and Harry escape on their bicycles, with Don exclaiming: "It's not our own skins we've got to bother about; we've got to warn the nation!" Our hero does just that, and Don is reunited with his mother and sister as the Germans are repelled. But his father and brother are dead, and he asks: "Tell me about the Navy. What has become of the North Sea Fleet? Why have they allowed the Germans to invade us?" The question taps into the fear that Britain was ill-prepared should she have to go to war with any of her European neighbours. The theme is re-visited in countless other tales, such as **The Boys' Herald**'s 1911 story "While Britain Slept". The reader is told that "Britain was doomed!... The Germans, taking advantage of the fact that a rebellion – even worse than the one in '57 – had broken out in India, despatched an army of a million to the shores of Old England." The heroes of the tale were, once again, the boys and young men of England, with the leader of the Otter Patrol of Boy Scouts, Dick Halliday, at the forefront. But for many Boy Scouts in Britain in 1911, an unimaginable fate awaited; the fear of war – if not invasion – was about to be realised.

"IN SUCH A WORLD OF CONFLICT, A WORLD OF VICTIMS AND EXECUTIONERS, IT IS THE JOB OF THINKING PEOPLE NOT TO BE ON THE SIDE OF THE EXECUTIONERS"

Albert Camus (1913-1960)

CHAPTER THREE
THE WAR TO END ALL WARS...

THE START OF THE GREAT WAR, in August 1914, also signalled the start of a new publishing boom. The Boer War had shown the proprietors and editors of newspapers and boys' story-papers how eager the British public was to keep up-to-date with events on the battlefield. In that momentous summer of 1914 publishers were quick off the mark; a huge number of new titles were launched within weeks of the outbreak of the war. They included *The Penny War Weekly*, *The War Illustrated*, *The Illustrated War News*, *The Graphic War Budget*, *British Heroes of the War & Their Gallant Deeds Illustrated*, *The War Pictorial*, *The War Budget*, *The Great War*, *The Great War in Europe*, *The War of the Nations*, *The Times' History of the War*, *Nelson's Portfolio of War Pictures* and *T.P.s Journal of Great Deeds of the Great War* – to name but a few.

The Penny War Weekly hit the streets on 5 September 1914, a little over a month after Britain declared war on Germany. At 24 pages, it was packed with facts, figures and stories about the war, highlighting both the bravery of our boys and the treachery of the foe. Unashamedly patriotic, it was the sister publication to the already successful *The War Illustrated*, which cost two-pence; both were published by Amalgamated Press. In the launch issue, the editor of *The Penny War Weekly* set out the paper's aims: "It will seek to gather together those invaluable 'human documents' which in other great wars have been supplied by private letters of

Left *Pluck* was quick to produce Great War stories – this issue is dated 5 September 1914, just over a month after the outbreak of the war

Facing page A dramatic cover from *The Boy's Own Annual*, dated 1914/15

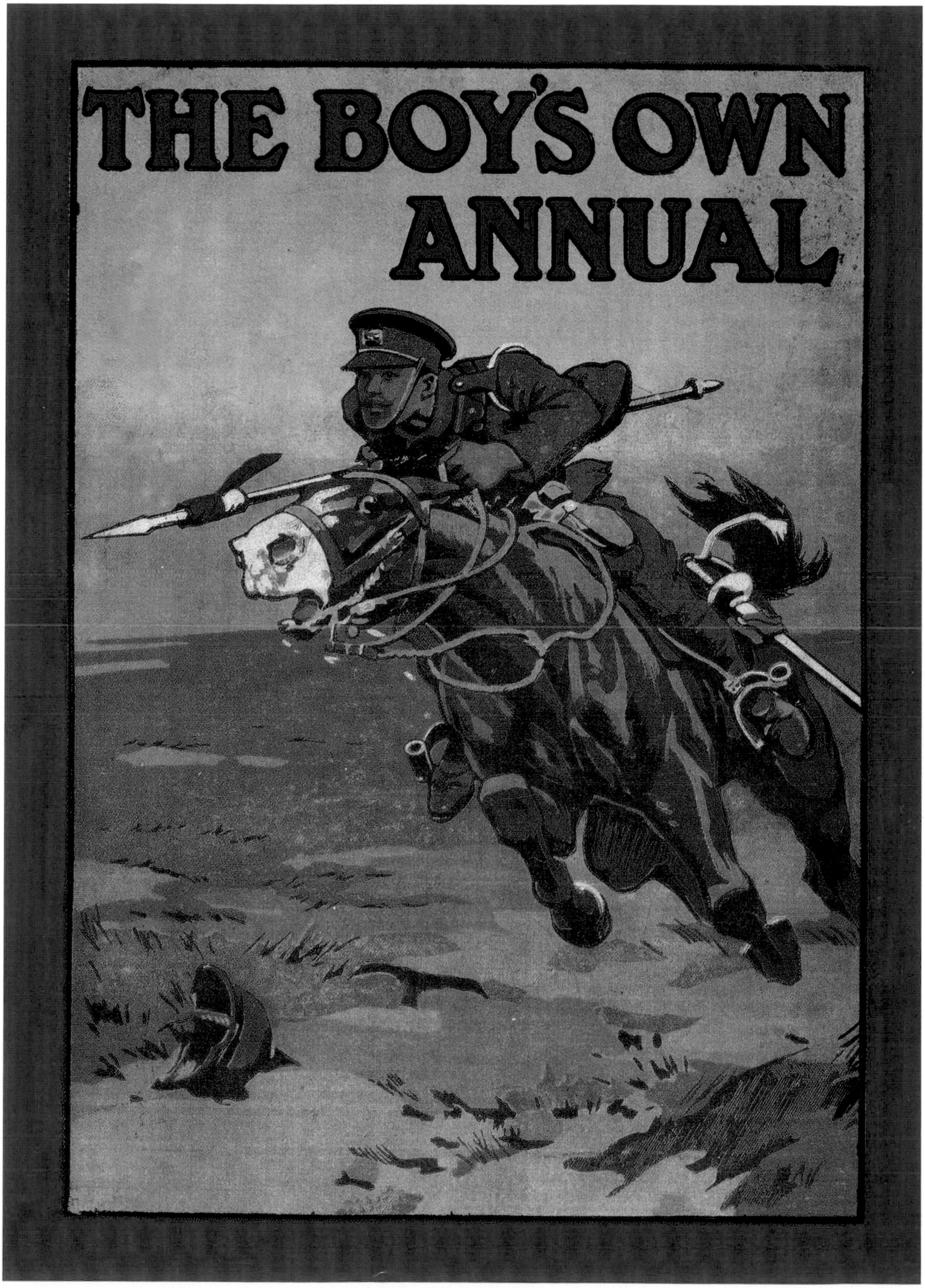
THE BOY'S OWN
ANNUAL

The Penny War Weekly, September 19th, 1914.

No. 3.

PACKED WITH VIVID WAR PICTURES

THE PENNY WAR WEEKLY

"WOMEN AND CHILDREN FIRST"—GERMAN VERSION.

At Aerschot, in Belgium, women with babies in their arms and little children clinging to their skirts were seen in front of the German forces, pushed forward to act as a shield for their advance guard.

SECTIONAL PLAN OF A GERMAN TRENCH.

A, Shelter.   B, Drain for water outlet.

the men on active service. It will devote special attention to illustrating the events at home, episodes of interest in the raising and training of our great new army of freedom, while, at the same time, no salient features of the War operation abroad will be omitted from its pages. It will also seek to interest the young people by stating in the plainest language what happens from week to week, and thus fulfil a useful educational function, as it is vital to the future of the British Empire that its young citizens should grow up with their minds vividly impressed by the ghastly truths of this awful time..."

The Penny War Weekly combined facts and stories about the war with fictional stories for the younger reader. In its "Items of Interest About the War" column readers are told that "The men of the British Expeditionary Force are supplied with a half-sheet typewritten French-English dictionary"; that "The Prince of Wales is now a Second-Lieutenant in the 1st Grenadier Guards"; and that "The British Columbia Fruit Growers' Association will give 100,000 barrels of apples to the British troops in the field." But the paper's real strength was its illustrations; both the covers and many inside pages were filled with graphic representations of events on the battlefield. Stories of German atrocities were particularly prevalent in the early days of the war; they stirred up a hatred of the enemy and fuelled the passion to serve. German war crimes in occupied Belgium – dubbed "The Rape of Belgium" – were strongly featured. On the cover of issue 3 (dated 19 September 1914) was an illustration of brutal German soldiers forcing Belgian women and children to march in front of their lines. The cover reads: "'Women and Children First' – German Version. At Aerschot, in Belgium, women with babies in their arms and little children clinging to their skirts were seen in front of the German forces, pushed forward to act as a shield for their advance guard." Indeed, on 19 August 1914, German troops entered Aerschot, encountering no

Facing page *The Penny War Weekly*'s depiction of 'the violation of Belgium', in the issue dated 19 September 1914

Above left Factual snippets about trench warfare were regular features in the boys' story-papers. This one about a German trench appeared in *The Boy's Own Annual 1914-15*

Below *The New York Times* reported, in March 1915, that the "violation of Belgium" was a decisive factor in David Lloyd George's decision to support the war. He became Prime Minister in 1916

LLOYD GEORGE NEARLY QUIT

Violation of Belgium Convinced Him of England's Duty to Go to War.

Special Cable to THE NEW YORK TIMES.

LONDON, March 9.—The Yorkshire Post today says that Premier Asquith was evidently disinclined yesterday to discuss the statement of Chancellor of the Exchequer Lloyd George that, but for the violation of the neutrality of Belgium, he would not have been a party to the war.

"The Prime Minister," says The Post, "can hardly at this stage be expected to reveal the differences that existed in the Cabinet at the end of July, but it is generally believed in political circles that at least seven members of the Government were prepared to resign and start an anti-war agitation until Germany began to send her armies through Belgium.

"That made all the difference. It was not only a case of our pledged word, but of high British policy, and every speaker who has addressed a public meeting since the war began agrees that it is the violation of Belgium that most aroused the British people to the necessity of taking up arms."

TO ALL MY READERS.

❮ Have you any relative or friend serving his King and Country either in the Royal Navy, the Regular Army or the Territorials?

If so, send me his photograph so that I may reproduce it on my

SPECIAL PAGE FOR PATRIOTS.

Address all photographs to The Editor, "Dreadnought & War Pictorial," The Fleetway House, Farringdon Street, London, E.C.

THE EDITOR.

Above The *Dreadnought & War Pictorial* editor wants his readers to get involved. The appeal was published on 26 September 1914

Below right Fighting in Belgium in the pages of *Dreadnought and War Pictorial* dated 10 October 1914

Facing page A call to arms, in *The Boy's Own Annual*, 1914

resistance from the Belgian army. A contemporary Belgian Government Commission report said: "...the Germans took every man who was inside of Aerschot; they led them, fifty at a time, some distance from the town, grouped them in lines of four men, and, making them run ahead of them, shot them and killed them afterwards with their bayonets. More than fifty men were thus found massacred."

The violation of Belgium continued throughout the summer, and gave the Allied forces a massive propaganda boost. The Germans justified their actions by claiming Belgian guerrilla fighters, or franc-tireurs, were attacking their troops, and their reprisals against civilians were the only way of tackling the problem. Other targets included Andenne (211 dead), Tamines (383 dead) and Dinant (665 dead). On 25 August, the city of Leuven was attacked; the University's library of 230,000 books was destroyed, 248 residents were killed and the entire population of 42,000 people was forced to evacuate.

Fictional stories were an important part of the mix for *The Penny War Weekly*. Issue six (dated 10 October 1914) carried the story "A Place in the Sun – A Superb Romance of the Great War". As the war progressed it ran more and more "Tales from the Front". The issue dated 2 January 1915 contained "Ministering Angels: Their Sorrow and Joy"; "Fighting Above the Clouds – An Aeroplane Duel"; and an illustration captioned: "Captive Briton Punishes A Prussian Bully".

The Penny War Weekly morphed into the *Vivid War Weekly* on 6 February 1915, but carried on pretty much as before, with a mixture of war reportage, illustration and story fiction.

SPECIAL WAR SUPPLEMENT.

Exclusive Pictures of War Events.

THE BRAVE DEFENCE OF OUR ALLIES.

The re-capture of the town of Aerschot by the Belgians so enraged the Germans that they organised a strong assault on the town; but our Allies, although outnumbered by four to one, successfully withstood the onslaught for over 12 hours, and to save themselves from complete annihilation they retired during the night, leaving the Germans to enter the town unopposed next morning. As our illustration shows, there were occasions when the Germans almost succeeded in gaining their object. It is this pluck and tenacity of the Belgians that has excited the admiration of all Britishers.

SEE THAT YOUR CHUMS READ THIS PAPER.

IN·THE·RANKS

I.

COME! lads from the village, and lads from the
    town,
    Your Country and King make the call;
The path that we follow leads on to renown—
    The goal that is envied of all.
The land with the fever of glory is ripe,
    And the air is alive with its hum—
The phil-a-loo-loo of the spiriting fife,
    And the rub-a-dub-dub of the drum.

Chorus.

So, lads, if you long for a glorious life,
    Join in with our ranks as we come
To the phil-a-loo-loo of the spiriting fife,
    And the rub-a-dub-dub of the drum.

II.

From Waterloo's plains to the sands of Khartoum
    It has quicken'd the march of our feet,
Thro' the furnace of war with its glare and its
    gloom,
    Whilst our hearts ever higher have beat.
We have trod to its tone under stars, over snows,
    By mountain, and valley, and waste—
A welcome to friends and a warning to foes
    Wherever our Empire is placed.

Chorus.

III.

And now we are fighting the cause of the just,
    With right and religion in hand,
And for innocent blood which appeals from the
    dust
    Of a ruin'd but resolute land.
The German invader is ruthless in fight,
    And he toasts to "The Day" he will shine
As Cæsar of Europe, and tyrant of might,
    But we'll roll him back over the Rhine.

Chorus.

DRUID GRAYL.

JOHN SAXON OF THE SECRET SERVICE

THE SIGHTLESS SUBMARINE.
BY LADBROKE BLACK.

Above John Saxon adventure of espionage and warfare in *The Vivid War Weekly*, issue dated 3 April 1915

Below Saxon is about to save the day, *The Vivid War Weekly*, 3 April 1915

The issue dated 3 April 1915 contained the first instalment of "John Saxon of the Secret Service" in a tale called "The Sightless Submarine". A regular character, Saxon features in "A series of magnetic short stories recounting the unusual adventures of a big, brawny man who presumably thinks more of playing golf than enlisting to fight his country's foes. Yet all the while he is John Saxon, a Secret Service agent. He is friendly with Gillian – commonly called Jill – Greenwood, the pretty niece of Richard Gurden, a wealthy man of leisure." "The Sightless Submarine" is a German vessel, the U18, which is destroying British shipping in the Irish Sea. Concern centres on the submarine's ability to re-fuel and re-stock supplies without returning to a German port.

Saxon travels to Callan in Ireland and his suspicions are aroused by the actions of the Danish-registered *Haakon*. Saxon follows the *Haakon* out to sea, in a tug manned by rescued British seaman, where she rendezvous with U18. Saxon and his men board and capture the *Haakon*. Saxon then boards the U18 and disables her by shooting out the lenses of the periscopes. "We've put out the eyes of your submarine for you," Saxon reports to the Callan harbour master.

Saxon's adventures continued in the next three issues. In the story "With the Coming of Spring" (issue dated 10 April 1915) Saxon foils a plan by German spies to blow up trains carrying newly trained troops from the barracks to Southampton, shooting two of the conspirators in the process.

In "The Master Spy" (17 April 1915) Jill Greenwood is

Running down from the bridge, Saxon rushed to the rail and, judging his distance nicely, vaulted over it so that he dropped on to the conning-tower of the German submarine.

suspected by Saxon of being a spy for the Germans; it transpires that the real spy is Richard Gurden, whose real name is Gottenburg. Gurden tries to flee the country. In "The Last Flight" (24 April 1915), Gurden/Gottenburg flees to Hendon aerodrome, where he steals an aircraft. But Saxon manages to destroy the aircraft, Gurden's only means of escape. Gurden takes Jill hostage; in exchange for her life Gurden wants Saxon to aid his escape. Saxon refuses, following pleas from Jill that she is "prepared to die for her country".

A BARBED WIRE PATROL.

The timely arrival of armed police and soldiers saves Jill's life and denies Gurden his escape; he is shot in the ensuing fight.

Another serialisation, "The Airman's Bride", was the story "...of Burleigh Holt and the wonderful aeroplane he invented, and of Lucy Ivrette, used as a decoy to steal his plans by a gang of German agents".

The Boy's Own Paper, too, was putting its considerable weight behind the war effort. In 1913, the editor, Arthur Haydon, scrapped the weekly edition, which had in effect been competing with the monthly compendium issue. So the paper became a 64-page sixpenny monthly. In *Take a Cold Tub, Sir!*, the story of *The Boy's Own Paper*, author Jack Cox explains the new pressure this move created: "One result of this was the need to choose serials with a strong story-line, characters and background bold enough to live in the mind for four weeks at a stretch, and neatly spaced climaxes tailored to keep the reader's interest going, month by month."

Below It's competition time, in *The Vivid War Weekly*, 20 February 1915 – £500 was a huge sum to win at that time. Competitions played an important role in the circulation war, with publishers trying to outdo each other with the value of their prizes. This competition was also running in *The Vivid War Weekly*'s sister publication, *The Union Jack*

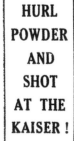

HURL POWDER AND SHOT AT THE KAISER !

POWDER & SHOT

FIRST PRIZE £500

HURL POWDER AND SHOT AT THE CROWN PRINCE!

2ND PRIZE - £100   3RD PRIZE - £50

4th Prize - £25   5th Prize - £20   6th Prize - £17 10s.

7th Prize - £15   8th Prize - £10

9th, 10th, 11th, and 12th Prizes, £5 each.   13th, 14th, 15th, 16th, 17th, 18th, 19th, 20th, 21st, and 22nd Prizes, £2 10s. each.

1,000 HANDSOME PRIZES IN KIND

UNIFORMS OF THE BRITISH NAVAL AND MILITARY FLYING CORPS SERVICES.
Private. Bluejacket. Lieut. Naval Lieut. Mechanician. Sergeant.
Officer (flying kit.) (Army.) (over eight years' service.)

The Royal Flying Corps.
By V. WHEELER-HOLOHAN.

Haydon was happy to use the paper's influence to fight the good fight; he had previously edited the patriotic **Boys of Our Empire**, with its heavy emphasis on war stories. Like its rivals, **The Boy's Own Paper** mixed fictional stories with news from the front and features about a wide and varied range of war-related subjects. The editor himself contributed the story "For England and the Right!", subtitled "A Tale of the war in Belgium". Starting in January 1915, it features the adventures of 15-year-old Roddy, a British boy holidaying on a farm in Belgium when the Germans invade. He is forced to hide in the hayloft while the Uhlans – Prussian cavalrymen – do their terrible work: "He moved across the loft to the little window that looked down upon the yard and peered cautiously out.

There was no one to be seen. Only a solitary fowl pecked among the rubbish in a corner by the stable. In the opposite direction his eye fell upon the blackened, smouldering ruins of the farm-house where, until that day, he had been a welcome visitor. The German soldiers had done their work thoroughly. 'Poor old M. Dupuis!' said Roddy – it did him good to hear his own voice in this desolation; 'what a home-coming for him! House burnt – horses carried off – a clean sweep of everything!" We hear how Roddy had "heard the Uhlans clatter into the yard and take possession of the place. By their shouts he could follow pretty well their movements; how they had feasted and drunk from old farmer Dupuis's store; how, having satisfied themselves in this direction, they had proceeded

Examining Shell Noses

80

The Penny War Weekly, September 12th, 1914.

TWENTY-FOUR PAGES PACKED WITH WAR PICTURES.

THE PENNY WAR WEEKLY

No. 2.
Vol. 1. **THE FIRST ENCOUNTER BETWEEN GERMAN AND BRITISH CAVALRY.** 12 September, 1914.

"We came plump upon them round a corner in a little village near Charleroi. It was absolutely a proper cavalry charge, like you see in the pictures. First thing I knew was my sword was sticking through a German's elbow, and his was through my wrist."—*Extract from a British Hussar's letter.*

A GERMAN VULTURE BROUGHT TO EARTH.

Above A typically action-packed front cover from *The Penny War Weekly*, in the issue dated 11 October 1914

Right *The Boys' Realm* recreates the danger and heroism of the trenches, in the issue dated 21 February 1921

to destroy the farm house." The story follows Roddy's adventures in escaping the German dragnet, and eventually he escapes back to England.

Alongside *The Boy's Own Paper*'s fictional output were articles designed to motivate young readers to contribute to the war effort. Typical of the genre was "British Boys' Work in War-Time", which described "What Boy Scouts, Cadets, and other Youthful Members of well-known Organisations are doing for their King and Country on Land and Sea". It begins: "Surely the spirit of the boys of the nation is the natural expression of the true heart of its people – the heart that is and is to be. In this great war, the boys of Britain have proved that they are ready and willing to help to their uttermost." The story records how former scouts have proved themselves heroes on the battlefield. "When Lance-Corporal Arthur Daphne, London Rifle Brigade, late assistant scoutmaster, 5th North London Troop, was called to higher service, he was trying to save a wounded comrade in action. Private Leslie Caulder, London Scottish, ex-scout, 1st Weybridge Troop, though fatally wounded himself, went out from his trench and brought back another wounded soldier. At the time of writing only one decoration had been earned by a scout. This was awarded to Albert Edward Bentley, who left the 1st Cheshunt Troop to enlist in the 1st Bedfordshire Regiment. One day, towards the end of October last, he was badly wounded in the thigh; in fact, if it had not been for a tin chocolate-box in his tunic pocket, he would have been in a very serious plight indeed. In spite of his wound he stayed behind for eight hours, all the while under fire, and during that time, with wonderful coolness and ability, he dressed the wounds of three men whom it was impossible to move. For this act of signal bravery he has

IN THE FACE OF THE ENEMY!

received the Distinguished Conduct Medal. It was worthy of special note that he learnt surgical dressing while he was with the Cheshunt Scout Troop." Other topics along similar lines included "Boy Heroes of the War" and "VC Heroes of the War"; practical subjects tackled included "How Big Guns are Made" and "With the Wireless in War" and "Tommy Atkins A-Wheel". This was "An Account of our Soldier Cyclists and of warriors on Wheels in other Lands. A Chat with 'The Father of Military Cycling'." In it we read how the humble push-bike "has recently so effectively taken the field in the cause of right and justice, for the reparation of wrongs, the relief of peoples oppressed, and the glorious defence alike of our nearer homeland and our far-flung empire overseas. Britain's warrior wheelmen – Army, Territorial, and Navy too – have been, and still are, each burning and eager in striving their splendid utmost to keep the grand old flag triumphantly flying." We learn that "for the Italo-Turkish campaign of

Below Bicycles were extensively used in the Great War – here a messenger-cyclist is put through his paces, from *The Boy's Own Annual* 1914–1915

1912, the Italian Minister of War ordered 6,000 bicycles, and these rendered more efficient service in Africa than camels...", and that "during manoeuvres, the French general staff were much impressed with the freshness of the wheelmen after give-and-take rides of eighty or ninety kilometres". Incidently, "The Father of Military Cycling" was Lieutenant-Colonel A.R. Savile. He was Professor of Tactics at the Royal Military College, Sandhurst, who, in 1887, described the bicycle as "a machine capable of great possibilities in the future of actual warfare". In the same year he organised the first series of military cycle manoeuvres in England.

Despite *The Boy's Own Paper*'s commitment to the war effort, the publication stuck to its school-yarn roots with a number of school-based war stories. "How the War came to Fountainbury" (August 1916) was a typical example. As the story opens a group of schoolboy chums are

HARD PRESSED!

A Cyclist Despatch Rider: An Exciting Moment during Manœuvres.

(Drawn for the " Boy's Own Paper" by A. E. HORNE.)

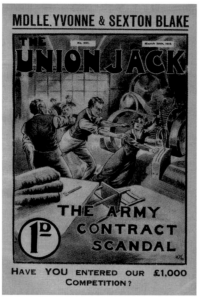

bemoaning the action of a new master, Solomon, an American, who has been promoted because so many other masters have "gone to the war". We know Solomon is a thoroughly bad chap because he has banned the boys from playing sport. Worse still, he is organising German zeppelin raids, using a wireless set secreted in his study. He is exposed by the pals, goes on the run, and is eventually captured. He is revealed to be Seligmann, a German American spy, who "paid the penalty of his crime in the Tower of London". Indeed, the Tower of London was used as a prison during the Great War for the first time since the early 19th century; between 1914 and 1916, eleven spies were executed in the Tower.

Like *The Boy's Own Paper*, *Dreadnought* was keen to show its support for the war effort after the outbreak of hostilities in mainland Europe. Launched in March 1912, prior to August 1914 the story-paper's military tales had titles such as "The New Year's Concert – A Tale of Boy Best of the Royal Navy" (3 January 1914); "Sealed Orders – A Grand Tale of Humourous and Dramatic Adventures Encountered by Midshipman Bob Hardy" (10 January 1914); and features such as "Shall I Enlist? The Advantages of the Army from a Boy's Point of View" (10 January 1914). The emphasis changed quickly. The issue dated 24 August 1914 carried a "Special War Page" featuring a debate on conscription, called "Compulsory versus Non Compulsory".

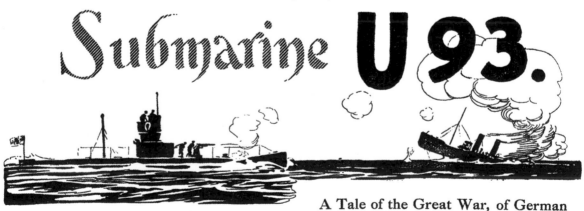

[NOTE TO THE READER.—In this story fact is blended with fiction. The account of the battle in the North Sea, in which the "Blücher" was sunk, is as historically accurate as is possible with the details at present available. On the other hand, it would be well to point out that the description of the pursuit of the "Dresden" in mid-Atlantic is wholly fictitious.]]

A Tale of the Great War, of German Spies, of Naval Warfare, and of all manner of Strange Adventures.

By CAPTAIN CHARLES GILSON,

THE EYE OF THE ENEMY.

"Who Will Rule the Waves –
A Feature on Naval Artillery"
(5 September 1914) continued the
factual vein; while "My First Time
Under Fire – A ceaseless rain of
bullet and splinters" (19 September
1914) was by Corporal Chupin, a
member of the *Chasseurs à Pied* of
the French Army (the *Chasseurs à
Pied* were elite French Light
Infantry troops).

By the following week
(26 September 1914), the
story-paper had become *The
Dreadnought and War Pictorial*, a
sign that sales were not healthy (the amalgamation of story-papers and comics
was a tell-tale sign of all not being well). The new title carried on as before – the
issue dated 3 October 1914 was a "Special War Supplement", carrying the story
"With the Flag to Belgium". This tale introduced Bill Stubbs, a Cockney
fighting hero who appeared in a number of subsequent stories.

On 31 October 1914, the publication changed its name once again, this time to
The Dreadnought and Boy's War Weekly; but on
2 January 1915 it reverted back to plain *Dreadnought*.
But for *Dreadnought* the war was over; after the issue
dated 12 June 1915 it merged with Amalgamated Press
stablemate *The Boys' Friend*.

Left Action at sea in the pages
of *The Boys' Realm*, dated
18 November 1922

Below Despite the devastating
and prolonged nature of the
fighting, there seemed to be no
let up in the demand for images
of the great conflict. This *War
Ilustrated* cover is dated
1 June 1918

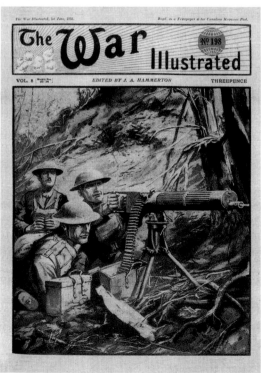

The merging and closing of titles was common practice
in the publishing world, but the pressure on
publishers during wartime was increased by paper
shortages, which hit harder as the war progressed.

In his book *Managing Domestic Dissent in First World
War Britain*, Brock Millman wrote: "Paper shortages,
caused by the increased demand produced by the war
and the lack of shipping, became endemic by 1917.
Imports of newsprint were something like one-quarter of
what they had been before the war (2,000 tons imported
in 1917 compared with 8,000 tons in 1914). Available
stocks were divided up between consumers on the basis
of ratios of pre-war circulation. By its nature, this

CHAPTER THREE: THE WAR TO END ALL WARS...

"What about a bit of cold steel?" yelled Sniper Sid, leaping on to the parapet and leading the attack.

Above By the late 1920s, more and more stories about the Great War were appearing in the story-papers. This action is from *The Boys' Friend*, dated 17 November 1927

Below Peace at last – the armistice is portrayed in this understated way on the cover of *War Illustrated*, dated 4 December 1918

system favoured the patriotic Beaverbrook-Northcliffe combine... the press lords were in a much better position... to obtain extra newsprint." But, as the example of **Dreadnought** shows, the bigger publishers struggled, too.

But the propaganda and recruiting value of the boys' story-papers was so important that, despite paper shortages, publishers were encouraged to keep on publishing. As the terrible toll of killed and injured continued to mount, the story-papers redoubled their effort to raise their readers' morale. The emphasis became less on fiction and more on real-life stories from the trenches and in the skies – aerial warfare in particular had captured the British public's imagination. As Michael Paris points out in his book *Over the Top: The Great War and Juvenile Literature in Britain*, the boys' story-papers were continuing to run features exalting this exciting and daring new occupation.

While many publishers struggled to keep their heads above water, the situation changed for the better after the end of the war; indeed, the boys' story-papers and comics enjoyed a boom in the early 1920s. Freed from the restrictions of the paper shortages, publishers piled into the market re-invigorated after the austerity of wartime. In 1921, a bold new entrant came into the market. D.C. Thomson, based in the Scottish city of Dundee, was a successful

MARINE

TURCO

ZOUAVE

ARTILLERY OFFICER

MOROCCO REGT

CHARGE OF ZOUAVES

FRENCH DRAGOON

INFANTRY

ALGERIAN SHARPSHOOTER

ENGINEER

FIGHTING UNDER THE TRICOLOUR.
Types of soldiers of the French Army.

Above The troops of the French Army, as seen in *The Boy's Own Annual* of 1915-16

GERMANY'S VENGEANCE ON GREAT BRITAIN!—For over forty years Germany has watched and waited, schemed and plotted, for the Great Day—the day on which she intends to take her revenge for the great defeat of 1918. And now, in the year 1962, the time has come! In this Magnificent New Serial you will read of what is supposed to happen when the new German Emperor blares forth his impudent challenge!

The WAR of REVENGE!

BY LESLIE BERESFORD.

ILLUSTRATED BY ARTHUR JONES.

Above Germany plots its revenge... from *The Champion*, 11 March 1922

Facing page and below *The Champion*'s tale of undersea warfare, 6 July 1929; and a story with a similar theme in *Adventure*, 7 July 1928

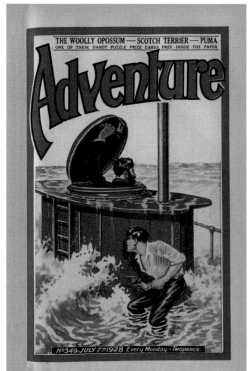

newspaper and magazine publisher, having launched the hugely successful *Sunday Post* in 1914. D.C. Thomson dipped its toe into the water with *Adventure* (launched 17 September 1921), which, as the title suggests, focused mainly on adventure stories, with a smattering of sports-based tales added for good measure. It was joined on the nation's newsagents' shelves by *The Rover* (launched 4 March 1922) and by *The Wizard* (23 September 1922). Both titles aped *Adventure*'s successful mix of tales of derring-do and sport, and all three offered their readers competitions, jokes, features and, importantly, giveways. The debut issue of *The Rover* offered "Two Real Photos given every week with each copy"; while *The Wizard* promised "Something Absolutely New – Hand Coloured Real Photos Free with each copy". But it seems the war was not considered suitable subject matter; the new comics tended to look to the future rather than the past.

The Champion, launched 28 January 1922 to counter the impact of the Scottish publisher's new titles by Harmsworth's Amalgamated Press, promised "Mystery–Adventure–Sport" and billed itself "The Tip Top Story-Paper for Boys". It offered readers the standard-issue adventure/thriller/sports mix, but one of its early serialised stories harked back to the "invasion literature" genre that had been so popular a decade or more earlier. "The War of Revenge" (issue dated 11 March 1922) concerned "Germany's revenge in 1962". "Germany's vengeance on Great Britain! – For over forty years Germany has watched and waited, schemed and plotted,

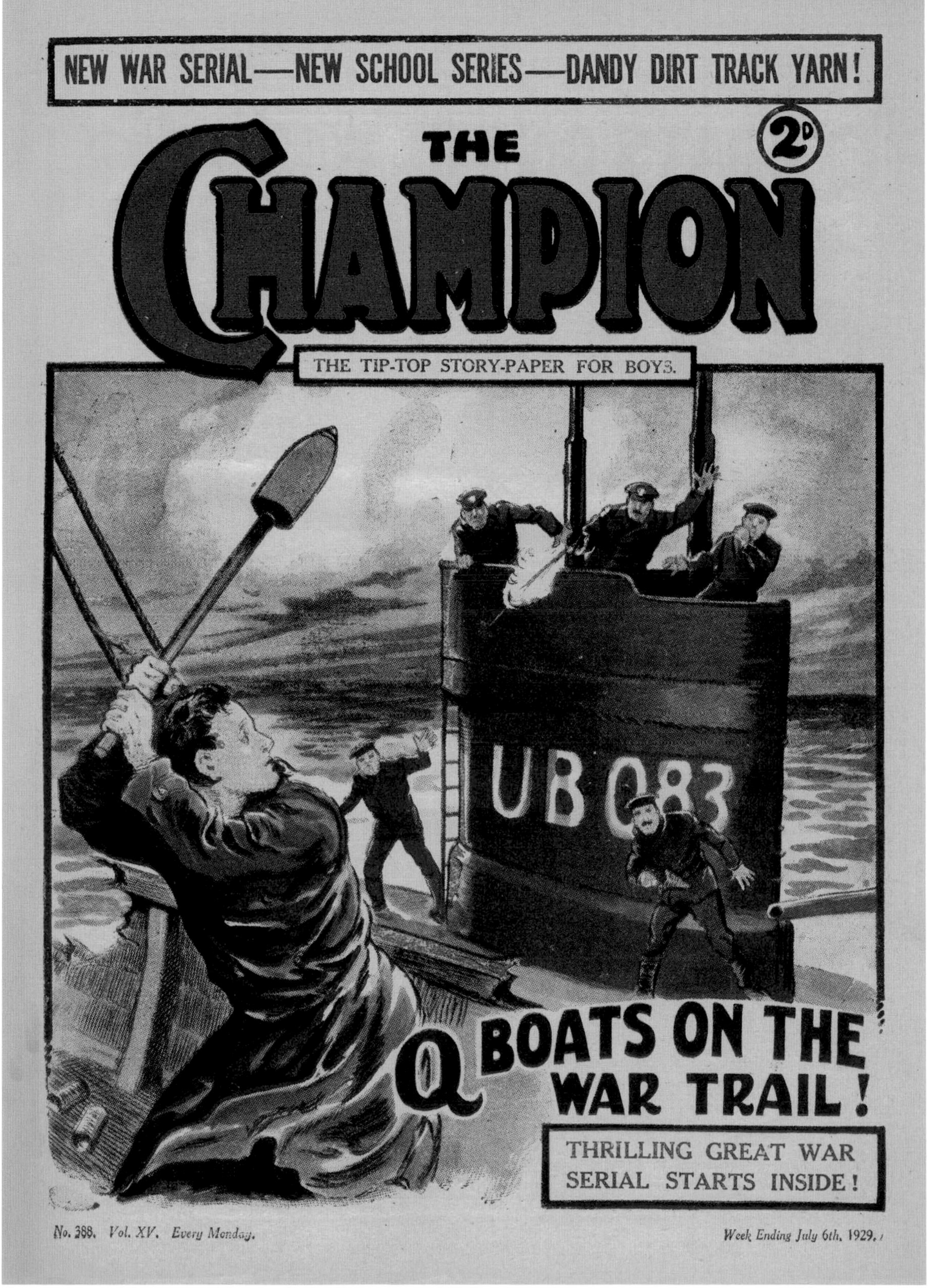
NEW WAR SERIAL—NEW SCHOOL SERIES—DANDY DIRT TRACK YARN!
THE CHAMPION
2D
THE TIP-TOP STORY-PAPER FOR BOYS.
UB 083
Q BOATS ON THE WAR TRAIL!
THRILLING GREAT WAR SERIAL STARTS INSIDE!
No. 388. Vol. XV. Every Monday.
Week Ending July 6th, 1929.

IN ACTION WITH

THE MYSTERY SHIPS!

The grim menace of the blockading German U-boats had to be fought tooth and nail. Old methods were a failure—so the mysterious Q boats were introduced by the British to sweep the enemy submarines from the seven seas. This is the story of Pete Cutting, who commanded Q boats, and of the astounding adventures he had.

THRILLING NEW SERIAL

OF THE GREAT WAR!

Q'BOATS ON THE WAR TRAIL!

PETE

Specially Written for THE
CHAMPION
By DICK SHAW.

for the Great Day – the day on which she intends to take her revenge for the great defeat of 1918. And now, in the year 1962, the time has come! In this Magnificent New Serial you will read of what is supposed to happen when the new German Emperor blares forth his impudent challenge." At the start of the tale we read how Britain's cities mysteriously came to be plastered with posters

THE FLYING FOX!
Spot it on the U-boat's
conning-tower? That
sign is going to enthrall
you, pals!

that read: "In retaliation for the humiliating Peace treaty of 1919, which the German government was forced to sign, the hour has come when German honour must be avenged. Ignored by the signatories of the Washington Conference of forty years ago, and therefore not pledged to the Peace, the Imperial Government considers itself fully justified in announcing that on and from the morning of Tuesday, April 13th, 1962, a State of War will exist between Germany and Great Britain unless the conditions imposed by the Imperial German Government and handed to the British Ambassador at Berlin a week ago – namely, on April 1st, 1962 – have been accepted by Great Britain." Germany's demand – for £10,000 million – was considered a huge joke, but it was no laughing matter when Britain's cities came under bombardment.

In "The War of Revenge", which ran until 27 May 1922, Germany invades England, landing on the East Coast. Led by the brilliant but evil scientist Von Helzen, the invaders use terrifying and bizarre weapons that cause death and disaster. The most terrible of the German weapons are the huge walking-machines that stalk the streets, belching out bullets and gas. German domination is total, with British forces reduced to fighting a guerrilla war.

Harry Davenport, a young officer in the Intelligence Corps, and his chum Paul St. Cloud, manage to infiltrate the German lines, and there discover the German Imperial Staff experimenting with a terrible new weapon called the "Green Ray", which is designed to burn up everything within its radius. The ray is used with devastating results.

Facing page, both images
The "Q Boats" in action, *The Champion*, 6 July 1929

Below *The Champion* took to the skies with this Great War story, in the issue dated 21 September 1929

B ut British pluck is never to be underestimated and the fight back against the occupiers begins. The newly created army, under the command of the young Duke of Manchester, rallies and starts to destroy the Germans' scientific weapons, including the 'Green Ray'. Captured ray guns are used against the enemy – "offering them a taste of their own medicine". Eventually, the Germans are driven back to the sea, and vast numbers are killed at sea by the mighty British Amphibian, a terrifying machine developed by the British scientists. The massive loss of life causes the German High Command to accept the terms of surrender offered by the British. The evil Von Helzen, along with his henchmen, die in a shoot out with Davenport and St. Cloud.

The Boys' Realm of Sport and Adventure also avoided stories directly related to the Great War, but, in an interesting departure, based one of its post-war serials on another major world event – the Russian Revolution. In "The Boy Adventurers; or, Braving the Bolshevists", our heroes Dick and Jimmy Lane are sent into Russia by their father, Sir Ralph Lane, to rescue Paul Orloff, son of Sir Ralph's friend Alec, murdered by the Bolshevists.

As the 1920s progressed, the story-papers' editors began once again to see the military as a source of new material. While stories set in the Great War were considered by some editors as "out of bounds", soldiers, sailors and particularly airmen featured in adventures set in peace time. Often these stories combined the

STUPENDOUS NEW SERIAL OF THE GREAT WAR!

This, pals, is a story of the gallant airmen who battled above the wastes of No-Man's-Land. Menaced by the vicious fire of anti-aircraft batteries, they slashed the air searching for enemy fighters, scouts and bombers. Fierce battles were waged far above the clouds—battles filled with a thousand thrills. Here you will read of the part played by a daring young airman named Mick Winton.

SKY-FIGHTERS OF THE HOT TRIANGLE!

military with sport; typical of these is ***The Boys' Realm of Sports & Adventure***'s "The Flying Fighter" (issue dated 3 December 1927). Readers are told: "Here's a new pal this week, Lads! Meet Dan Dare – he's out to make good as boxer and airman. Start right away on this gripping serial of wing and ring." The story centres on an 18-year-old new RAF recruit – yes, he really is called Dan Dare –

who has designs on winning the Services Boxing Championships.

By the tenth anniversary of the Armistice, editors and proprietors were far more relaxed about using the Great War as the backdrop for their stories. Many such tales were to be found in the pages of both *Chums* and *The Champion*.

The latter's "Thrilling Great War Serial" was "Q Boats on the War Trail!", which kicked-off in the issue dated 6 July 1929. The scene is set: "The grim menace of the blockading German U-boats had to be fought tooth and nail. Old methods were a failure – so the mysterious Q boats were introduced to sweep the enemy submarines from the seven seas. This is the story of Pete Cutting, who commanded Q boats, and of the astounding adventures he had." It ran until 21 September 1929, but was more a tale of adventure and mystery than war. It was replaced in the pages of *The Champion* the following week by a story that used the Great War as a backdrop – "Sky-Fighters of the Hot Triangle!" "This, pals, is the story of the gallant airmen who battled above the wastes of No-Man's-Land. Menaced by the vicious fire of anti-aircraft batteries, they slashed the air searching for enemy fighters, scouts and bombers. Fierce battles were waged far above the clouds – battles filled with a thousand thrills. Here you will read of the part played by a daring young airman named Mick Winton", was how the tale was described to eager readers.

In *Chums*, war-based stories started to appear from the mid-1920s. "When the War-God Walks Again" (October 1927) is one example, where "All the atmosphere of modern war is to be found in this, the first of the magnificent series of stories from the pen of Mr. F. Britten Austin. Here you will find the drone of 'planes, the racket of machine gun fire, and the heavy tension of approaching battle." But this was not a story of the Great War – it was the story of warfare to come. While echoing many features of the First World War – gas attacks, trenches – it predicted the dominance of tank and aircraft. As one of the characters remarks: "We've seen the last of infantry, and unprotected, limber-drawn artillery on a battlefield... we've inaugurated a new era, and who knows what will be the end of it? Landships as big as dreadnoughts, perhaps,

Facing page The story "When the War-God Walks Again", which appeared in *Chums* in October 1927, might look like a Great War story, but in fact it predicted a future war dominated by tank and aircraft

Below *The Champion*'s popular "Q Boats" story, 13 July 1929

fighting high-speed battles of manoeuvre across every sort of country short of a mountain or a marsh."

Chums was published both weekly and monthly, with the monthly edition consisting of the weeklies, minus front and back covers, but with added content. Amid the school, sports and tales of adventure was a smattering of war stories, including a serialisation called "For Lawrence of Arabia", based on the exploits of T.E. Lawrence. Many war stories were complete rather than serialised, however. One example was "A Battlepiece Old Style", the story of an attack on enemy trenches. Graphic and violent, the story pulled no punches in its vivid description of the horrors of war: "Behind a wrecked trench parapet, an infantry subaltern, faceless and grotesque in a gas-mask crouched with his eyes upon the dial of his wrist-watch. In the semi-fluid mud of the depression between one crumbled traverse and another, crouched some of his platoon, similarly anonymous and grotesque in their masks – weird figures divorced from humanity in a demoniac world divorced from normality. Each had a hand upon the weapon of his job – bayonet-tipped rifle, the divided paraphernalia of Lewis guns, bags of bombs. Among them, rolled on to his face, was the body of a man half-covered with a remnant of sack. The mud under him was red, and very fluid. A shell had landed in the trench just before. Two other men had completely vanished in its flash and smoke and stunning detonation." The subaltern in question has been ordered to reach a section of enemy ground – N 25 C – and capture it. The countdown begins: "He looked at his watch again. Six minutes. Quite a time yet. Curse these gas-masks! One could not breathe in them. The nose-clip already hurt him. He shivered with a cold that soaked into his bones. That was a nice comfortable billet, that last one. Duck your head! – down! CRASH! Fragments all gone over? – Yes. Sickening sound, that hissing rush as it arrives." In those anxious few moments the whole conduct of the war is questioned: "Staff officers – yes – supposing they had to attack, too – they wouldn't be so glib then with their 'at all costs'" ... "Politicians at home, sleeping also in nice white beds, getting up to shout 'Win the war at all costs'." And then the attack: "What

Below *Chums'* story of going "over the top" – "A Battlepiece Old Style" – graphically described the terror and violence of trench fighting. It appeared in October 1927

"Wonderful how quick it was—fellow was alive then, dead now."

followed was a dream – a phantasmagoria that had no reality. Those faceless men who dropped around him were not killed – or were phantoms who had never lived. The little groups of tanks that lurched and plunged like ships in a rough sea were prehistoric creatures of a nightmare. The earth leaped up, almost at his feet, in quick red flash, black smoke and studding concussion – leaped up all around him, in front, behind, on either side. The enemy counter-barrage. He wasn't killed. A vaguely apprehended miracle. Worst of it was these confounded shell-holes – couldn't hurry up – up to his waist in water that time – nice job for his servant cleaning off the mud! What was that insistent hissing, like an engine letting off steam, audible through the infernal din? Must get on – at all costs – N 25 C. Look at all those fellows throwing themselves down, taking cover! They weren't going to move. Kick 'em forward? Silly ass! Casualties. Hissing was machine-gun bullets.

Marvel he wasn't hit. Charmed life. Thank God, enemy wire blown to bits. Enemy trench just beyond – hell erupting in it – no one visible. Anyone following? Yes. Scattered figures emerging through the smoke. Good chaps. He waved to them. In their trenches. Ghastly mess. What a lot of blood a man has – never believe it – running down in a stream like that. The faceless snouted figure that had popped up from a hole. His revolver had gone off automatically at it. Figure had dropped. Wonderful how quick it was – fellow was alive then, dead now. What's that coming over? Bombs! Down in the mud – face down – can't help what it is. Ugh! Bang-bang-bang! Close call that!"

Above and below Thrills-and-spills in the sky were hugely popular with readers; the action here is depicted in *The Champion*, on 5 October 1929, above, and in a promotion for a new story to come, In the issue dated 21 October 1929

While more and more Great War stories were appearing in the comics and story-papers, few were as hard-hitting as "A Battlepiece Old Style"; in its gritty portrayal of the physical and psychological horrors of warfare it was ahead of its time – as we shall see.

"NEVER, NEVER, NEVER BELIEVE ANY WAR WILL BE SMOOTH AND EASY, OR THAT ANYONE WHO EMBARKS ON THE STRANGE VOYAGE CAN MEASURE THE TIDES AND HURRICANES HE WILL ENCOUNTER"

Sir Winston Churchill (1874-1965)

CHAPTER FOUR
KEEPING THE HOME FIRES BURNING

THE CIRCULATION WAR BETWEEN the old-guard Amalgamated Press and the Scottish newcomer D.C. Thomson intensified in the early 1930s, fuelled by two new launches from the Dundee publisher: *Skipper*, on 6 September 1930, and *The Hotspur*, which first hit the newsagents' shelves on 2 September 1933.

D.C. Thomson's new publications followed the same formula that had been such a success with **Adventure**, **Rover** and **Wizard** a decade earlier; their stories were exciting, fast-paced and innovative, and collectively the titles came to be known as "The Big Five". Many of the characters in the Big Five comics had superhero qualities, and the stories often had a strong element of either science fiction or the supernatural – or both. Cowboy, spy, crime, school, adventure and sports stories jostled in the comics' pages with the occasional war-related tale. As the author E.S. Turner wrote in his book, *Boys Will Be Boys*: "Plausability and probability never worried the writers from beyond the Tweed… their chief concern seems to have been to avoid any charge of conventionality." R.D Low, the managing editor of the Big Five, certainly seemed to have his finger on the pulse; by the late 1930s *Wizard*'s circulation peaked at 800,000 copies sold each week.

But Amalgamated Press was not prepared to surrender its market share without a fight, and its story-papers beefed up their content in response. One of its more popular titles, *Triumph*, carried a whopping 52 pages each week, costing 2d, by the time *The Hotspur* launched in 1933. *Triumph*'s stories included the mystery adventure "Sinister Island"; "Know-All Noel", another adventure yarn; the cowboy "Poker-Face Peters"; "Catch-'em-Alive Carr" (an adventure story); and "Yukon Ken, the Arctic Postman", which was "No 1 of

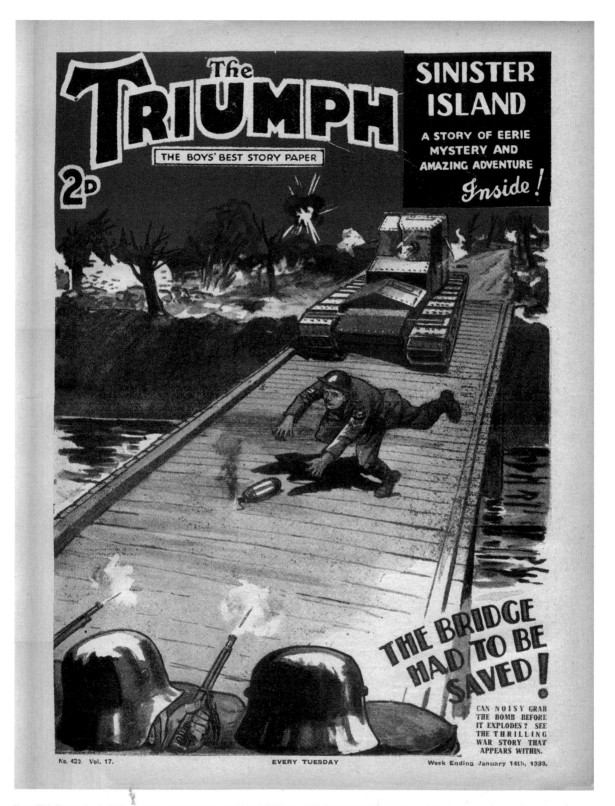

Above "Noisy" saves the day in the story "The Whippets O' War", in *Triumph*, 14 January 1933. **Facing page** The Red Baron's legend lives on, in the pages of *Boys' Magazine* dated 21 February 1931. The story, "Richthofen's Rival", was "our-red-hot-real-life thriller of the war on wings". The editor boasted that the story was "Crammed with Excitement, Drama and Heroism Sky High, this Startling Epic Tale Has Been Specially Penned from Authentic Records by a Famous Author-Airman".

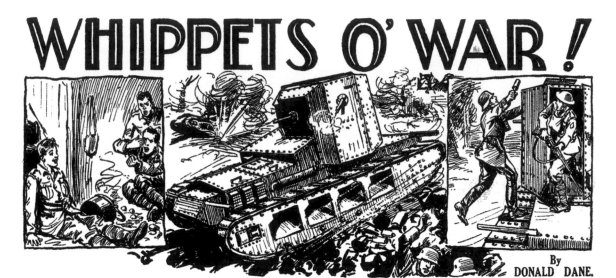

WHIPPETS O' WAR!

By DONALD DANE.

Above "The Whippets O' War" in *Triumph*, 12 November 1932

Below As paper shortages impacted on the publishing industry, W. Barton of Central Street, London E.C.1, devised a series of story-papers called *The Mighty Midgets*. Each was 36 pages long and measured just 95mm by 63mm

a thrilling new series" (issue dated 25 March 1933). The following week's postal-services-related story was "Rivals for the Mexican Mail". *Triumph* also published many war-based stories, among the best of which was "The Whippets O' War", by veteran story-paper writer Donald Dane. Like many war stories in the boys' story-papers, it is set against a backdrop of the Great War. It featured the exploits of Corporal "Noisy" Nelson of the Whippet Tanks, "the lad with the biggest record for bad luck in the whole British army", along with his mate Tex Murphy. Each weekly episode was a self-contained adventure within a longer narrative. In the issue dated 7 January 1933, our hero Noisy catches one "Sergeant Stone" in the act of blowing up an ammunition dump that had been captured by the Whippet Tanks. Stone is a German infiltrator and spy, who is thwarted in his act of sabotage and eventually shot by the pals. In the following week's issue the Whippets are ordered to attack a fortified mill between

Baupaume and Peronne, on the Western Front. Their progress is halted at a narrow bridge when a desperate German hurls a bomb onto the narrow wooden structure. The bridge had to be saved – and cometh the hour, cometh the man: "Noisy threw open the tank door and leaped from the rattling vehicle on to the bridge of death. Bullets by the score were screaming through the air, but for once Noisy's luck held good. Like a greyhound he burst for the sizzling bomb, gripped it, and hurled it back towards the barricade. There had only been two inches of fuse left when the missile soared from Noisy's fingers, and at sight of their engine of death coming back at them the Germans yelled in horror. As the Whippet lurched forward there came an appalling explosion from behind the wall of brick and sandbags. Boom! Earth, bricks, men and machine-guns were blown up in one terrific gush of flame, and as others tried to flee out of the holocaust the Whippet's right gun took deadly toll."

The story was replaced in **Triumph** by "The Fighting Freelance" (issue dated 28 January 1933), written by Herbert Macrae. It was "the amazing exploits of a young Aussie who 'smuggled' himself on to the battlefield" because "they wouldn't let him enlist – but they couldn't keep him out of the war!". Kit Carson runs away from home in the Australian Outback to sign up, but he is turned away from the recruiting office because he is too young: "'To hear you fellows talk one 'ud think there wasn't a war on at all!' he barked. 'Here's the Germans marching on Paris, and yet you turn your noses at a willing volunteer! It's enough to make a cobber sick – square dinkum it is!'" Undeterred, Kit stows away on a troop ship bound for France with the aim of finding his elder brother, Major Sam Carson, who is fighting on the front. Kim sees action in the trenches on the Western Front, but he is believed to be a spy and has to escape the dreaded Military Police. He ends up in Gallipoli fighting with his Australian comrades, where he single-handedly captures a key Turkish trench. Kit is badly wounded, but, reunited with his brother, the tale has a happy ending.

Apart from stories centred on trench and aerial warfare, the other popular genre of Great War stories concerned military intelligence and espionage. A typical example was "The Secret Squadron", which appeared in **Modern Boy** (issue dated 28 November 1936). It was a tale about how "The squadron without a number drops spies behind

Below Strewth! The Fighting Freelance in action in the pages of *Triumph*, 11 March 1933

enemy lines", for the "Secret men are playing a desperate, perilous game!" A complete, one-off story, it concerns a pilot, Scotty, who is ordered to drop a French spy behind enemy lines. But the plane crashes and the spy is killed. In a bid to escape from behind enemy lines Scotty swaps identities with the dead man, but is intercepted by the Germans. They believe him to be the dead Frenchman, who, it transpires, was a double-agent and working for the enemy. The quick-witted pilot manages to persuade the Germans that he knows plans for a huge British bombing – one that the Germans could intercept, and thus destroy the British aerial threat in one fell swoop: "His words thrilled his three hearers. For this was the dream of the German High Command – to shatter the hated power and superiority of the British squadrons on the Western Front."

Scotty manages to persuade them to let him fly a Fokker to escort the high-ranking Von Blohm to Berlin; instead, he doubles back to France, taking Von Blohm with him. Scotty is a hero; as well as saving his own skin he has put paid to a German spymaster! Scotty was to appear in many more *Modern Boy* adventures in subsequent years.

Above Scotty deals the enemy a crushing blow – in more ways than one – in the story "The Secret Squadron" in *Modern Boy*, 28 November 1936

Right Tiger Wallace, "The Master Spy", thrilled readers of *Rover* with his bravery and cunning in the Great War. This cover is dated 22 April 1939

Facing page Hiding out in occupied territory is easier if you have friends to help you. This was from *Skipper*, dated 23 December 1939

According to *Triumph*, John Silence was the "King of Spies" (story started in issue dated 22 April 1933); he was given free rein to uncover the enemy's war plans on the Western Front; the yarn was in a similar vein to "The Hooded Spy", which appeared in the launch issue of *Skipper* – "They seek him low/They seek him high/But cannot find/The Hooded Spy". The story centred on "No 29 of the British Secret Service", aka Major Walter Rand: "All his life he had run risks. He had prospected in the

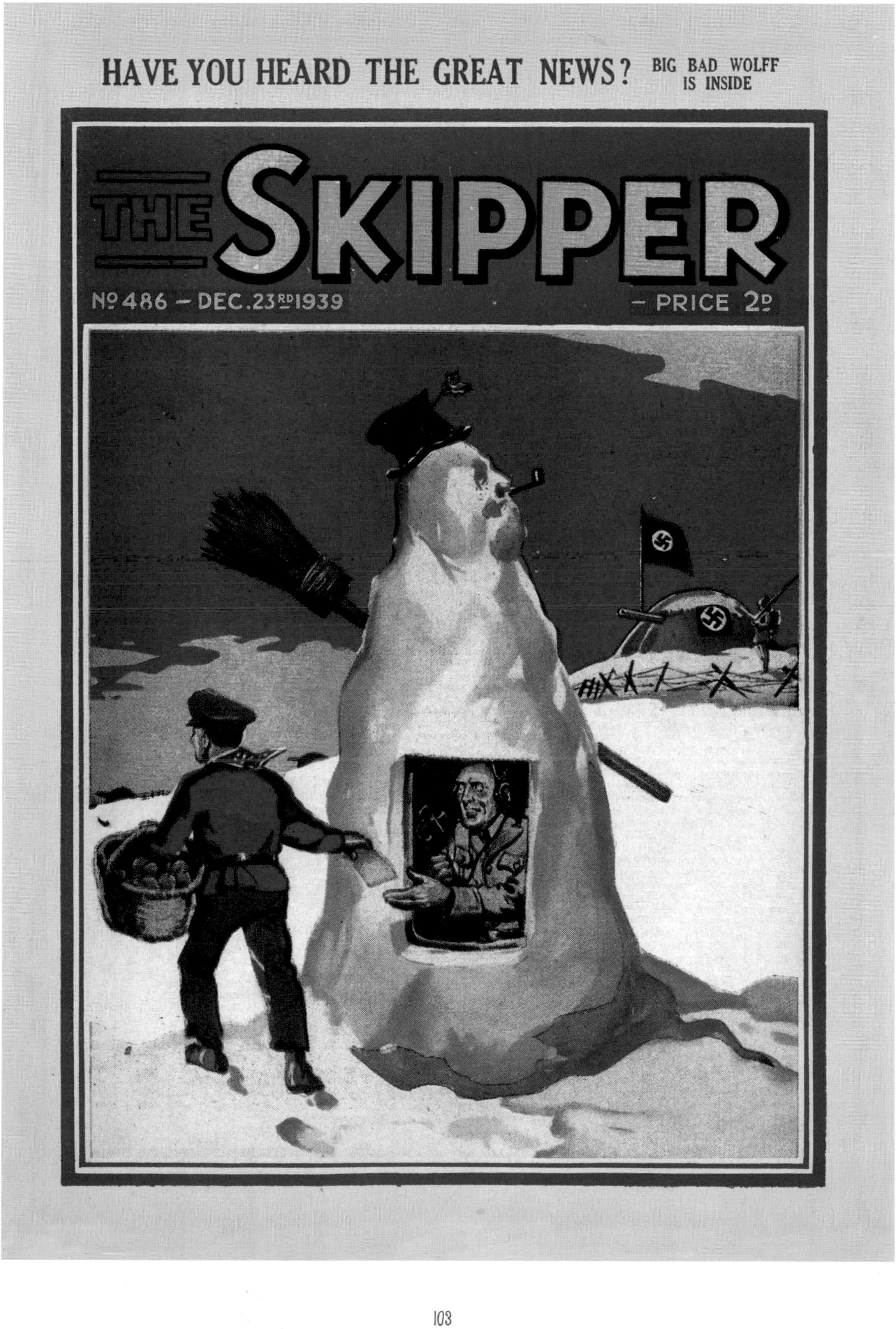
HAVE YOU HEARD THE GREAT NEWS?
BIG BAD WOLFF IS INSIDE
THE SKIPPER
No 486 – DEC. 23RD 1939
– PRICE 2D

HERBERT MACRAE'S Latest and Greatest Thriller Begins Below.

Above John Silence was "The King of Spies", *Triumph*, 22 April 1933

Below "'Stop! I'm English!' As the British soldier rushed at him with fixed bayonet, Tiger Wallace, dressed in German uniform, held up his hand and cried that he was English", for "The Master Spy" is in trouble in this *Rover* story dated 17 June 1939

Yukon; he had shot big game in Africa; had explored the Himalayas; had walked and worked in almost every country in the world. He was as hard as nails. In addition, he was known as the finest revolver shot in the army, and probably the world." But he was not the "Hooded Spy" – that was Baron Vortz – "the master spy of the German Secret Service". Interestingly, Vortz was not portrayed as an archetypal WW1 German villain: he was brave, cunning, resourceful, intelligent and generally to be admired. As well as adventure, issue one of *Skipper* also featured real-life action stories, including "The Man who Fell Six Miles" – "Major Schroeder went blind when his 'plane was 35,000 feet above the ground – his eyes froze solid!"

As the decade progressed, the boys' story-papers began to feature more and more stories of the "invasion literature" type that appeared in vast numbers in their counterparts in the run-up to the Great War. The genre had never entirely disappeared – *Modern Boy* (issue dated 8 August 1931) featured

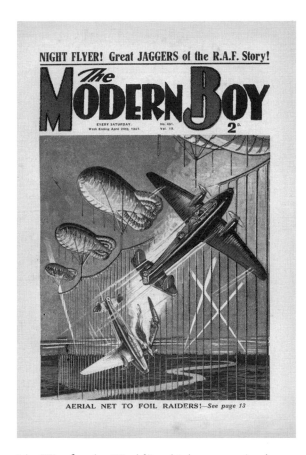

Above Two classic *Modern Boy* covers, both from 1937

"At War for the World", which was set in the year A.D. 2500. The story opens with a terrorist attack that devastates New York City – the work of Peran-Wisa, "the crazy Persian who would make himself Master of All the Earth".

Fortunately for the Western world, he had Andy Fox, a detective and inventor, on his trail. "At War for the World" was typical of the futuristic war fanatasies that appeared at the time, and the re-appearance of "invasion literature" stories reflected the growing tension that was developing in Europe throughout the 1930s. Hitler's rise to prominence and his consolidation of his power base in Germany, coupled with the Reich's aggressive talk of military expansion, created a new paranoia in Britain less than 20 years after the end of the Great War. Fear of aerial attack was widespread, with the threat of invasion by air and the bombing of British cities particularly acute. While there had been sporadic air raids during the Great War, huge technological advances meant an invasion by air was thought a strong possibility. *Modern Boy* (24 April 1937) had an idea of how to beat the foe – an "Aerial net to foil raiders!" Readers are told: "A barrier of steel wires, suspended from balloons, stretched across the sky; a giant net to trap enemy aeroplanes raiding Britain! That is one of the possible defence measures now being discussed. The idea is not

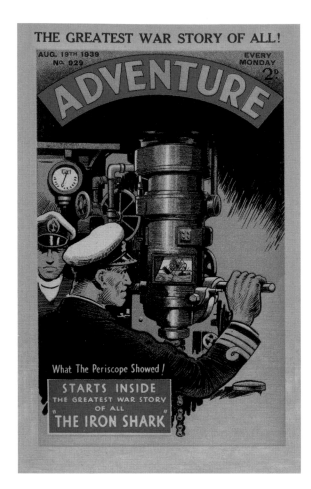

Above *Adventure* covers, both from 1939. "The Iron Shark" story was pre-war (dated 19 August) and was centred on the Great War; "The School of Deadly Secrets" appeared on 14 October, after war was declared, and related to the Second World War

new. In the Great War these "aprons", as they were called, were flown over London. As dusk fell, the captive balloons rose into the air, raising up the great net of steel wires, and when darkness came they were invisible. Nine thousand feet up in the air they went, and towards the end of the War they were planned to go to 12,000 feet. Now the idea is brought forward again, and it is suggested that an aerial screen stretching for hundreds of miles could be sent up. Climbing performances of bombing planes have increased tremendously since the War, but only the Government experts know how high the balloons could go. Only one plane was caught by the net during the War. But it is reckoned that the very existence of the net discouraged the raiders: the dread of being caught like a fly in the spider's web!"

This fear of aerial invasion was apparent in *Hotspur* story "The Secret of the Hated Hunchback". The story was set in Belwood School, where the "hated hunchback" was Huncher Newman, a teacher with a big secret. For "Great Britain was in danger! There were rumours of war in the air. A certain foreign power was likely to attack Britain at any moment now, for all efforts to keep peace seem to have failed. The newspapers were filled with gloomy reports and grim warnings. There would be no real declaration of war, they said, but one night enemy aircraft would fly over Britain and bomb the biggest cities. London would be blown to pieces. Newcastle, Leeds, Manchester, Glasgow, Edinburgh, Cardiff and Birmingham would be paralysed. In the big cities people went around with fear in their hearts. But at Belwood School, in the centre of the country, war seemed to be very far away. Belwood was a lonely place, surrounded by moorland, and the nearest village was four miles away. The boys of Belwood little dreamt that their school was now the most important part of Britain! The safety of the whole country depended on the working of an invention which was hidden in the school. In fact, only one man knew the secret of the strange invention which had been installed in Belwood by the British Government. This was the Fifth Form master, the man known as Huncher Newman because of the hump on his back. He was hated by the boys of his class, and disliked by the other masters. His bad temper and rudeness had made everyone believe that he was a sour, discontented man. Not

Above An all-action *Triumph* dated 15 April 1933

Below What is Huncher Newman's deadly secret? The story appeared in *Hotspur* throughout 1939

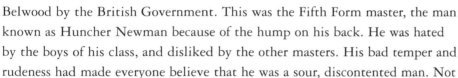

a soul in Belwood could claim Huncher Newman as his friend. However, Huncher Newman had a reason for making everyone hate him. He was the man in charge of Britain's strange invention and had been sent to Belwood at the command of Britain's Defence Chiefs. Huncher Newman, master of the Fifth Form, was also No. 473 in the British Secret Service! The secret apparatus was really a powerful electric ray which would bring enemy aeroplanes crashing to the ground before they could drop their deadly bombs."

The story-papers continued with this diet of Great War, invasion and spy stories right up to September 1939; sometimes the tales were a mix of all three, with a large dollop of science fiction thrown in. Understandably, with the exception of the Great War stories, the enemy were invariably fictional or nameless. All this changed with the outbreak of the Second World War, when scorn was poured on Nazi Germany. *The Rover*'s story "The Terror over the Nazis" (issue dated 2 December 1939) featured "The superman of the skies with a secret air base inside the German frontier!" Declaring on its title page in bold letters that "It's about the present war!", "The Terror over the Nazis" features the Steele family, who are on holiday in an Austrian castle when war is declared. They are stranded in enemy territory: "Castle Glockner had belonged to the Litzenhofen family for hundreds of years. Once they had been rich. But when the power-drunk Hitler had marched into Austria, his Nazi agents had whisked Count von Litzenhofen off to a

BIGGLES FIGHTS ALONE!

The whereabouts of the enemy's base is a secret no longer, but it is touch-and-go whether BIGGLES will live to reveal it!

Left Biggles was a hugely popular character who appeared in a number of comics. "Biggles Fights Alone" was in *Modern Boy*, issue dated 28 November 1936. In the story "the whereabouts of the enemy's base is a secret no longer, but it is touch-and-go whether Biggles will live to reveal it!"

Below The "Q" Squadron engages the enemy in the pages of *Hotspur*, 2 December 1939

Facing page Jerry Steele dons his schoolcap to drop bombs on the Germans from an aircraft piloted by his brother Richard. The story, "The Terror over the Nazis", first appeared on 2 December 1939 in *Rover*

concentration camp on some false charge of stirring up the people against the Reich. No more was heard of von Litzenhofen. He was said to have died within a month, a victim of the cruel Nazi system. Franz was the last of his family. There was now a strange look in his eyes – a look that one did not usually see in the eyes of a boy of thirteen. 'Oh, I don't think we shall be drawn into it, Franz,' remarked Mr Steele. 'The whole affair will be smoothed over as it has been before.' 'And Poland will disappear down Hitler's throat, like my own country, like Czechoslovakia, like the whole world if we do not watch!' said Franz, jumping down from the parapet, on which he had been sitting, his legs

This is the greatest school story ever written—

It tells about the adventures of 200 evacuated schoolboys at Britain's most famous school

It Starts To-Day

DR JEROME CARRYING ON

DEAD-WIDE DICK STILL SKIPPER OF THE SCHOOL

MR A. SMUGG AUX. FIRE CAPTAIN

THIS WEEK'S RED CIRCLE SCHOOL STORY

DIXIE DALE – ON SECRET SERVICE

SERGEANT COGG ON ACTIVE SERVICE.

KIT KIMBERLEY – ON SECRET SERVICE

AND HERE ARE RED CIRCLE'S NEW PUPILS – 200 EVACUATED BOYS FROM A BIG TOWN. READ ABOUT THEIR ADVENTURES AT THE FAMOUS SCHOOL

RED CIRCLE IN WARTIME

Above Pupils at Red Circle School had to share with evacuees "from a big town" in this wartime story dated 21 October 1939

Below Turbulence in Asia was the focus of the story "Ken Carries On" in *The Boy's Own Paper Annual* 1938-39. It was a story of the Second Sino-Japanese War, which started in July 1937. Ken's father, a doctor, was murdered by the Japanese; here, Ken confronts Chinese troops looking for injured Japanese soldiers being treated in the hospital

dangling into space. 'It is cruel – wicked! Why does not someone stop this mad German?'" Soon a gyroplane lands in the grounds of the castle, piloted by the Steele's eldest son, Richard, who uses the castle as a base from which to attack the enemy – the "terror over the Nazis".

War in the air was also the theme of *Hotspur*'s wartime story "Reckless Men of 'Q' Squadron", about "the secret air-fighters who dare death in the skies to battle for Britain". The "Q" Squadron are all members of Blade's Flying Circus, pre-war daredevil flyers who had "formed a barnstorming team which travelled from place to place giving aerobatic performances in small towns all over the States". They are captured by German troops but escape, joining up with the Polish Air Force before quickly being recruited to the "Q Squadron". Their leader, Dan Blade, is told: "'…you can fight for your country in a service for which your special talents make you admirably suitable. I mean the Secret Service, of course.' 'I'm an airman, not a

Above "The Fighting Free-lance" in typically belligerent mood, on the cover of *Triumph*, dated 11 March 1933

WAR SAVINGS CERTIFICATES OFFERED FREE TO READERS!

MAY 11TH 1940 — EVERY MONDAY — No. 967 — 2D

ADVENTURE

WHAT WILL LORD HAW-HAW SAY ABOUT THIS?
READ ABOUT IT IN THIS WEEK'S 'SLIPPERY SLINK'

Above As the war progressed the comics began to mercilessly lampoon the Nazi hierarchy, especially Hitler, as this *Adventure* cover demonstrates, dated 11 June 1940

Facing page Seeing the funny side, in *Adventure* dated 20 November 1943

Below Paper was a vital commodity and wartime – and in short supply. Readers were urged to recycle their comics to help the war effort, as this appeal in *Adventure* in the issue dated 2 January 1943 shows

detective, sir!' 'We need airmen, for our Q squadrons.' 'Q squadrons?' 'Yes. Squadrons that play a bigger game than shooting down enemy aircraft. The air arm has become as vitally necessary to the Secret Service as it is to the Army or the Navy. And its work is of such a delicate, dangerous nature that only specially picked men can be used, men like yourself, Blade – may I say rather reckless – fellows who stick at nothing!'"

But the war was to take its toll on British boys' story-papers and comics; by 1940 paper was in extremely short supply and a number of long-established and much-loved titles were forced to cease publishing. So a fond farewell was bade to, among others, *Triumph*, *Skipper* and *Chums*, while *Modern Boy* was axed just six weeks after the outbreak of the Second World War. *Triumph* ran for 814 issues over more than 15 years and was Amalgamated Press's companion paper to *The Champion*. *Triumph* had incorporated three titles over the years: *The Rocket* in 1924; *The Boys' Friend* in 1928; and *Gem*, on 13 January 1940. Soon after this merger, *Triumph* also succumbed and was subsumed into *The Champion*, on 25 May 1940. Previously, *Modern Boy* had been incorporated into *Boys' Cinema*, on 21 October 1939. *Chums*, launched in 1892 by Cassell, was sold to Amalgamated Press in 1927. It became a monthly publication in August 1932; by 1934 it had become an annual. In 1941 it ceased publication, as did *Skipper*, the first of D.C. Thomson's "Big Five" titles to be closed down.

As the war progressed war stories dominated the comics and story-papers. Both *The Boy's Own Paper* and *The Scout* ("The only official organ of the Boy Scouts") mixed fictional stories with features and articles focusing on both

ANY OLD MAGAZINE WILL HELP TO FILL HIS MAGAZINE!

Our snipers will take care of the Huns if you take care of the waste paper.

SAVE EVERY SCRAP!

the fighting overseas and the home front. So while Scouts were urged to do all they could to help the war effort, readers of *The Boy's Own Annual* 1938-39 were treated to articles on "Helping the A.R.P. – Jobs that you can do". Boys should... "make the acquaintance of your nearest A.R.P. warden. You can

NEWS ABOUT "The Last White Boy In Singapore."

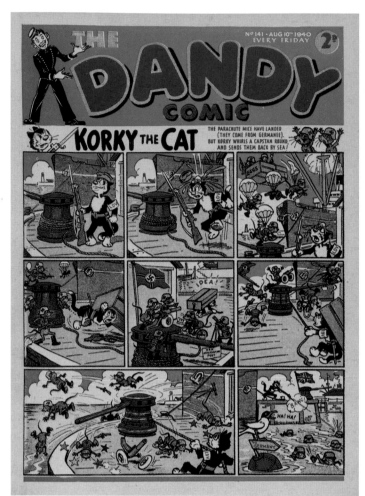

easily find him by the plate on his house. It's pretty certain he'll be glad to know he can call on you for any little odd jobs he needs doing, and he may give you tips on things you can do right away. Probably he's a busy man, so don't worry him unduly; but in any emergency take care to be on hand if he thinks he will be able to use you."

Above The children's comics wasted no opportunity to stick it to the enemy. Here Korky the Cat takes his revenge in *The Dandy* on a band of Nazi "parachute mice", issue dated 10 August 1940

Below Lord Snooty knows exactly how to deal with the Fuhrer, in *The Beano* dated 16 November 1940

The children's comics joined in the fun, too. Both *The Dandy* (launched 4 December 1937) and *The Beano* (launched 30 July 1938) mercilessly lampooned the enemy, in stories such as "Musso the Wop" ("He's a big-a-da flop") and "Addie and Hermy". Big Eggo, Desperate Dan, Pansy Potter and Lord Snooty never missed an opportunity to stick it to the enemy. As D.C. Thomson's own *The History of the Beano* relates, the Fuhrer was not best pleased "at the incessant mockery. This suggestion is backed up by intercepted wartime records of a planned German invasion which stated that a list of prominent newspaper editors and publishers were to be captured and made answerable to Hitler for the crime of 'gross disrespect'. This list included the Editor of *The Beano* as well as the prodigious artist Dudley Watkins, who was held back from active military service due to the irreplaceable positive impact he was deemed to be making on the nation's morale."

D.C. Thomson's *Adventure* took a global approach to the conflict; its stories

were set in the European, African and Asian theatres of war, and even in the United States. The story "The Yellow Ghost", which appeared throughout 1943, concerned the attempts of fugitive German and Japanese plotters living in California to sabotage the US military effort. They are aided by "The Yellow Ghost", an invisible spy; and the allies have their work cut out to thwart his dastardly efforts, as described to Robert Lewis O'Brien of the US Secret Service by a government attorney: "'You won't believe me when I tell you. I can hardly believe it myself,' he said, 'but they've got the Boeing 77 plans and specification in their hands, and plan to have someone present at the demonstration of the new mortar tomorrow.' Bob O'Brien leapt to his feet with a growl. There was a good deal of the bulldog about him when he looked like that. 'Are they magicians?' he roared. 'Almost, or at least one of them is. They have a man they call The Yellow Ghost, undoubtedly a Jap who is their star turn for spying. The blighter is invisible!'" (issue dated 22 May 1943).

Above Italian dictator Mussolini was constantly in the firing line in *The Beano*. This episode is dated 28 June 1941

Below Hitler and Goering are the "nasty Nazis", in *The Dandy*, dated 14 December 1940

While set on a different continent, the story "The Last White Boy in Singapore" also focused on the war with Japan. Alan Shand is a 14-year-old British lad whose father is fighting a guerilla war on the Malayan Peninsular against the Japanese – with the help of Alan and the Australian forces. Alan captures a Japanese officer and hands him over to his father: "'It's me, Dad, and I've got a prisoner, a Japanese officer.' 'That's dinkum!' came a growl from one of the figures in the boat. Where is the yellow rat?' Alan Shand pointed, and a burly, ragged figure slithered over to fetch the prisoner. No one in Malaya hated Japs with more intensity than Sergeant Seaton of the Australian Forces. He would have cut their throats on sight if he could have had his way" (issue dated 4 December 1943).

"Seven Iron Crosses" was a story of espionage set in Berlin. Captain Kruft, working for the British, manages to steal a top-secret code, but is caught before he can pass it on to his British contact. But Kruft manages to scratch the "Panzer Code" on a series of Iron Cross medals. Kruft is killed, and the medals are distributed, and it is left to Major Elton of the British Secret Service to recover them from the seven recipients and piece the code together. The story ran until 24 September 1943, when Elton completes his task, and communicates the information to his superior officer: "'This is Elton, sir, and I've got it. There's no need for me to wait to come to see you. Take it down now, sir. Here it is – 65487612. That's the last line of numerals that we needed.' At the other end of the wire, where the head of the Secret Service sat, came a low gasp of delight. 'Magnificent, Elton!' he cried. 'Good man!' That was all, but Major Elton went to the bed provided for him at the aerodrome with the knowledge that from now onward the famous German Panzer Code was an open book to the British Government."

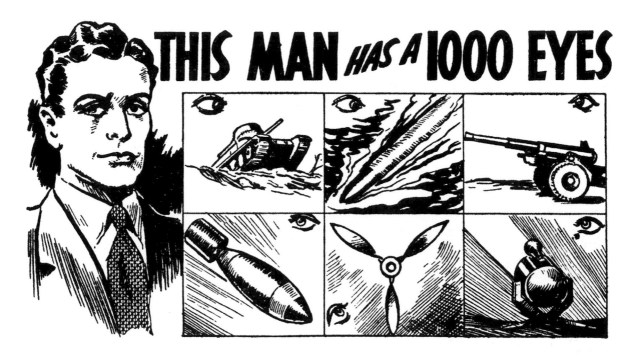

THIS MAN HAS A 1000 EYES

In the pages of **The Hotspur**, the pupils of the ever-popular Red Circle School were also doing their bit for the war effort. There's no need to explain the premise behind the story entitled "The Yanks are Coming!" (issue dated 2 January 1943), but "there was great excitement at Red Circle School. The news had just come out that a large number of American soldiers were coming to the district and that many of them were to be billeted at the school itself."

Above Hidden cameras gave top spy Royd Murray a huge advantage over his opponents, in *Wizard*, dated 11 December 1943

Below Guerilla war against the Japanese was the subject of the story, "The Last White Boy in Singapore", *Adventure*, 4 December 1943

The comic retained its focus on schoolboy stories throughout the war. Bob Deane, a 16-year-old schoolboy, was the hero of the story "The Seven Bullets" – he "has to go to school in Germany to help the British Secret Service". His father, in a German prisoner of war camp, has invented a high explosive that will change the nature of aerial warfare. But his secret is discovered and rather than hand over the secret powder to the Germans,

Adventure

THE LAST WHITE BOY IN SINGAPORE

THE WOLF OF KABUL

Bob's father explodes it, blinding himself in the process. He is sprung from the prisoner of war camp by the Secret Service, and Bob is sent to Germany to meet with his father and bring back the formula.

The "Q" Squadron, whom we met at the start of the war, continued to fight the good fight in the pages of *The Hotspur* for the duration. Dan Blade and company were at the controls of a unique new weapon known as "The Flying Crusher" (story started 17 July 1943). The pals are staggered by the enormous, weird contraption, but soon set to work, using the machine's giant pincers to crush an E-boat that was going about its deadly business. "Krantz looked up. He uttered a gasp. A strange huge shape was descending from the mist. It hovered above the E-boat. Two fantastic arms of steel began to close. It was the Crusher. 'Hard aport!' shouted Krantz, and the boat heeled over with a violence that bowled over torpedo men and gunners. 'Himmel!' The jaws shut. There was a grinding and a smashing as the teeth crunched into the the hull of the E-boat. Aloft, Dan Blade stared downwards. He shifted the lever, and slowly the Crusher began to ascend. The rotors spun ever more rapidly, and… the doomed E-boat was lifted from the waves. Higher, higher it was carried like a victim in the claws of an eagle. Then from a hundred feet Blade let it go. The E-boat hit the surface of the sea and smashed into fragments."

Weird and wonderful inventions were a common feature of many wartime yarns in the boys' comics and story-papers — although some were more realistic than others. *The Wizard*'s story

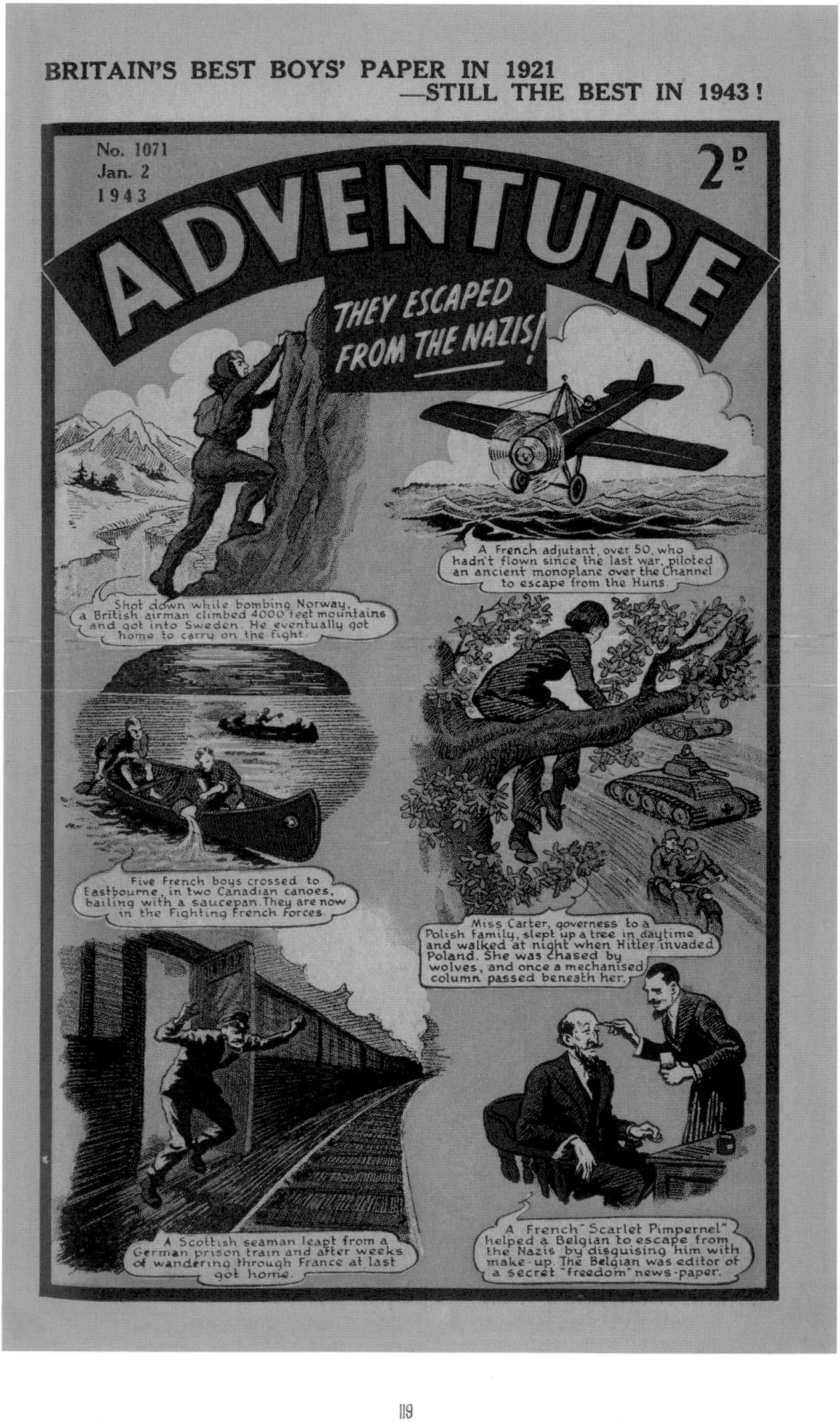
BRITAIN'S BEST BOYS' PAPER IN 1921
—STILL THE BEST IN 1943!
No. 1071
Jan. 2
1943
2D
ADVENTURE
THEY ESCAPED FROM THE NAZIS!
A French adjutant, over 50, who hadn't flown since the last war, piloted an ancient monoplane over the Channel to escape from the Huns.
Shot down while bombing Norway, a British airman climbed 4000 feet mountains and got into Sweden. He eventually got home to carry on the fight.
Five French boys crossed to Eastbourne, in two Canadian canoes, bailing with a saucepan. They are now in the Fighting French Forces.
Miss Carter, governess to a Polish family, slept up a tree in daytime and walked at night when Hitler invaded Poland. She was chased by wolves, and once a mechanised column passed beneath her.
A Scottish seaman leapt from a German prison train and after weeks of wandering through France at last got home.
A French "Scarlet Pimpernel" helped a Belgian to escape from the Nazis by disguising him with make-up. The Belgian was editor of a secret "freedom" news-paper.

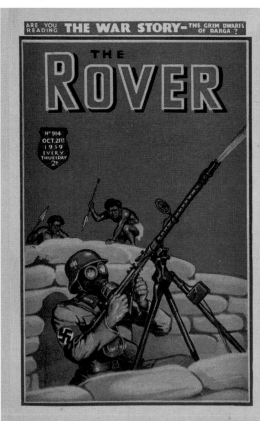

"This Man has a 1000 Eyes" (started issue dated 11 December 1943) features "a British spy who collects secret information by miniature cameras!" The hero, Royd Murray, was the inventor of the tiny cameras which were secreted in cap badges and other items, providing a steady flow of intelligence to the Allies.

Rover's story "Raiders from the Depth" is set in German-occupied Russia (started issue dated 23 January 1943). But the Russians have "human torpedoes" on their side; a crack commando unit who are "fired" from a submarine, who "moved with the speed of torpedoes, but they were living men, clad in padded rubber garments, wearing helmets of special design".

In a propaganda fantasy story in *Rover*, called "The Ghost Voice Speaks" (6 March 1943), a mystery man who goes by the name of "Nemo" has technology that enables him to interrupt radio broadcasts – an opportunity the "Ghost Voice" is keen to exploit. Hiding out in a copse with his transmission equipment, Nemo waits for Propaganda Minister Goebbels to broadcast to the German nation: "The man in the copse continued to listen, until suddenly the voice of the announcer came over the air. 'In exactly fifty seconds, Herr Goebbels, Press and Publicity Minister of the Reich, will be speaking to you. Stand by for Herr Goebbels!' 'And for his lies!' said [Nemo] clearly and distinctly into the microphone. 'In less than thirty seconds you will hear Herr Goebbels trying to explain our defeats on the Russian front.' He spoke in fluent German, quietly and distinctly, and the apparatus before him was capable of carrying his voice to the powerful power wave on which Goebbels was about to address the whole of Germany." Later Nemo interrupts: "Already we have had more casualties than we had in the whole of the Great War of 1914 to 1918. This is Nemo giving you the facts that are hidden by Goebbels.'"

The stories in the comics and boys' story-papers continued through the war in much the same vein; mixing high-tech fantasy with espionage and schoolboy heroics. So in *The Hotspur* in 1945 readers were treated to "The Walkie-Talkie Warrior" (issue dated 13 January 1945), in which Major Jock Brett, aka "the Vanishing Major", directs air operations from the ground with the aid of "a cylinder about a foot long, with a mouthpiece and an earpiece like a telephone receiver. There was a dial on one end and one or two knobs and switches. It was, in fact, an amazingly compact radio telephone, called a Walkie-Talkie." Indeed, the Walkie-Talkie was a new invention – it was developed by Donald Lewes Hings, a Canadian inventor. In 1937 he created a portable radio signalling system which he called a "packset", but which later

Above Gemany was taunted by a "ghost voice" on the airwaves in this *Rover* story, 6 March 1943

became known as the "Walkie-Talkie". It was used by the military from 1940 onwards, and was often called the "Handie-Talkie". The "Q" Squadron made a reappearance in the issue dated 6 October 1945, this time flying "The Smasher" in the story "'Q' Squadron's Flying Smasher". This new-fangled aircraft featured a "long and ponderous gun-barrel extending forward over the cockpit from a 'hump' on top of the fuselage. A second glance showed that the barrel

Left A Japanese soldier as depicted in *The Boy's Own Annual* 1945

Facing page "The Grim Dwarfs of Darga" formed the personal bodyguard of African hunter Lee White. He had the details of a "duralanite" mine, a light metal that was stronger than steel and which could be used to build superior fighters and bombers. So it was vital he returned to Britain with the information. The *Rover* story followed White's adventures with the Grim Dwarfs as they headed for Blighty

was in actuality a hollow tube for firing a rocket and open at the rear to permit the discharge of the gases."

After the Allies' victory in Europe, in May 1945, *Adventure* continued publishing war stories, switching to the Pacific theatre with the story "The Tank with the Purple Heart", a "smashing yarn of the war in Burma". *The Boy's Own Paper* was quick to publish a retrospective of the main events of the war in an article headlined "The Way We Came Through" (June 1945).

Of greater interest is the *Adventure* story "They'll Try It Again!" The tale, which first appeared on 27 March 1945, was a "new and thrilling story of another World War!" Readers are told that: "We didn't finish the Germans in 1918 – They rose again in 1945. If we don't finish them in 1945 – THEY'LL TRY IT AGAIN!" Bizarrely, it was a story of the "invasion literature" genre, predicting a Nazi conquest of the United States in 1965 as a prelude to an invasion of Britain – yet the fighting in Europe at the time it was published was still going on. In the story, the US is saved by a British counter-invasion, and once more the Nazis (this time the "Fifth Reich") are defeated.

Below "Invasion literature" returned with this story from *Adventure*, dated 26 March 1945, predicting Germany's re-emergence as a military power in 1965

The Second World War ended in Europe on 8 May 1945; in the comics and story-papers, its battles were to be fought and re-told and its heroes remembered for the following five decades.

THE HUN HUNTER OF 1965!

Above "Rockfist" Rogan, the fighter pilot and boxing star, was a hugely popular character in *Champion* who went on to appear in many other comics over the years. This cover is from the issue dated 4 November 1944

"I DON'T KNOW WHETHER WAR IS AN INTERLUDE DURING PEACE, OR PEACE AN INTERLUDE DURING WAR"

Georges Clemenceau (1841-1929)

CHAPTER FIVE
FIGHT THE GOOD FIGHT

THE PRIVATIONS OF THE Second World War were keenly felt by the publishing industry, with acute paper shortages accounting for a number of titles. D.C. Thomson emerged from the war in the strongest position of all the publishers; the Dundee firm's only casualty was *Skipper*. The surviving four of the "Big Five" – *Adventure*, *Rover*, *Hotspur* and *Wizard* – prospered into the 1950s. The decade is often described as the "Golden Age" of British comics, and that was certainly true for D.C. Thomson; the company's children's comics, especially *The Beano* and *The Dandy*, enjoyed huge sales. Its rivals, notably Amalgamated Press, were trailing in the market, and looking at ways of recovering lost ground.

The first major launch of the 1950s was eventually to become one of Britain's best-loved and critically praised comics, and one that did much to popularise the comic-strip format. Yet the *Eagle* had an unusual provenance, for its existence owed everything to an eccentric priest from Lancashire. Reverend Marcus Morris was already making waves far beyond his Birkdale patch by producing probably the most unusual parish magazine anywhere in Britain, *The Anvil*. A far cry from the typical parish magazine, *The Anvil* was lively and thought-provoking, and its fame spread far and wide. C.S. Lewis, Prime Minister-to-be Harold Macmillan and the cartoonist Norman Thelwell all contributed to it at different times.

But as a firm believer in the power of the written word, a new phenomenon was beginning to concern Morris. As he wrote in his history of the comic, *Best of Eagle*, he was concerned by the "rise and rule of the comic in America", and having studied what British children were reading, came up with

ANOTHER SMASH-HIT RED CIRCLE STORY INSIDE

No. 876—AUG. 22nd, 1953

THE

HOTSPUR

EVERY THURSDAY   PRICE 3d

VIVE LA FRANCE

The PHANTOM ARCHER STRIKES AGAIN

Above The "Phantom Archer" had the Nazis occupying France in a panic in the story "I Was a Secret Flyer", which appeared in *Hotspur*. This cover is dated 22 August 1953.
Facing page The hero of "I Was a Secret Flyer" was Nick Waring, a 17-year-old pilot stranded in France, where he linked up with the local Resistance force. Here Nick encounters a spot of bother while trying to escape the Nazis in a battered old van belonging to the French freedom fighters. The story appeared in the issue dated 29 August 1953

THE LONE COMMANDOS in OPERATION GUNFIRE

By EDWARD R. HOME-GALL

DURING THE WAR, LONDON AND SOUTH-EAST ENGLAND WERE THE TARGET FOR GERMANY'S FLYING BOMBS. THEY CROSSED THE CHANNEL IN HUNDREDS, TO WRECK BRITISH HOMES AND TO BRING DEATH TO BRITISH PEOPLE. THE BOMBS WERE LAUNCHED FROM RAMPS IN NORTHERN FRANCE; AND IT WAS TO DESTROY THOSE RAMPS, AND THE STOCKS OF FLYING BOMBS NEARBY, THAT A FORCE OF BRITISH COMMANDOS LANDED NEAR CALAIS TO TAKE PART IN "OPERATION GUNFIRE". WITH THEIR JOB WELL DONE, THE COMMANDOS STARTED TO RETURN TO THE SHIPS WHICH WERE TO CARRY THEM BACK TO ENGLAND. THEY KNEW THAT OTHER TROOPS HAD HAD THE JOB OF DESTROYING ALL THE GERMAN COASTAL GUNS IN THE DISTRICT. THIS WOULD ENSURE THAT THE SHIPS WOULD BE ABLE TO SAIL IN SAFETY

AMONG THE COMMANDOS WHO HAD TAKEN PART IN THE RAID ON THE FLYING BOMB SITES WERE TWO PALS –– SGT. ROY TEMPEST AND PTE. JACK STEEL. SITTING IN A JEEP. THEY WERE NOW SPEEDING TOWARDS THE BEACH TO BOARD A LANDING CRAFT

WELL, SERG, IT LOOKS AS IF THE SHOW HAS BEEN A BIG SUCCESS, AND THAT THE BOYS WILL BE ABLE TO MAKE AN EASY GETAWAY. NOT A SINGLE GERMAN GUN IS FIRING

I GUESS ALL THE GUNS HAVE BEEN PUT OUT OF ACTION, JACK –– HELLO, WHAT'S THAT?

Above and facing page, bottom
"The Lone Commandos" were popular heroes in the pages of *Lion* throughout the 1950s. Here they appear in a story called "Operation Gunfire", in the *Lion Annual* 1954

the idea for *Eagle*. He wrote: "Many American comics were most skilfully and vividly drawn, but often their content was deplorable, nastily over-violent and obscene, often with undue emphasis on the supernatural and magical as a way of solving problems. But it was clear to me that the strip cartoon was capable of development in a way not yet seen in England except in one or two of the daily and Sunday newspapers and that it was a new and important medium of communication, with its own laws and limitations. Here, surely, was a form which could be used to convey to the child the right kind of standards, values and attitudes, combined with the necessary amount of excitement and adventure."

Morris was on a mission – to make the concept fly. For the next 16 months the *Eagle* was in development, although the response from publishers was lukewarm. Eventually, Hulton Press agreed to publish it, and the first issue hit the streets on 14 April 1950. The gamble paid off – at the height of its popularity *Eagle* was selling just under one million copies a week, and its influence was apparent on every other British boys' comic.

War fiction was not a major feature of *Eagle* – the emphasis was on adventure and fantasy. Its most famous character was "Dan Dare, Pilot of the Future". But there were plenty of "true-life" features – "The Happy Warrior", which throughout 1957 and 1958 was "the true life story of Sir Winston Churchill".

Eagle's success galvanised Amalgamated Press and the company rose to the challenge with the launch of two titles: *Lion* in 1952 and *Tiger* in 1954. *Lion*'s launch issue, dated 23 February 1952, came with a free gift of a "sports star" album, and featured the war story "The Lone Commandos". The fighting men of the title were Sergeant Roy Tempest and Private Jack Steel, and their mission was "to destroy a German radar station at La Vaste, in Nazi-occupied territory, fifty miles inland from the French coast". They are sent off with their commanding officer's words ringing in their ears: "There's none of my men I would rather trust with this job than you, Sergeant, and you were right to ask for Private Steel to go with you. He's tough – tough as steak. Goodbye – and good luck! And blow that radar station to little pieces."

Above "The Lone Commandos" are in a tight spot having just blown up a German radar station, in *Lion*, issue dated 26 July 1952

AT BUSTER'S OMINOUS WORDS, STEVE AND DUSTY WHEELED ROUND

STUPID BRITISHERS! OUR RADAR FOLLOWED YOUR EVERY MOVE TO THIS ISLAND. IF YOU TRY TO ESCAPE, YOU WILL BE SHOT. NOW PLEASE TO ACCOMPANY HUMBLE SELF. MARCH!

Above "The Naval Castaways" are captured by the Japanese, *Lion*, 9 August 1952

Below, and below, facing page Escape was the ambition for the prisoners of Calitz Camp, *Lion*, 25 July 1953. The story continues on pages 132–133 and 134–135

But the pals' plane is shot down and they are forced to bail out on the coast, and have to make their way fifty miles through dangerous countryside to get to their target. Mission accomplished, the duo are rescued by helicopter from certain death when they are trapped on an aerial surrounded by burning trees (issue dated 26 July 1952).

"The Naval Castaways", a "powerful war picture story" written by Joe Colquhoun, who had served in the Navy in the war, was set in the South Pacific (started issue dated 2 August 1952). Steve Hazard, Dusty Miller and Buster Brown are shipwrecked on a desert island when their cruiser, *HMS Newley*, is destroyed by Japanese dive-bombers. But unfortunately for the friends, the island is occupied by the Japanese, who are using it as a base to launch their own version of the devastating "V2" rocket.

No one could accuse the *Lion*'s story-writers of conventionality. "Frogmen Are Tough!" was by Edward R. Home-Gall, a prolific writer of boys' stories who also wrote under the pen-name Edwin Dale. Set in Second World War Italy, Don Drew and Nobby Pounds were two British frogmen who volunteered to find "some powerful secret weapon [that] was being used

THE SECRET TUNNELLERS of CALITZ CAMP

By REX KING

SERGEANT WILSON WAS THE LEADER OF A PARTY OF BRITISH SOLDIERS WHO WERE CAPTURED DURING THE WAR.
THEY LIVED IN HUT 13 AT CALITZ PRISON CAMP, IN THE HEART OF GERMANY.
DETERMINED TO BREAK FREE, THEY PLANNED TO DIG AN ESCAPE TUNNEL FROM BENEATH A BANDSTAND IN THE COMPOUND.
IN THE HOPE OF FINDING SOMETHING TO DIG WITH, SGT. WILSON AND TWO OF HIS MEN — TUBBY AND ANDY — CREPT THROUGH THE DARKNESS TO THE FOOD STORE.
TWO GERMANS WERE IN THERE, BUT ANDY LURED THEM INTO THE ADJOINING COOKHOUSE BY MAKING SOME SAUCEPANS BOIL OVER

NERVES TENSED, SGT. WILSON AND TUBBY STEPPED SWIFTLY INTO THE FOOD STORE

THERE DOESN'T SEEM TO BE A SPADE HERE, SERG

SHH! YOU WATCH THAT DOOR, TUBBY, IN CASE THOSE JERRIES RETURN I'LL HAVE A QUICK LOOK ROUND. WE'VE GOT TO ACT FAST, OR WE'LL BE CAUGHT

SPOTTING SOME PIES ON A TABLE, TUBBY COULDN'T RESIST HELPING HIMSELF TO ONE AND TRYING IT

I EXPECT THESE WERE MADE FOR THE GERMAN OFFICERS' MESS. MMMM! THEY'RE GOOD! I'LL TAKE SOME BACK FOR THE BOYS

by the enemy. For Allied ships, carrying vital supplies, were being mysteriously sunk to the north of Sicily".

Lion's editors were keen to present different aspects of the war, and Rex King's "The Secret Tunnellers of Calitz Camp" did just that. Set in a prisoner of war camp in the heart of Germany's Black Forest, legend had it that no one had ever escaped from Calitz. But Andy "The Trickster" Ellis had other ideas, and hatched a plan to dig a tunnel from the unused bandstand in the middle of the camp (story started 27 June 1953). "Lost Pals of 9 Platoon", written by Cliff Hooper, was set in Italy and featured Joe Dale and Shorty Brown (story started 6 February 1954). Operating behind enemy lines, their mission was to destroy German "radio guns" that were being operated from a secret location and were holding up the Allied advance across Europe. An all-action comic-strip story, the "Lost Pals" proved extremely popular and the characters appeared in many comics and annuals throughout the 1950s.

Above There was trouble in store for pals Joe and Shorty, in the story "The Mystery House in No-Man's-Land", *Lion Annual* 1956

Above "The Tough Frogmen" in action, *Lion*, 30 August 1952

Below and below, facing page Trouble in Calitz Camp, *Lion*, 25 July 1953. More from this story on pages 134–135

The avid **Lion** reader for whom 52 issues a year was not enough could always turn to the annual for another fix of war stories. For the reader these stories had the advantage that they were complete, and many favourite characters enjoyed further adventures in the pages of the annuals. In the **Lion Annual** 1956 the "Lost Pals" Joe and Shorty appeared in a tale set on the Italian front called "Mystery House in No-Man's-Land". A patrol is ordered to destroy a derelict cottage that German snipers are exploiting, but they fail to return from their mission. When this happens twice more, Joe and Shorty are ordered to investigate. In the cotttage the pair stumble across a secret passage, hidden behind an old fireplace and leading to the German trenches, in which the lost patrolmen are found, trussed up. The men are freed and an ambush is set – when the Germans return they are captured and the tunnel – and the "Mystery House" – are destroyed.

Don Drew and Nobby Pounds, the "Tough Frogmen", appeared in another undersea adventure in the *Lion Annual* 1955. The tale was called "Operation Frogman!" – "During the war, the Germans built a submarine parent-ship of a new and deadly type. Its task was to service a fleet of U-Boats which, hoping to sink all Allied ships, surrounded the British Isles. The German parent-ship was based in a Norwegian fjord, and so well-protected was it that the enemy were convinced that it was safe from attack."

A similar story appeared in the *Lion Annual* 1959, with the "Frogman Pals in Operation Torpedo!". The two young hero marines are Nobby Clark and Bert Bradley, whose mission was to destroy a German submarine base from which the enemy was launching U-Boat attacks on shipping convoys.

Above A fuming Führer in rages after 'Battler' Britton outwits the Luftwaffe, *Sun Weekly,* 4 October 1953

In the same year, *Lion* incorporated a title called *Sun*, which was launched in January 1948 as *Fitness and Sun* by independent publishers J.B.Allen. The comic started as a fortnightly publication and after just four issues it dropped the word "Fitness" to become *Sun*. It was sold to Amalgamated Press on 24 May 1949 and on 20 May 1950, *Sun* became a weekly publication. *Sun Weekly* is notable for being one of the first titles to switch entirely to a comic-strip presentation, abandoning traditional text-based stories (issue dated 10 September 1955). On the war front, the most notable character in *Sun Weekly* was the punningly-titled "Battler Britton", a Wing Commander in the RAF in the Second World War. The comic's cover star, Battler was involved in much

Above 'Battler' Britton in action, *Sun Weekly*, 12th July 1958

Below and below, facing page The conclusion of "The Secret Tunnellers of Calitz Camp", *Lion*, 25th July 1953

aerial high-jinx and dog-fight action; in one instalment he captures "a new secret German plane, complete with its pilot, the German air ace Karl Neubolt" (issue dated 4 October 1953). In the final frame we see a furious Adolf Hitler cursing as he hears the news, broadcasted into Germany by the BBC.

The air ace's run came to an end when, on 24 October 1959, after 558 issues, *Sun Weekly* was incorporated into *Lion*. In its lifetime it was known variously as *Fitness and Sun*; *Sun*; *Sun Comic*; *Sun Adventure Weekly*; *The Cowboy Sun*; and *Sun Weekly*.

Spurred on by the success of *Lion*, Amalgamated launched a companion paper, *Tiger*, on 11 September 1954 (the comic's full name was *Tiger – The Sport and Adventure Picture Story Weekly*). While *Tiger* looked a tad old-fashioned compared with *Eagle* and *Lion*, carrying traditional text stories as well as comic strips, it was an instant success. Its primary focus was sports stories – this was, after all, the comic in which "Roy of the Rovers" first appeared – but action, adventure and war stories were also included.

"Fugitive Flyers in Enemy-Held France" (9 October 1954) was one of a series of "Daring Escape Stories" by Frank S. Pepper – the man who created "Roy of the Rovers". The "fugitive flyers" were "brought down behind enemy lines!

Their plane a mass of flames! Hunted by German patrols! Mike and Terry's plight seemed hopeless. But they were determined to avoid capture – and to save the gallant Frenchman who helped them."

Some of *Tiger*'s output seemed to hark back to the pre-war story-papers. One such example was "Tales of Whitestoke School" (27 November 1954). A Nazi fighter plane crashes into woods close to the school and the boys become "The Schoolboy Nazi-Hunters".

The success of *Tiger* was such that it soon became the dominant

ROCKFIST ROGAN–
Secret Flyer of Squadron X

Above "Rockfist" Rogan, boxing champ and air ace, was a very popular character, first in *Champion* then later in *Tiger*. The illustration above is from the *Champion Annual 1954*

title in Amalgamated Press's stable. This was apparent when the long-running *Champion* was incorporated into *Tiger*, on 19 March 1955. *Champion* was a product of the post-Great War boom in story-papers, launching on 28 January 1922 and running for 1,729 issues. Derek Birnage, who edited *Champion* immediately after the Second World War, was also the launch editor of *Tiger*, so he knew exactly what he was getting. There's no doubt that *Tiger*'s roster of stories was strengthened by the arrival in its pages of the hugely popular "Rockfist Rogan", one of *Champion*'s star attractions. Rockfist, a boxing champ as well as ace pilot, first appeared in *Champion* in 1938. The stories were

penned by Hal Wilton – a pseudonym used by Frank S. Pepper. Birnage wasted no time in getting Rockfist stories into the pages of *Tiger* – his debut was in the issue dated 26 March 1955, in a Second World War story. *Tiger* readers are told what *Champion* readers already knew, that: "Rockfist and his pals were members of the Freelance Squadron, a specially picked group of ace pilots, trained to fly many different types of aircraft and capable of taking on vital flying duties wherever the need was greatest. At the moment the most desperate task was to beat back the swarms of enemy raiders who were trying to smash Britain's air defences and clear the way for an invasion. Rockfist, Curly and Archie were three among the gallant and unconquerable few who were flying and fighting almost continuously round the clock, battling against odds of ten to one." The cast of regulars was completed by Dizzy Dyall, "Rockfist's scatter-brained batman". He was "the most muddle-headed airman on the station. He wore his forage cap sideways, his clothes would have disgraced a scarecrow; yet

Below "The Lone Commandos" were far from alone during this raid on a German stronghold, *Lion*, 26 July 1952

INFANTRYMEN are trained in the use of the mortar. In the hands of a skilled crew, it is a weapon of deadly precision.

A CLOSE action weapon of deadly effect is the hand grenade. Here's how the infantryman trains to use it.

TO make the infantryman tough and able to overcome all sorts of obstacles, his training includes exercises over this fearsome-looking assault course.

IN war, a careless sound can betray a surprise attack and cost lives. In this fieldcraft training exercise, infantry men are being trained to creep forward silently while others, in blindfolds, strive to pick up their approach.

COLD steel has won many a battle. The infantryman must be an expert with his bayonet, and this is how he trains to use it to its most deadly effect.

A LESSON the infantryman quickly learns is that when caught under fire on exposed ground he has to dig in quickly. Here, in training, one man of a Bren gun team works swiftly with an entrenching tool while his mate gives covering fire.

he was devoted to Rockfist and always tired so hard to make himself useful that Rockfist hadn't the heart to get rid of him."

Tiger readers took to their new hero and his all-action adventures from his very first adventure in *Tiger*: "Rockfist and his pals speared straight into the heart of the Nazi formation with guns flaming. The Nazis scattered in desperate panic. Suddenly Rockfist saw a Messerschmitt dart across his sights. In a flash he thumbed his firing-button. Brrrrttt-tt-tt! Flames spouted from the nose of the enemy plane and were followed by a gush of sooty smoke as the machine went into a howling dive. Next moment Rockfist's own plane was being swept by a storm of bullets. A Nazi fighter was hammering down on his tail. Rockfist kicked his plane into a desperate slideslip. Then he hauled on the stick, stood his battered kite on its tail, and went over in a loop as the Nazi swept past him. Rockfist caught the Messerschmitt with a short burst as it tried to pull clear. Bits flew off the enemy aircraft.

Above Be a good soldier with this *Wizard* guide, issue dated 23 May 1959

Below Rockfist Rogan in action in the *Tiger Annual* 1957

THANKS TO ROCKFIST'S SKILL, THE PALS WEREN'T INJURED IN THE CRASH

UP INTO THE TURRET, CURLY. WE MUST STOP THEM GETTING OUT OF THE WADI AGAIN UNTIL OUR TANKS GET HERE

Despite mortal wounds, John Travers Cornwell, boy sightsetter on a cruiser at the battle of Jutland, refused to desert his post. He was awarded the V.C.

Above *Lion* ran features about real-life feats of herosim. This snippet tells the story of "Jack" Cornwell, who was awarded the VC for his gallantry at the Battle of Jutland. He died as a result of his wounds on 2 June 1916, aged just 16 (issue dated 22 March 1952)

Below Nick Waring proves he is an ace on two wheels as well as in the cockpit, *Hotspur*, 8 August 1953

The wings of the crippled enemy kite began to churn like windmill sails as the machine sunk earthwards. Rockfist snatched a moment for a quick look around. Curly and Archie had both claimed a victim. The rest of the enemy formation, now scattered over the sky, were beginning to run for it. They had had enough."

At *Hotspur*, war stories were part of the mix, along with western, adventure, crime and tales from the ubiquitous Red Circle School. Typical of *Hotspur*'s war output was the story "I Was a Secret Flyer" (29 August 1953): "The might of the German Army, soldiers, motor-cyclists, armoured cars and dive-bombers, is out hunting one small green van! Why?"

The Editor explains all: "This is the personal diary of Nick Waring, the seventeen-year-old Battle of Britain pilot who was shot down over France while taking the place of his cowardly step-brother, Wilf, who had deserted. Nick escaped the Germans by posing as Nicholas Varen, the nephew and pupil of Mathieu, the schoolmaster at the village of Vion. Later, Mathieu was replaced by Marbot, another loyal Frenchman. Nick also met Daniel, the working manager of a sawmill, and Alf Chumley and Kitch Perks, two RAF ground crew, who had been in hiding since the Battle of France. A Hurricane fighter, left behind in the British retreat, had been hidden in a cave by Alf, Kitch and the local French Resistance men. Nick operated the fighter from an old airstrip in a glade, and acting under the instructions of the Resistance leader, the mysterious Archer, struck telling blows at the Germans. A Blenheim, after a bombing raid, crashed in flames near the sawmill. The pilot was rescued by the

resistance and he told them that he believed the Germans were using a secret radar device to help shoot down raiding British planes. Helped by Pinette, a French actor, the Resistance try to get into the radar station to steal the apparatus. They are foiled the first time, but disguised as men inspecting the drains, they later pull off the coup and are just making their getaway when the Germans discover the trick. Motor-cyclists set out in pursuit of Nick, Pinette and Vaux, another Frenchman, who are in a battered old green motor van."

To keep up the pretence of the diary's authenticity, the Editor interjects at various points in the narrative to explain certain details to the reader – "The rate of fire of a Hurricane or Spitfire was 10,000 rounds a minute. Pointing slightly inwards, the eight guns concentrated this storm of fire about 300 yards ahead of the plane. – Ed."

Above W.E. Johns' much-loved Biggles character frequently appeared in the pages of *The Boy's Own Paper*. The story "Biggles Follows On" (April 1952) was serialised in the story-paper prior to its being published as a novel

Below Another tale of true-life heroism in *Lion*, dated 22 March 1952

Meanwhile, ***The Boy's Own Paper*** carried on serenely, seemingly oblivious to the developments taking place in the boys' comics market. Yet with list of dedicated subscribers all over the world – in the late 1950s it was mailed to some 55 countries – and a top-notch roster of writers, ***The Boy's Own Paper***'s future was secure. The mix of school and adventure stories was complemented with features on hobbies, history, travel, sports and science. Story writers during the 1950s included Elleston Trevor, Hammond Innes and Geoffrey Morgan; in the sports department, contributors included cricketer Len Hutton, football star Stanley Matthews and boxer Freddie Mills. Furthermore, Captain W.E Johns' "Biggles" stories and C.S Forester's "Hornblower" tales were perennial favourites.

Interestingly, the Editor at the time, Jack Cox,

Determined to get his messages through the inferno of the London air-raid "blitzes," Ronald Heys, an Auxiliary Fire Service boy messenger, defied bombs and fire. Blown off his bicycle by a near-miss, he remounted and carried on.

The POLE-VAULT PRISON-BREAK!

Above "The Pole-Vault Prison Break!" was the story of "a daring escape from a Nazi war-time prison camp" that appeared in the *Tiger Annual* 1957

Below Boys could experience the drama of aerial warfare with the game "Targette", as advertised in *Rover*, 8 September 1956

solicited readers' opinions of the publication – and was not afraid to publish their responses. In the March 1952 issue the letters column contained such opinions as: "Most school stories are improbable rubbish, with the notable exception of Talbot Baines Reed – J.D.Lannin, Grimsby"; and even more damningly: "School stories in general are a hideous waste of time and paper, being unreal and made-up by old-fashioned authors who write a lot of ballyhoo about what might happen in a school if the masters were stupid enough to allow the boys to behave so badly – 'B.O.P. Reader', Sleaford, Lincs".

Despite these criticisms *The Boy's Own Paper* marched on; in March 1954 it celebrated its 75th anniversary, a milestone rarely reached by any boys' story-paper or comic in any era.

As the 1950s progressed the fight for market share intensified and, for the comics' editors, war-related stories continued to be a vital part of the mix. In *Lion*, the importance of war stories was illustrated in 1957 when its front-page story for its first five years, Captain Condor (its take on the *Eagle*'s Dan Dare), was replaced by a war one. The all-action new cover star was Second World War fighter pilot "Paddy Payne". His star status was reinforced by the fact that his story was three pages long; most comic-strip stories in *Lion* at that time were two pages in length. Paddy stayed on the front cover until the early 1960s.

At D.C. Thomson, both *Rover* and *Hotspur* carried war stories, but the best of the action was to be found in the pages of *Wizard*. *Rover*'s characters included Stormy Winter, the "ace test pilot of the Fleet Air Arm"; and "The Worst Shot in the Regiment", the Gurkha Rana Narayan. He is "no good with a rifle, but when he goes into battle it's the deadly kukri he wields" (issue dated 8 September 1956). The story was one of a series called "The Men Behind the Weapons", complete stories of both human interest and the weaponry of war. The reader is informed that the kukri is the favourite weapon of the Gurkha soldier, "a heavy, curved knife with a single cutting edge. It weighed four pounds, and was about two feet in length. The kukri made 'Johnny Gurkha' the terror of the

Above High drama with "Rockfist Rogan", in the pages of the *Champion Annual* 1954

battlefield." Rana put the kukri to bloody effect while fighting the Japanese in Burma: "Rana Narayan loaded and fired until his rifle was smoking and his eyes sore. The Japs came in swarms, and as fast as they were shot down, more came from out of the trees and pressed the assault right home. A screeching little monkey-faced man poised himself above Rana and dug down at him with a bayonet, and as the Gurkha parried the thrust his own rifle was jolted out of his hands. Suddenly, Rifleman Narayan felt free. With an exultant yell he flicked

This Kite's a Killer!

Above Britain's latest top-secret military aircraft – the "Warbat" – is not all it's cracked up to be, in the *Hotspur* story "This Kite's a Killer!", in the issue dated 4 January 1958

Below "Lucky Chance – Pilot of the Unarmed Raider" is a Mosquito pilot in trouble on a raid over Germany, in the *Lion Annual* 1958

the kukri out of its sheath. He grasped the Jap by his baggy breeches and pulled him into the trench, on to the kukri. Then it was kill, kill, kill – with no quarter asked or given on either side. The Japs came and the Gurkhas slew them, and then it was all finished again. The jungle was silent, except for the frenzied screeching of the birds and the screams of the monkeys."

In *Hotspur*, the story "This Kite's a Killer!" was an aerial combat story with a difference: "It's 1942 – Britain needs a new fighter plane to win the war in the air! Here is the new plane – the Warbat – and no pilot will fly it!" (issued dated 4 January 1958). This was because the Warbat was prone to engine failure – and the story followed the determined efforts of Squadron-Leader Rudd to get to the bottom of the problem.

Wizard's war stories took pride of place in the comic; towards the end of the 1950s many of *Wizard*'s covers featured tales of men at war. A hugely popular story "V for Vengeance", a reprint of a 1942 story, was "The most amazing story of the Second World war – the story of the Deathless Men, the grim, grey fighters whose vengeance the Germans feared" (issue dated 3 January 1959). "The Deathless Men" were underground fighters who had escaped from German prison camps to wreak vengeance against leading Nazis. Each had the codename "Jack" followed by a number; their leader, Colonel Von Reich, second-in-command to Himmler in the Black Guards, was

WE'RE GETTING TOO LOW TO BALE OUT. I'LL HAVE TO PUT HER DOWN SMACK IN THE MIDDLE OF THAT NAZI DROME

"Jack One". In the opening episode, Otto Leben, chief of the Gestapo in Paris, is murdered in his car, the first act of vengeance by the Deathless Men: "There was no doubt about it. Herr Leben, the Butcher of Paris, was dead. Pinned to his chest was a slip of paper which was carried inside to be read. At the head of the page was a blood-red letter V, and underneath this was printed in German – V for Vengeance. The free peoples of Europe strike again. This murderer is only one of many who will die. The oppressed peoples of France, Poland, Belgium, Yugoslavia, Czechoslovakia, Greece, and the other occupied countries have long cried for vengeance. The Deathless Men are answering the call. It is now the turn of the tyrants, the murderers and the torturers to tremble. Before long all the under-mentioned will share the fate of Leben. They cannot escape us. Their time is coming. Then followed a long list of names of gauleiters – traitors put in charge of districts of their own countries by the Germans as rewards for their treachery – police officials, commanders of concentration camps, German governors of captured cities, notorious members of the Gestapo, and Nazi officials of various ranks both in occupied countries and Germany. The list finished with the three leaders of the Nazi party – Joseph Goebbels, Minister of the Interior; Hermann Goering, Marshal of the Luftwaffe, the German Air Force; and Adolf Hitler, Dictator of Germany. The name of Otto Leben was at the top of the list, but it had been crossed off already with a red line."

The victims came thick and fast – one of them was Dr Kurt Kruger (issue dated February 21 1959): "Within the gates the two sentries lay dead. Just within the passage leading from the side entrance to the surgery stood four grim figures clothed in grey, four Deathless Men. Silently, the Deathless Men stood.

Below The "Deathless Men" were out for revenge in the *Wizard* story "V for Vengeance", issue dated 25 April 1959

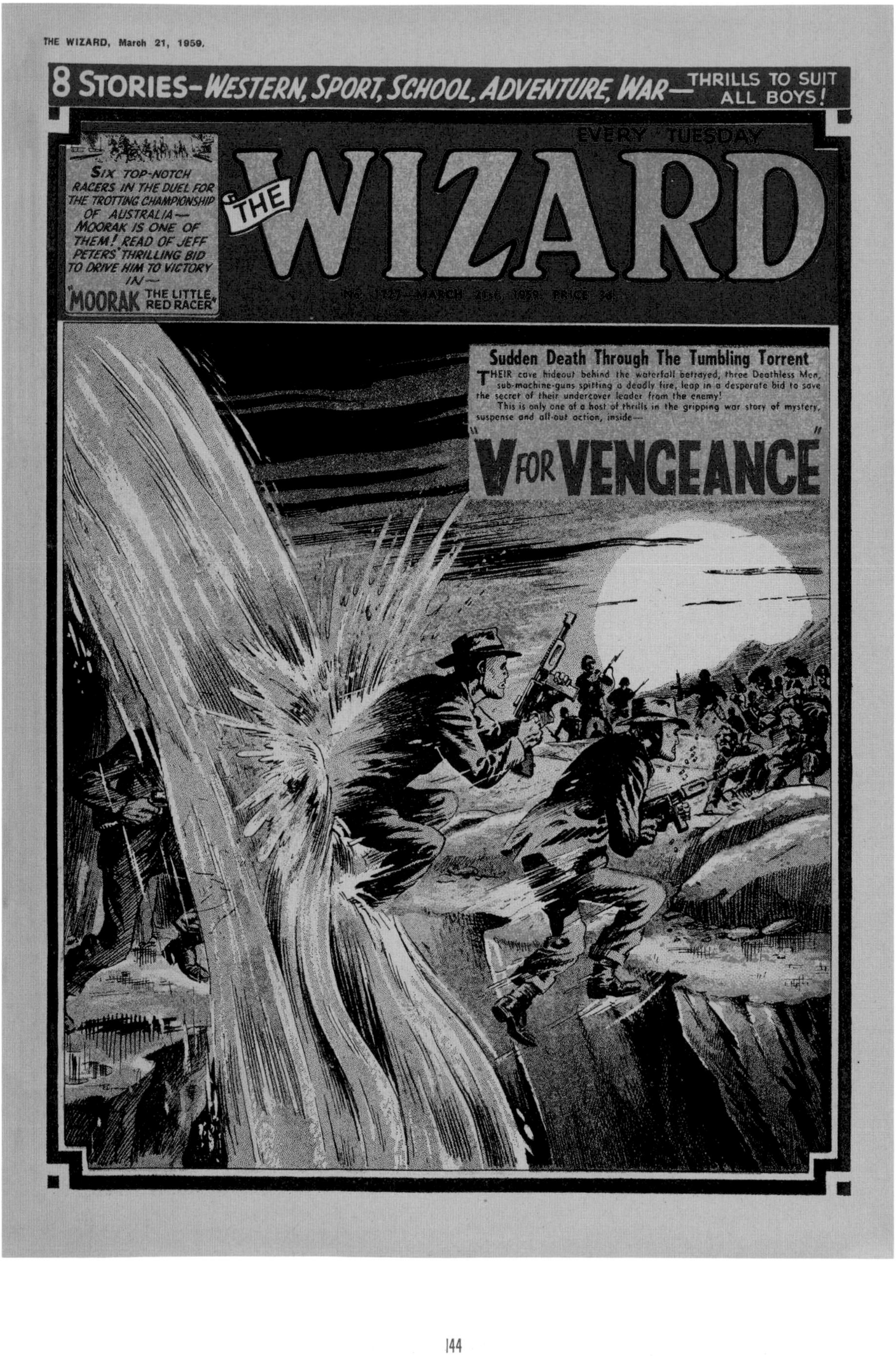
THE WIZARD, March 21, 1959.
8 STORIES–WESTERN, SPORT, SCHOOL, ADVENTURE, WAR–THRILLS TO SUIT ALL BOYS!
EVERY TUESDAY
THE WIZARD
SIX TOP-NOTCH RACERS IN THE DUEL FOR THE TROTTING CHAMPIONSHIP OF AUSTRALIA— MOORAK IS ONE OF THEM! READ OF JEFF PETERS' THRILLING BID TO DRIVE HIM TO VICTORY IN—
"MOORAK THE LITTLE RED RACER"
Sudden Death Through The Tumbling Torrent
THEIR cave hideout behind the waterfall betrayed, three Deathless Men, sub-machine-guns spitting a deadly fire, leap in a desperate bid to save the secret of their undercover leader from the enemy!
This is only one of a host of thrills in the gripping war story of mystery, suspense and all-out action, inside—
"V FOR VENGEANCE"

'LUCKY' CHANCE, PILOT OF THE UNARMED RAIDER

BY MARK ROSS

DURING WORLD WAR II, AT THE HEIGHT OF BOMBER COMMAND'S DEVASTATING ATTACKS ON THE ENEMY, SQUADRON-LEADER "LUCKY" CHANCE WAS THE DARING YOUNG PILOT OF A MOSQUITO PLANE. HIS ACE NAVIGATOR WAS JOHN GREEN. ONE DAY THEY WERE TOLD TO REPORT TO THEIR WING-COMMANDER'S OFFICE, TO RECEIVE DETAILS OF AN AMAZING AERIAL MISSION -- AN UNARMED FLIGHT TO A MYSTERIOUS TARGET IN THE HEART OF NAZI GERMANY!

GRIMLY THE WING-COMMANDER OUTLINED THE OPERATION TO LUCKY AND JOHN

GENTLEMEN – I'LL COME STRAIGHT TO THE POINT. OUR SCOUT SERVICE IN ENEMY-OCCUPIED TERRITORY HAS DISCOVERED THAT THE NAZIS ARE MAKING SECRET WEAPONS WHICH MAY WELL MENACE THE ENTIRE ALLIED WAR EFFORT

Above "Lucky Chance" is briefed for his next mission, *Lion Annual* 1958

Facing page "The Deathless Men" on the attack, *Wizard*, 21 March 1959

They were on guard, alert, their eyes watching the square outside, their ears striving to catch sounds from the surgery at the end of the passage. No sounds came, for the walls were thick, yet within that elaborately-equipped room Dr Kurt Kruger, of the German Medical Corps, fought in the grip of four other grey men. The grey men carried him to the operating table and stretched him out. There were straps for holding patients in position, and he was quickly bound and gagged. The grey men straightened up, and their eyes were hard through the slits in their masks. 'Kurt Kruger, you were present when Warsaw fell,' said one of them sternly. 'Many Polish wounded fell into your hands, but you refused them medical aid. You stood by and laughed at their dying agonies, Kruger, and for that reason you have been doomed by the Deathless Men!' went on the grey one remorselessly. Kruger could make no reply. He strained his neck to try to look towards the door, but no help was coming. When the Deathless Men had planned this vengeance raid they had known that all the troops in the barracks would be out searching for General Edler. The whole operation had been carefully planned by a man in a chateau in the forest about twenty miles outside the town. This man was known to the Germans as Colonel Von Reich, second-in-command of the Gestapo, but actually he was Aylmer Gregson, a British agent who had been "planted" in the Nazi party long before the war. 'You are going to die, Kurt Kruger,' said the grey man, picking up a surgical knife. 'We are not going to torture you, but you are going to die slowly, as those poor wounded men in Warsaw died.' Kruger's sleeve was ripped up, the man with the knife stopped for a moment, then made a deep cut. Kurt Kruger

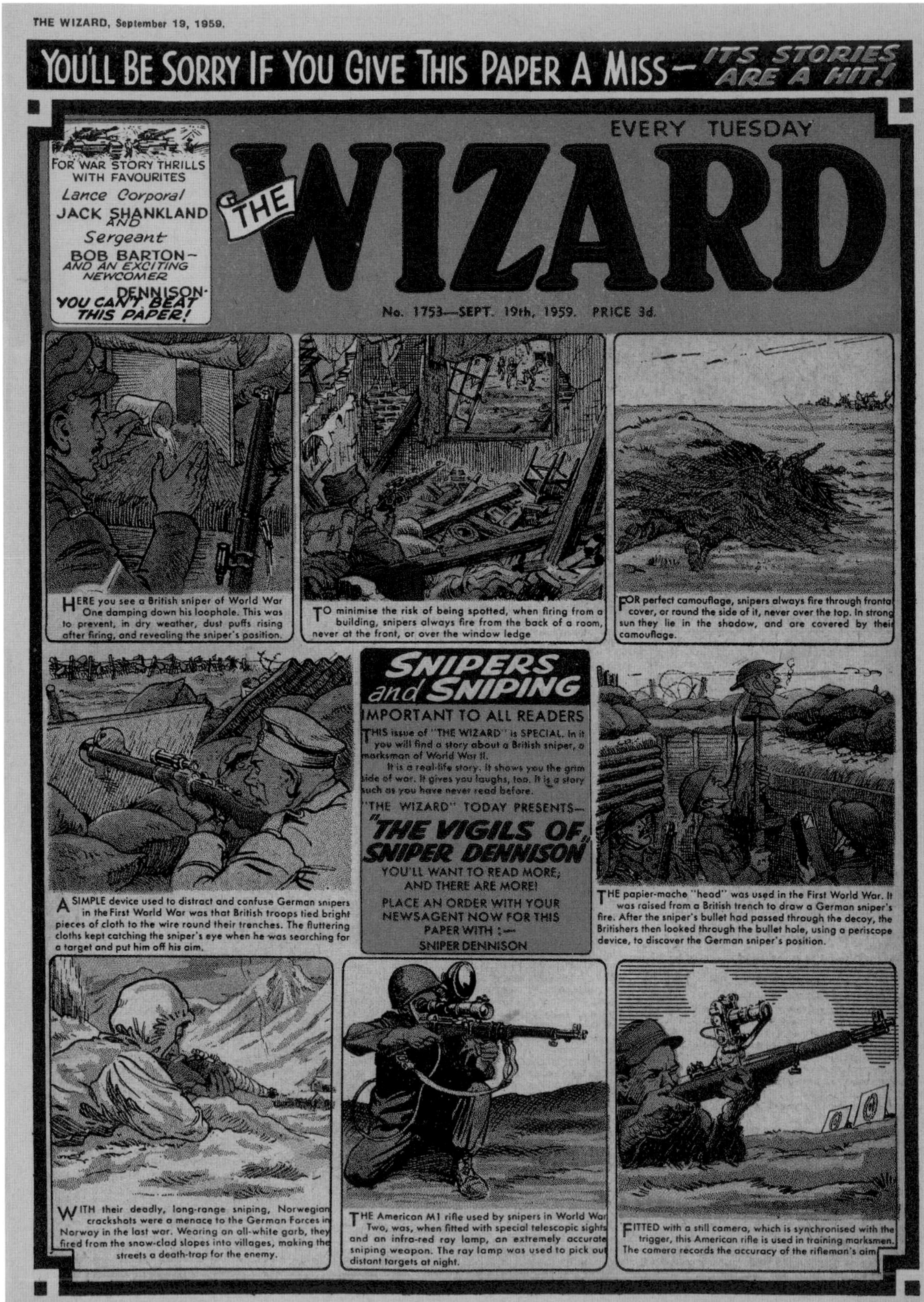
THE WIZARD, September 19, 1959.

YOU'LL BE SORRY IF YOU GIVE THIS PAPER A MISS– ITS STORIES ARE A HIT!

FOR WAR STORY THRILLS WITH FAVOURITES Lance Corporal JACK SHANKLAND AND Sergeant BOB BARTON– AND AN EXCITING NEWCOMER DENNISON· YOU CAN'T BEAT THIS PAPER!

EVERY TUESDAY

THE WIZARD

No. 1753—SEPT. 19th, 1959. PRICE 3d.

HERE you see a British sniper of World War One damping down his loophole. This was to prevent, in dry weather, dust puffs rising after firing, and revealing the sniper's position.

TO minimise the risk of being spotted, when firing from a building, snipers always fire from the back of a room, never at the front, or over the window ledge

FOR perfect camouflage, snipers always fire through frontal cover, or round the side of it, never over the top. In strong sun they lie in the shadow, and are covered by their camouflage.

A SIMPLE device used to distract and confuse German snipers in the First World War was that British troops tied bright pieces of cloth to the wire round their trenches. The fluttering cloths kept catching the sniper's eye when he was searching for a target and put him off his aim.

SNIPERS and SNIPING

IMPORTANT TO ALL READERS

THIS issue of "THE WIZARD" is SPECIAL. In it you will find a story about a British sniper, a marksman of World War II.

It is a real-life story. It shows you the grim side of war. It gives you laughs, too. It is a story such as you have never read before.

"THE WIZARD" TODAY PRESENTS—

"THE VIGILS OF SNIPER DENNISON"

YOU'LL WANT TO READ MORE; AND THERE ARE MORE!

PLACE AN ORDER WITH YOUR NEWSAGENT NOW FOR THIS PAPER WITH :—

SNIPER DENNISON

THE papier-mache "head" was used in the First World War. It was raised from a British trench to draw a German sniper's fire. After the sniper's bullet had passed through the decoy, the Britishers then looked through the bullet hole, using a periscope device, to discover the German sniper's position.

WITH their deadly, long-range sniping, Norwegian crackshots were a menace to the German Forces in Norway in the last war. Wearing an all-white garb, they fired from the snow-clad slopes into villages, making the streets a death-trap for the enemy.

THE American M1 rifle used by snipers in World War Two, was, when fitted with special telescopic sights and an infra-red ray lamp, an extremely accurate sniping weapon. The ray lamp was used to pick out distant targets at night.

FITTED with a still camera, which is synchronised with the trigger, this American rifle is used in training marksmen. The camera records the accuracy of the rifleman's aim.

THE WORST SHOT IN THE REGIMENT

shivered, blood began to well out, and the avengers stepped back. The Deathless Men had cut one of Kruger's arteries. He would bleed to death. It was a terrible vengeance, but then Kurt Kruger had been a terrible creature without mercy."

For *Wizard*, 1959 was a vintage year for war stories, for "V for Vengeance" was followed by "Your Best Friend is Your Rifle!" (first appeared issue dated 16 May 1959) and "The Vigils of Sniper Dennison" (issue dated 19 September 1959). Private Jack Shankland of the Second Battalion, Royal Midshire Regiment, was "the fearless, fighting infantryman whose motto is – your best friend is your rifle!". The regiment was fighting a rearguard action in northern France in 1940, trying to hold the Allied line at the Somme for advancing Germans. Jack's unit have to counter-attack after the Germans break through the line: "Sprawling in the lane were the bodies of several soldiers in French uniforms. Evidently they had been ambushed from behind the roses. Shankland saw three Germans. Two sat behind the machine-gun and the other, who had a pair of field-glasses, was standing behind the machine-gun and looking round. Shankland's practised eyes gauged the range. "Two hundred yards," he murmured and adjusted the sight of his rifle. He pushed his left arm through the sling and brought the butt up to his shoulder. He aimed at the German with the field-glasses. Crack! Shankland squeezed the trigger and the Jerry spun round and then pitched over

Above Gurkha Rana Narayan was "no good with a rifle, but when he goes into battle it's the deadly kukri he wields". The story appeared in *Rover*, issue dated 8 September 1956

Facing page The war from a sniper's perspective… an interesting and novel approach from in the story "The Vigils of Sniper Dennison", 19 September 1959

Below "Sniper Dennison" is dressed to kill, in the pages of *Wizard*

Above Lance-Corporal Jack Shankland would no doubt disagree with Gurkha Narayan – for the former "Your Best Friend is Your Rifle!", *Wizard*, 11 July 1959

Facing page Introducing the "Warbat" in the story "This Kite's a Killer!", *Hotspur*, 4 January 1958

backwards. The gunners jerked round in an attitude of utter surprise. As they did so, Shankland ejected the cartridge from the breech and fired again. One of the Germans toppled over sideways and before the survivor had time to throw himself down, Shankland's rifle cracked a third time, and the German slumped forward over the gun. A figure loomed through the drifting smoke as a fourth German came at a run from the other side of the cottage. Shankland picked him off as he ran. Then the deadshot Britisher lowered his rifle and watched for a full minute. No other German showed up. Shankland had wiped out the gun crew and the way was clear for him to push on a bit further with his section."

nother top story in *Wizard* was "The Vigils of Sniper Dennison". The story was written by Alan Hemus, who actually trained as a sniper in the Second World War. It was a riveting psychological exposé of the dark arts of the sniper: "Dennison lay motionless, hugging the baked ground like a lizard, and in the same way as a lizard he blended with his background. From a distance of ten paces his faded clothing, once-green webbing equipment and dust-caked boots began to take on the nondescript hues of the ground whereon he lay, and his uplifted head to merge with the outline of a scrubby bush that sprouted defiantly from the parched soil. At twenty paces it was difficult to discern Dennison. At two hundred yards, provided he continued to lie completely motionless, it was almost impossible. Dennison was aware of this and greatly comforted by the knowledge. Just two hundred yards before him, running laterally, was the double embankment of an irrigation ditch, and in that ditch were Dennison's enemies – Germans. Dennison was about his lawful business of the Second World War, the killing and harassing of the enemy. The butt of his rifle rested under his shoulder, his left arm thrust forward and twisted through the sling." Forced to play a waiting game, "Dennison continued to lie patiently in his hide. In the near side of the embankment directly before him was a drainage channel, a narrow slot just wide and deep enough to show the head and shoulders of a tall man passing along the ditch. Dennison knew that three times a day, on this quiet part of the line, there was movement along the ditch by the enemy to collect medals from their field kitchens. He had been in position since shortly before dawn, waiting for the chance of a shot. There had been opportunities

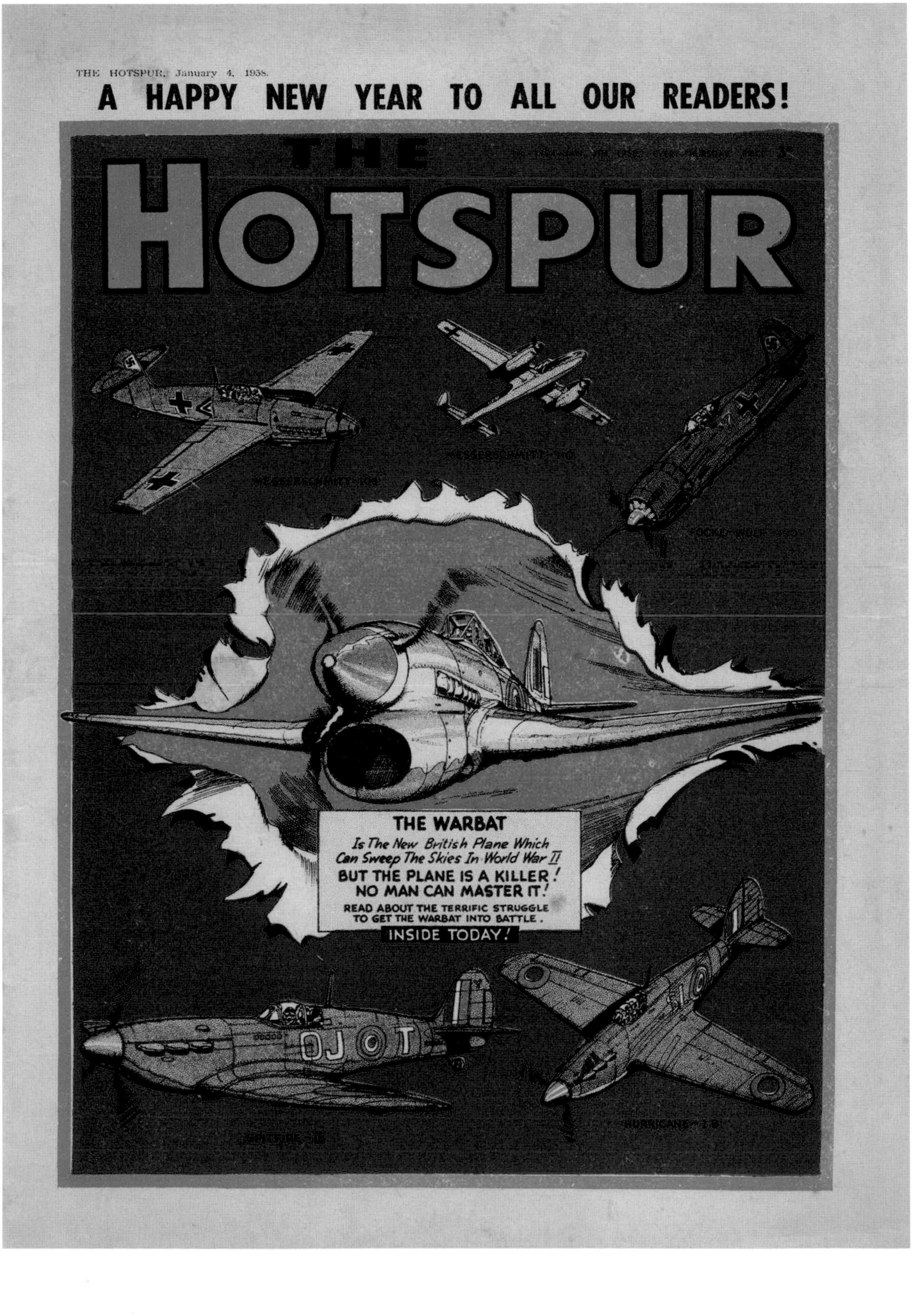
THE HOTSPUR, January 4, 1958.
A HAPPY NEW YEAR TO ALL OUR READERS!
THE HOTSPUR
THE WARBAT
Is The New British Plane Which Can Sweep The Skies In World War II
BUT THE PLANE IS A KILLER! NO MAN CAN MASTER IT!
READ ABOUT THE TERRIFIC STRUGGLE TO GET THE WARBAT INTO BATTLE.
INSIDE TODAY!
OJ T

THE SITTING DUCK OF DUNKIRK

when the breakfast meal was brought up, but the light then had been uncertain. Dennison preferred to wait until dusk and come back the following morning if necessary."

For Amalgamated Press, the success of *Tiger* continued apace, its mix of sports and action stories proving extremely popular. On the war front, towards the end of the 1950s, the "war slot" was shared by "Commando One" and "Spike and Dusty". The latter were Spike North and Dusty Minton, "Royal Naval frogmen in Word War II. The intrepid pair had undertaken many tough and dangerous missions and their skill and bravery beneath the waves led them to being chosen to take part in one of the most vital assignments of the war…" In the story "Destination Danger!" (issue dated 7 June 1958), the pair enter a Nazi stronghold to rendezvous with a French resistance fighter and collect stolen German documents that are vital to the Allied war effort.

"Commando One" was the story of Rex Royal, "famed as king of the Commandos… a fighting man who knew no fear. The tougher the task before him, the harder he fought, and the better he liked it! It was such courage as this that inspired men to follow his dashing leadership!" Rex Royal started life in *Comet*, a title launched on 20 September 1946 by J.B.Allen. A fortnightly publication, *Comet*, like stablemate *Sun*, was one of the first titles to adopt an all-comic-strip format (in March 1952). Like *Sun*, it also had many different incarnations, namely *The Comet*, *Comet Comic*, *The Comet Adventure Weekly*, *Comet Weekly* and, finally, *Comet*. Amalgamated Press finally bought *Comet*, and the rights to the characters, on 31 May 1959, and wasted no time in putting Commando One into the pages of *Tiger*. Amalgamated Press closed *Comet* on 17 October 1959, but Rex Royal survived. Indeed, he teamed up with Spike and Dusty in the story called, rather unoriginally, "Spike and Dusty and Commando One" – "Three of the country's top fighting-men picked for a vital Word War II mission" (issue dated 7 October 1959).

There was no sign that the popularity of the war story was on the wane; indeed, the opposite was true, for the 1960s was to see a further rise in the stock of the comic characters at war and their adventures on the battlefield.

Above *Wizard* regularly ran one-page complete war stories. "The Sitting Duck of Dunkirk" describes how a seaside paddle-steamer was pressed into action during the 1940 evacuation of British troops from Dunkirk. It was published on 17 January 1959

Facing page Action from the *Comet* story "Commando One", featuring the exploits of Rex Royal, in the issue dated 2 August 1958

REX LEFT AS HE HAD ENTERED... AND THE SENTRY WAS NONE THE WISER! LIKE A WRAITH, COMMANDO ONE DRIFTED THROUGH THE SHADOWY DEPÔT UNTIL HE FOUND THE ARTILLERY MEN'S LORRY... AND ITS DRIVER...

SORRY, CHUM. I'VE DECIDED TO TRAVEL BY ROAD FROM NOW ON!

HE DONNED THE UNCONSCIOUS DRIVER'S HELMET AND GREATCOAT.

THEY'RE ONLY INTERESTED IN WHO GOES IN...NOT WHO COMES OUT. AS FOR YOU, FRITZ... YOU CAN COME WITH ME ON A LITTLE TRIP TO DEAR OLD ENGLAND!

NEAR A SECLUDED COVE ON THE COAST REX PARKED THE LORRY, AND, CARRYING THE SENSELESS DRIVER, MADE FOR THE BEACH, WHERE A GUARDED TORCH SIGNAL OUT TO SEA BROUGHT AN ANSWER...

COR, WE'VE BEEN WAITING AN HOUR FOR YOU, SIR. WHY ARE YOU BRINGING THE SQUAREHEAD?

ONE GOOD TURN DESERVES ANOTHER...SO I'M TAKING HIM OUT OF THE WAR, PERMANENTLY!

ON THE DECK OF THE FAST MOTOR TORPEDO BOAT WAITING OFF-SHORE, REX ROYAL GLANCED AT THE LIGHTENING SKY AND GRINNED...

WHAT'S THE JOKE, SIR?

I'M JUST WAITING FOR THE JERRIES TO FIND OUT SOMETHING!

AT THAT VERY SECOND THE GREAT GUN IN LEQUOT BELLOWED... AND A MASSIVE SHELL WAS HURLED FROM IT... *BUT NOT VERY FAR!*

AFTER MUCH CHECKING AND RECHECKING, THE SHAKEN GERMAN OFFICER IN COMMAND DECIDED TO TRY AGAIN... *WITH DISASTROUS RESULTS...*

AAGH... MY BEAUTIFUL GUN IS RUINED. FOR TWO YEARS I MAKE THE WEAPON...THEN *POOF*... IT IS GONE! NEXT TIME...

THERE WILL BE NO NEXT TIME, HERR PROFESSOR. MY REPORT TO THE FUEHRER WILL SETTLE THAT! PAH... THE WHOLE IDEA WAS MAD!

THE THUNDEROUS EXPLOSIONS HAD BARELY REACHED THE SPEEDING M.T.B.... BUT THEY WERE JUST WHAT COMMANDO ONE HAD BEEN WAITING FOR...

...AS WE COULDN'T BOMB IT, I JUST FIXED THE TIME FUSES TO GO OFF AS SOON AS THE SHELLS WERE FIRED. I THINK THAT'S THE LAST WE'LL HEAR OF THAT NEW TOY OF JERRY'S!

SIR, YOU ALMOST TEMPT ME TO TRANSFER TO THE ARMY! AS COMMANDO ONE YOU SEEM TO FIND ALL THE FUN AND GAMES!

"WAR! THAT MAD GAME THE WORLD SO LOVES TO PLAY"

Jonathan Swift (1667-1745)

CHAPTER SIX
RAGIN' FURIES

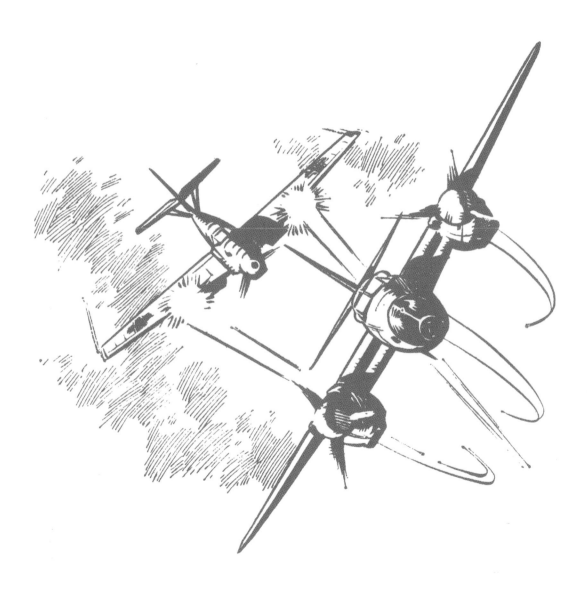

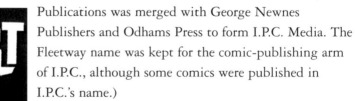

THE 1960S WERE A DECADE of tumultuous change – it was out with the old and in with the new. This was certainly the case in the thriving comics market. Comic publishing was enjoying a boom at the start of the decade, with publishers looking to build on the "golden era" of the 1950s and exploit the success of the new comics, which included *Eagle*, *Lion* and *Tiger*.

The early part of the 1960s saw a spate of new launches as D.C. Thomson and Fleetway Publications (the new name for Amalgamated Press) slugged it out for market dominance. D.C. Thomson struck the first blow with the launch of *Victor*, on 25 February 1961. This was followed onto the newsagents' shelves by Fleetway's *Valiant* (launched 6 October 1962), to which D.C. Thomson responded with *Hornet* (launched 14 September 1963). Fleetway made it two-all with *Hurricane*, the first issue dated 29 February 1964. (In 1963, Fleetway Publications was merged with George Newnes Publishers and Odhams Press to form I.P.C. Media. The Fleetway name was kept for the comic-publishing arm of I.P.C., although some comics were published in I.P.C.'s name.)

By the end of the decade, text-based story had all but disappeared (except for in the annuals, where they continued to be popular), and some very well-known titles had disappeared, too. D.C. Thomson's *Adventure* closed on 14 January 1961 after a 40-year run, when it was incorporated into *Rover*. *Wizard*, too, was shelved, on 16 November 1963, when it too was incorporated into *Rover*. *Wizard* ran for over 41 years, but was to be reborn on 14 February 1970 as a comic-strip publication. There were changes at *Hotspur*, too, where the title was renamed *New Hotspur* in October 1959; it reverted to plain *Hotspur* on 16 February 1963. The reason for the name change in 1959 was because

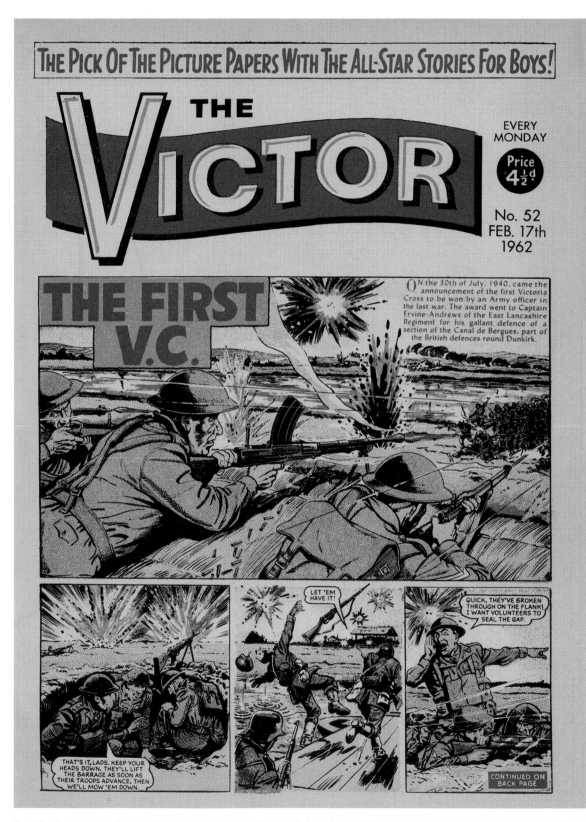

Above *Victor* frequently had stories of real-life herosim on its front cover, with the conclusion on the back. Particularly popular was its series focusing on winners of the Victoria Cross. The story above (continues on page 156) concerned Captain Ervine-Andrews, who won his V.C. in 1940. **Facing page** The "Picture Library" concept became hugely popular in the early 1960s. The single-story-in-a-pocket-sized-book took off with the launch of Fleetway's *War Picture Library* in 1958. There have been more than 2,000 issues of *War Picture Library*, while D.C. Thomson's *Commando Library* series has run to more than 4,0000 issues. Fleetway has also published more than 1,700 issues of *Battle Picture Library*

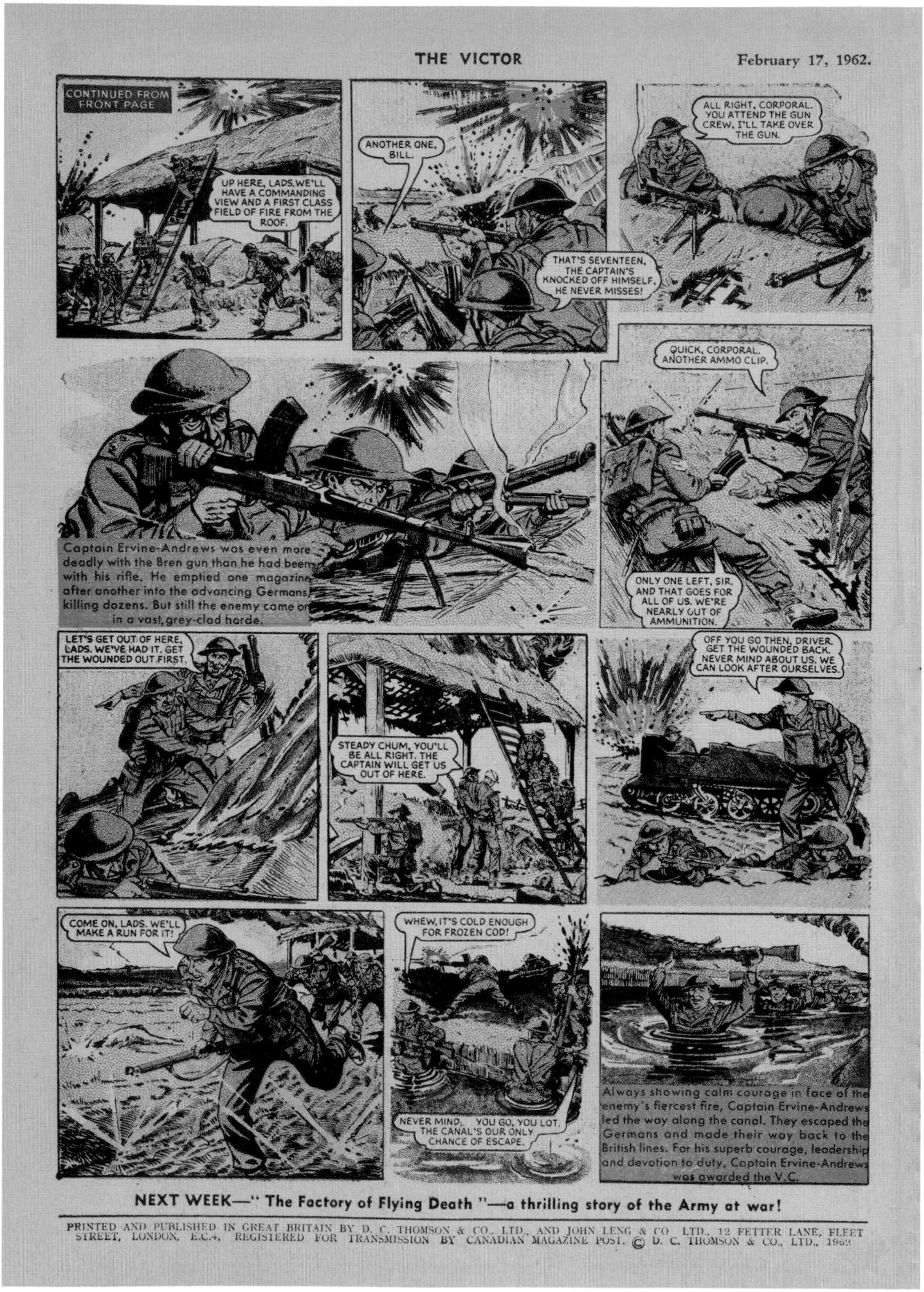
THE VICTOR
February 17, 1962.
CONTINUED FROM FRONT PAGE
UP HERE, LADS. WE'LL HAVE A COMMANDING VIEW AND A FIRST CLASS FIELD OF FIRE FROM THE ROOF.
ANOTHER ONE, BILL.
THAT'S SEVENTEEN, THE CAPTAIN'S KNOCKED OFF HIMSELF. HE NEVER MISSES!
ALL RIGHT, CORPORAL. YOU ATTEND THE GUN CREW, I'LL TAKE OVER THE GUN.
Captain Ervine-Andrews was even more deadly with the Bren gun than he had been with his rifle. He emptied one magazine after another into the advancing Germans, killing dozens. But still the enemy came on in a vast, grey-clad horde.
QUICK, CORPORAL. ANOTHER AMMO CLIP.
ONLY ONE LEFT, SIR, AND THAT GOES FOR ALL OF US. WE'RE NEARLY OUT OF AMMUNITION.
LET'S GET OUT OF HERE, LADS. WE'VE HAD IT. GET THE WOUNDED OUT FIRST.
STEADY CHUM, YOU'LL BE ALL RIGHT. THE CAPTAIN WILL GET US OUT OF HERE.
OFF YOU GO THEN, DRIVER. GET THE WOUNDED BACK. NEVER MIND ABOUT US. WE CAN LOOK AFTER OURSELVES.
COME ON, LADS. WE'LL MAKE A RUN FOR IT!
WHEW, IT'S COLD ENOUGH FOR FROZEN COD!
NEVER MIND. YOU GO, YOU LOT. THE CANAL'S OUR ONLY CHANCE OF ESCAPE.
Always showing calm courage in face of the enemy's fiercest fire, Captain Ervine-Andrews led the way along the canal. They escaped the Germans and made their way back to the British lines. For his superb courage, leadership and devotion to duty, Captain Ervine-Andrews was awarded the V.C.
NEXT WEEK—" The Factory of Flying Death "—a thrilling story of the Army at war!
PRINTED AND PUBLISHED IN GREAT BRITAIN BY D. C. THOMSON & CO., LTD., AND JOHN LENG & CO. LTD., 12 FETTER LANE, FLEET STREET, LONDON, E.C.4. REGISTERED FOR TRANSMISSION BY CANADIAN MAGAZINE POST. © D. C. THOMSON & CO., LTD., 1962

publisher D.C. Thomson re-launched *Hotspur* as a comic-strip-based publication, moving away from traditional text-based stories.

Indeed, both the Dundee firm and Fleetway were moving away from text-based story-papers, following the example of *Eagle*, with its emphasis on comic-strip stories. *Victor* was a case in point: its debut issue carried only two text-based stories, one of which was "I Flew with Braddock", a tale of ace airman Matt Braddock V.C., whose stories had previously appeared in both *Wizard* and *Rover* in the 1940s and 1950s.

A hugely popular character, Braddock, one of many characters given a new lease of life by the comic-strip format. He was tough and fearless, with superb piloting skills, yet uncompromising and disdainful of authority. He was fiercely loyal to the men who served him, especially his navigator, Sergeant George Bourne, the narrator of the stories when they were in text format. He remained at the rank of sergeant because he refused promotion to officer level.

The story "Braddock V.C." (issue dated 7 April 1962) is a typical tale. Readers are told that "Ranger flights have started and flyers of the Luftwaffe no longer

Above and below Matt Braddock, ace fighter pilot of the Second World War, graced the pages of many of the comics. The dogfight, above, appeared in *Victor*, dated 18 March 1967; while "Braddock Fought the Flying Saucers", the last original Braddock story ever written, appeared in *Rover and Wizard* on 23 July 1966

BRADDOCK FOUGHT THE FLYING SAUCERS

The men from Camp Z free a captured American pilot—by making a mountain " talk."

THE MEN FROM CAMP Z

Camp Z, the base of the Australian Special Duties Commando Unit, lay on a tiny island off the coast of Australia. Although they were used mainly as a deadly striking force against the Japs during the Second World War, many Allied fighters owed their lives to the daring and resourcefulness of the men from Camp Z. One such was Pete Hoskins, an American Navy pilot, who was returning to his carrier one day when the engine of his Hellcat fighter started to run rough.

Above The commandos from Camp Z on a mission in *Victor*, dated 4 April 1964

Below Features of the "Did-you-know-that?" variety were popular in all the boys' comics. This one about nuclear submarines appeared in *Valiant* on 5 May 1963

feel safe as Matt Braddock stalks enemy air crews in the skies over Germany!" Furthermore, "Sergeant Matt Braddock, V.C., was the greatest pilot of the last war. With Sergeant George Bourne, his navigator, his Mosquito was engaged on Ranger flights, daylight intruder raids over Germany. These flights were the idea of Squadron Leader Nolan Harland, the much-wounded air ace who was the commanding officer at Ropewell R.A.F. station. A second Mosquito, piloted by Flight Lieutenant Don Douglas, was to co-operate with Braddock on the Ranger flights. Braddock did not think Douglas was good enough for this hazardous job, but Harland over-ruled his objections, and now the two Mosquitos were flying to attack a German airfield on the first two-plane Ranger mission."

Unfortunately, Douglas's flying was not up to Braddock's standards and he made no secret of his dissatisfaction to his superiors. While those in authority refused to bow, Braddock was, ultimately and as ever, proved right.

The war story was an important part of the mix for *Victor*, and virtually no theatre was left untouched. "The Men from Camp Z" related the exploits of the "Australian Special Duties Commando Unit", based in Camp Z, on a small island off the coast of Australia:

Atomic power has brought us nearer to the 'ideal' submarine, a vessel which can stay underwater indefinitely. In August, 1958, the U.S.S. Nautilus made submarine history by passing over the North Pole under the Arctic ice pack. It also established a record by staying submerged for 14 days and 4 hours. Nautilus can travel 60,000 miles underwater on a supply of uranium little bigger than a golf ball.

"Although they were used mainly as a deadly striking force against the Japs during the Second World War, many Allied fighters owed their lives to the daring and resourcefulness of the men fom Camp Z." In one adventure, they set out rescue Peter Hoskins, an American Navy pilot, "who was returning to his carrier one day when the engine of his Hellcat fighter started to run rough" (issue dated 4 April 1964). Hoskins has to bail out and is captured on a remote island by the Japanese. There the indigenous people are subjugated by the invaders, and explain to the Camp Z men sent to rescue Hoskins that they cannot fight until their "god" speaks to them. Their god is a dormant volcano, which the men from Camp Z pack with explosives. When detonated, the explosion sounds like the volcano is erupting – and the "god" speaks. The natives are inspired and turn on the Japanese, driving them into the sea, enabling the Camp Z men to rescue the American pilot.

Greece was a more unusual setting for a comic-book war story. Crete was the backdrop for the story "The Phantom of the Fighting Fifth" (issue dated 28 July 1962). It concerns the adventures of four members of the Fighting Fifth Hussars, who decide to stay and fight after the Germans overrun the island, driving out the British army.

Victor also frequently delved into the archives to bring readers true stories of the Second World War – and other wars, too. These stories invariably started on the front cover and finished on the back. A typical story of this type was "The First V.C.", which celebrated the heroism of Captain Harold Ervine-Andrews of the East Lancashire Regiment, who won the first VC of the Second World War on 30 July 1940. Ervine-Andrews led the gallant defence of a section of the Canal de Bergues, near Dunkirk. Also in the series was the tale of "Piper Richardson V.C.", who won honours at the Battle of the Somme. James Richardson was the piper for the Manitoba Regiment, and led the Canadians into an attack on a German position at Regina Trench (issue dated 4 September 1965). Richardson won the Victoria Cross for

Above An advertisement for the Commando Library, in *Victor*, dated 28 July 1962

Left Nerve-jangling action in the story "Phantom of the Fighting Fifth", which appeared in *Victor* on 28 July 1962

continuing to play his pipes despite the Canadians being under heavy fire, and then leading an attack on a German trench. After that he helped evacuate the wounded before he was killed while retrieving his pipes from the raided trench.

The South American theatre of war was also on the radar of the *Victor*'s story writers. "Gordon of G Force" concerned Sub-Lieutenant Jim Gordon, a member of a Naval unit that has trapped the German pocket battleship *Graf Spee* in Montevideo harbour, the German vessel being damaged after the Battle of the River Plate (issue dated 26 September 1964). Because Montevideo was a neutral port the British could not attack the *Graf Spee* while she was in the harbour, and so chose to play a waiting game. However, the *Graf Spee* was a formidable fighting ship and, with only HMS *Ajax* and HMNZS *Achilles* in the immediate vicinity, would pose a serious threat to British Naval and merchant shipping if she sailed. In effect, despite having put pressure on the Uruguayan authorities to make the *Graf Spee* leave harbour, the British suddenly realised it was better if she stayed put. At this point the British concocted a cunning plan to convince the Germans that reinforcements in the shape of three more warships had arrived, and that even the *Graf Spee* could not take on five British vessels.

Facing page Piper Richardson's heroism is remembered in *Victor*, dated 4 September 1965

Below *Victor*'s take on the story of the *Graf Spee*, in the issue dated 26 August 1964. The denouement of the story is on page 162

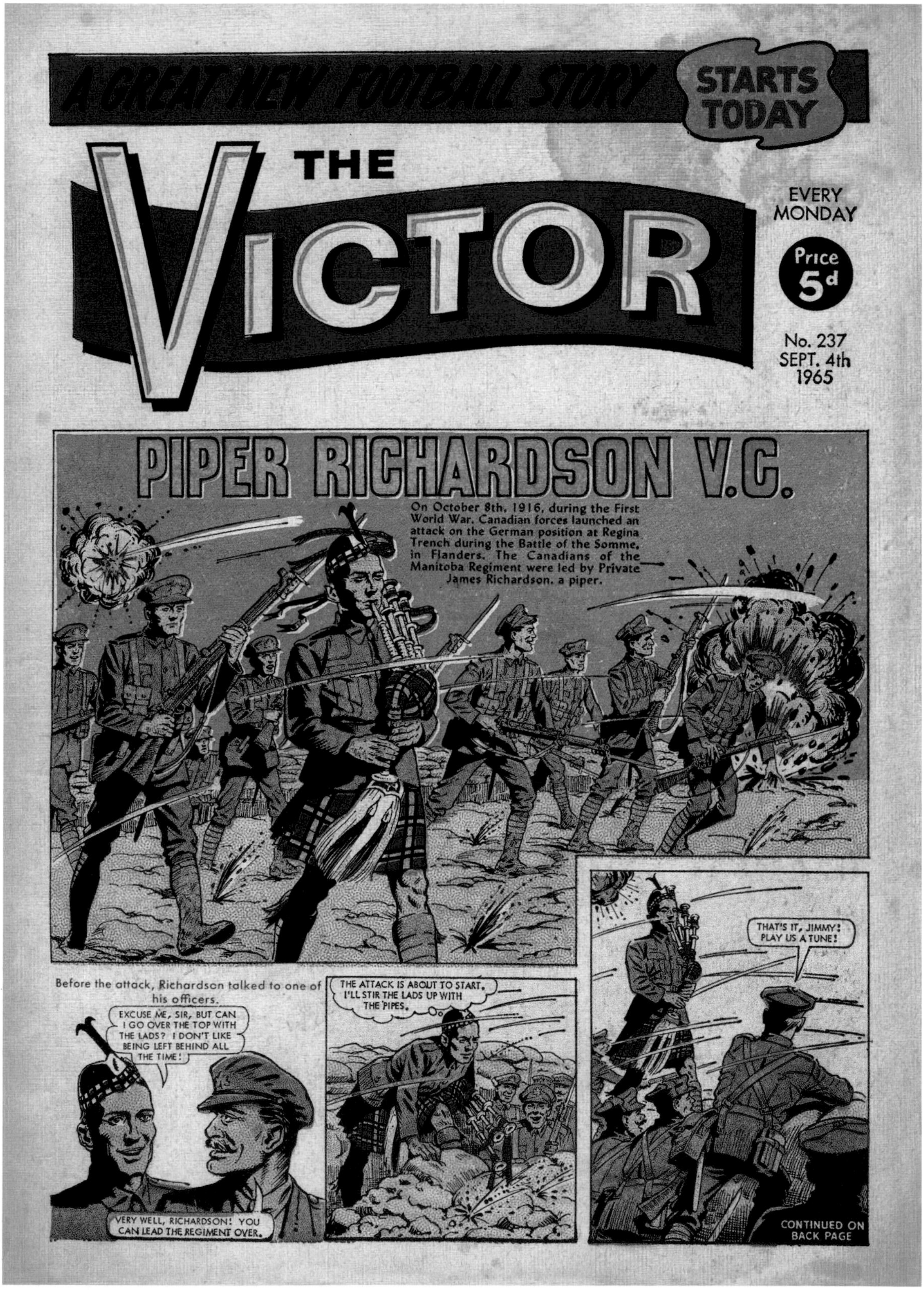
A GREAT NEW FOOTBALL STORY
STARTS TODAY
THE VICTOR
EVERY MONDAY
Price 5d
No. 237 SEPT. 4th 1965
PIPER RICHARDSON V.C.
On October 8th, 1916, during the First World War, Canadian forces launched an attack on the German position at Regina Trench during the Battle of the Somme, in Flanders. The Canadians of the Manitoba Regiment were led by Private James Richardson, a piper.
Before the attack, Richardson talked to one of his officers.
EXCUSE ME, SIR, BUT CAN I GO OVER THE TOP WITH THE LADS? I DON'T LIKE BEING LEFT BEHIND ALL THE TIME!
VERY WELL, RICHARDSON! YOU CAN LEAD THE REGIMENT OVER.
THE ATTACK IS ABOUT TO START. I'LL STIR THE LADS UP WITH THE PIPES.
THAT'S IT, JIMMY! PLAY US A TUNE!
CONTINUED ON BACK PAGE

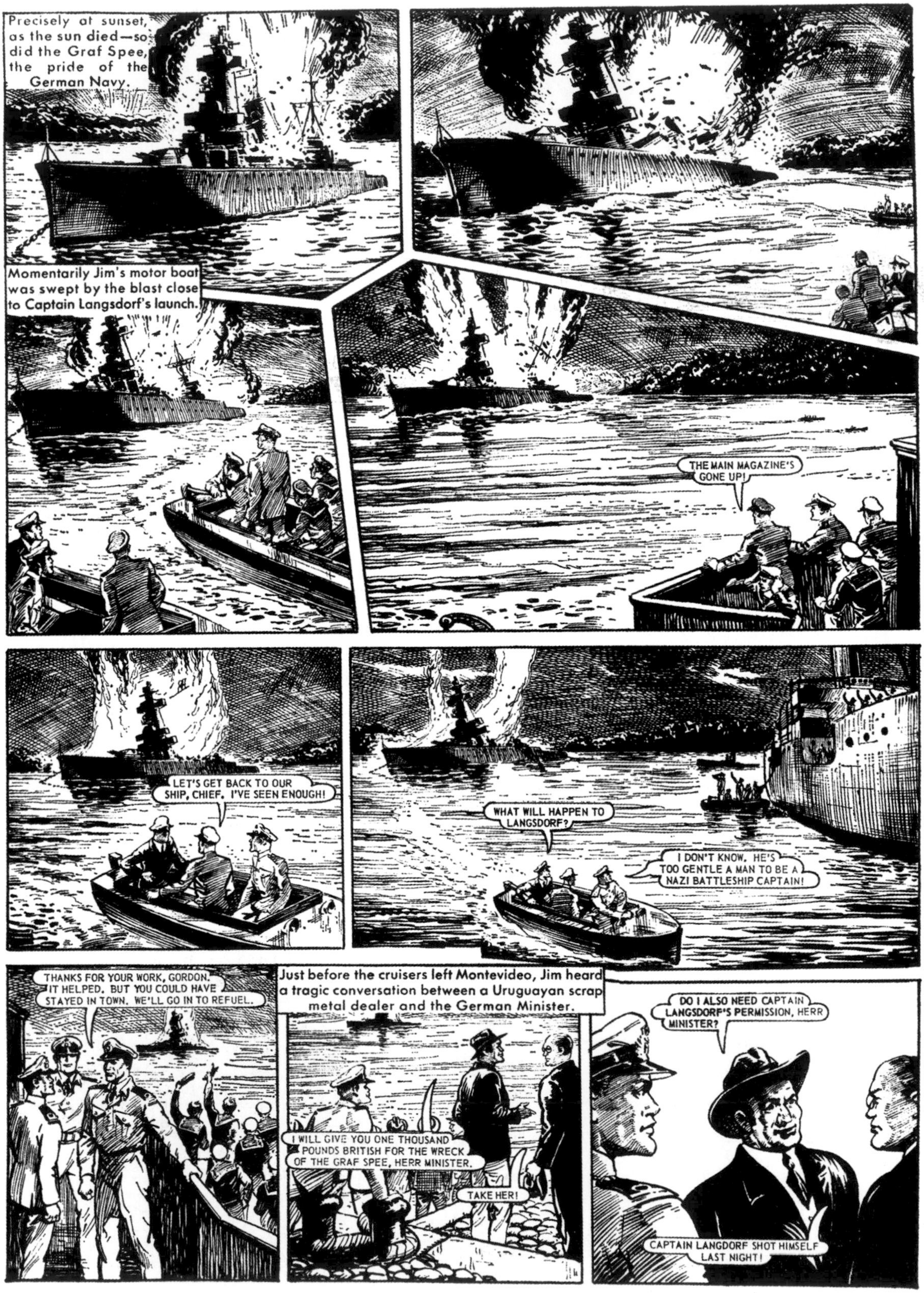
Precisely at sunset, as the sun died—so did the Graf Spee, the pride of the German Navy.
Momentarily Jim's motor boat was swept by the blast close to Captain Langsdorf's launch.
THE MAIN MAGAZINE'S GONE UP!
LET'S GET BACK TO OUR SHIP, CHIEF. I'VE SEEN ENOUGH!
WHAT WILL HAPPEN TO LANGSDORF?
I DON'T KNOW. HE'S TOO GENTLE A MAN TO BE A NAZI BATTLESHIP CAPTAIN!
THANKS FOR YOUR WORK, GORDON. IT HELPED. BUT YOU COULD HAVE STAYED IN TOWN. WE'LL GO IN TO REFUEL.
Just before the cruisers left Montevideo, Jim heard a tragic conversation between a Uruguayan scrap metal dealer and the German Minister.
I WILL GIVE YOU ONE THOUSAND POUNDS BRITISH FOR THE WRECK OF THE GRAF SPEE, HERR MINISTER.
TAKE HER!
DO I ALSO NEED CAPTAIN LANGSDORF'S PERMISSION, HERR MINISTER?
CAPTAIN LANGDORF SHOT HIMSELF LAST NIGHT!

Extra fuel for the ships was ordered and this information was leaked to the Germans. They fell for the trap, and thinking the *Graf Spee* might be captured ordered her skipper, Hans Langsdorff, to scuttle her. The *Graf Spee* sailed out of Montevideo with a skeleton crew on board, and just three miles out dropped anchor. Later, a huge explosion rocked *Graf Spee* – the ship was still burning four days later. Langsdorff had scuttled the ship, having allowed the crew to disembark, and the skipper committed suicide a few days later. The story "Gordon of G Force" was unusual in the modern comics in that, while fictional in terms of characters, it was actually based on a true story. Indeed, *Victor*'s version of the *Graf Spee* story was extremely faithful to actual events.

Above and below *Victor* story "The Roaring Rockets" tracked the progress of "Sparks" Howard and "Sleepy" Saunders, spotters for a flotilla of rocket-launching craft. They land in Italy, but not everything goes to plan, above. But Commander Hawkes and some men from the rocket flotilla save the day – and the Nazis have to flee for their lives (issue dated 11 September 1965)

The story "The Raid on Zeebrugge" followed the same format (*Victor*, issue dated 22 May 1965). The events and the main characters depicted in it were real – only the dialogue was imaginary. The Zeebrugge raid took place in April 1918, when the British attempted to bottle up German U-Boats in the Belgium port of Zeebrugge by scuttling three ships at the entrance to the Bruges canal. (While a huge propaganda coup at the time, the raid was not judged a great success, the Germans being inconvenienced only for a few days.)

Not all the *Victor*'s war stories were deadly serious, and occasionally comic characters turned up. One example was "Ticker Turner", who was "the soldier whose motto is 'A wangle a day keeps the sergeant at bay!'" (issue dated 6 June 1962). "Ticker Turner was an infantry private during the last war. He did his job well enough, but he was always on the lookout for ways to make life a bit easier for himself. Ticker was, in fact, the Army's champion wangler." The story charts

A RED MIST FLOATED BEFORE HERCULES HURRICANE'S EYES AND HE ERUPTED INTO A TERRIBLE "RAGIN' FURY"!

GREAT BLISTERIN' BULWARKS! YOU'LL PAY FOR THIS, FLANNEL-BRAIN! GET READY FOR THE CLOBBERING OF ALL TIME!

T-TAKE IT EASY, CAP'N! I-I ONLY MEANT TO 'ELP!

Above and below Captain Hurricane was unstoppable when he was goaded into a "ragin' fury". His adventures appeared in many different comic titles over the years: above, action from the *Valiant Annual* 1980; below, in earlier days, in the *Valiant Annual* 1965

Ticker's escapades at the beginning of 1945, as he was advancing through Holland with the British army.

Fleetway Publications' *Valiant* carried the same mix of stories as rival *Victor*, with sport, adventure and war stories the staple diet. One of its main covers features was "Famous Fighters", which profiled warriors from down the ages, but there is no doubt who the star of the show was – "Captain Hurricane". Hercules Hurricane was the captain of a tramp steamer until his ship was sunk by a German U-Boat; he and his first mate, "Maggot" Malone, were left in the sea to their fate by gloating German submariners (issue dated 6 October 1962). But the pair were picked up by a passing ship, and immediately enlisted in the Royal Marine Commandos, with revenge at the top of their agenda. As the Germans (and Japanese) were to discover over subsequent years, Captain Hurricane had a short fuse, and when roused to a "ragin' fury" he acquired superhuman strength.

Valiant had only been in existence for a few months when it incorporated the comic *Knockout* (on 23 February 1963). *Knockout* was first published in March 1939, as a response to D.C. Thomson's exciting new comics, *The Dandy* and *The Beano*. *Knockout* managed to survive the paper shortages of the war, incorporating the famous story-paper *Magnet* on 1 June 1940. *Knockout*'s characters included "Battler Britton", the air ace who first appeared in *Sun* comic, and Johnny Wingco, the "Master Pilot". Johnnie Wingco was

CAPTAIN HURRICANE

Before the war, Captain Hercules Hurricane, of the Royal Marines, had served in the Merchant Navy. He had been in Singapore many times, but never under such circumstances as he found himself in 1942, when the island was about to fall to the Japanese army.

SO HELP ME, IF I ONLY HAD MYSELF TO CONSIDER I'D STAY AND KEELHAUL A FEW OF YOU YELLOW WEEVILS!

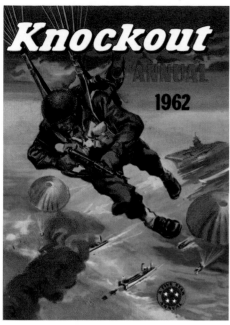

Commander Wingate-Cole, a civilian pilot with a military past.

Hot on the heels of *Valiant* came D.C. Thomson's *Hornet*, first published in September 1963. The title followed the trend of mixing sport, adventure and war stories with a smattering of "real life" features. *Hornet* recycled a number of stories that first appeared in other titles from the Scottish stable, including the excellent "V for Vengeance" – only this time the Nazis were being terrorised in comic-strip rather than text-based format.

Hornet also ran a sequel, called "The Voice of Berlin" (started issue dated 3 May 1969), in which "The Deathless Men" aim to settle matters with Basil Royce, a Lord Haw Haw-type figure ("Basil Royce calling! Basil Royce calling from Germany with the Voice of Truth!"). From a bunker in Berlin, Royce broadcasts propaganda to Britain. In one episode he claims that the city of Dundee – the home of D.C. Thomson – had been obliterated in an air-raid. Yet, "in the city of Dundee, hundreds of miles away, Royce's broadcast was heard by the citizens who listened to it with amazement, amusement and hoots of laughter, for there had been no air raid at all on the city the night before". However, the "news" has a devastating effect on exiled Dundonians, who believe their home city to be in ruins. But the Deathless Men were to gain their revenge for all Royce's distressing propaganda. They capture him in his broadcasting station, and force him to wear the grey shoes, overcoat and grey mask that is the uniform of the Deathless Men. Royce is then pushed down a flight of stairs, at the foot of which are waiting Nazi guards. They assume he is one of the enemy and riddle him with bullets – and the Voice of Truth is no more (issue

Above Johnnie Wingco escapes two German Messerschmitts with an unusual manoeuvre, from the *Knockout Annual* 1960

dated 17 May 1969). So who were the Deathless Men? At the end of this story readers are told that "they thought nothing of their lives. They considered themselves men who had died years before in the concentration camps. They considered their present lives only time borrowed in order to achieve vengeance."

Hornet's adventure/war/sport mix continued throughout the 1960s. Its war stories were almost exclusively of the Second World War. "Volts of Vengeance" (issue dated 6 September 1969) was "the amazing vengeance trail of the man the dreaded German Gestapo could not break – the man with sudden death in his bare hands". It concerned British Secret Service agent Eddie Harmon, who was parachuted in to help the French resistance – the "Maquisards". He is captured in an ambush and tortured. The Germans resort to electric shock treatment, but enraged by Harmon's seeming resistance, go on to massively raise the voltage. At this point they believe he is dead, and Harmon's body is removed to the morgue. There he comes back to life and discovers – as

Below The "Black Eagle" has his wings clipped when he fails to notice anti-aircraft barrage balloons, from the story "Strike the Black Eagle and Die", which appeared in *Hornet*, dated 21 June 1969

does an unfortunate sentry – that he can pass on lethal electric shocks with a touch of his hand. This he does to great effect.

Revenge was a common theme for *Hornet*'s war stories. In "Strike the Black Eagle and Die" (issue dated 21 June 1969), First World War pilot Lieutenant Harvey Wright seeks vengeance for a killed comrade, who was mown down by machine guns bullets having bailed out of his Sopwith Pup. Wright flies behind German lines to challenge the perpetrator – the so-called "Black Eagle" – to a duel. Revenge is gained on the treacherous German, who dies in a shell-hole trying to commit one last act of criminality.

"Ten Targets for the Gunnery Jack" was also a tale of vengeance – this time in *Hotspur* (issue dated 8 February 1969).

The premise was: "Wrongly accused of selling secret information to a foreign power, Lieutenant Mike Gray, a Royal Naval gunnery expert, or Gunnery Jack as they were called, had been convicted on false evidence and dismissed from the Service shortly before the outbreak of the Second World War. Determined to clear his name and get back into the Navy, Gray joined the Merchant Service and, with the help of Joe Kent, a young seaman, set out to hunt down the ten men whose lies had ruined his career." American Hiram B. Robey was the first target; he is working for the Germans as a spy and is exposed by Gray, who confesses to

Above "The Deathless Men" go about their deadly business in the story "V for Vengeance", in *Hornet*, dated 8 August 1969

Below There is a shock in store for this German sentry as British Secret Service agent Eddie Harmon comes back to life in the story "Volts of Vengeance" in *Hornet*, issue dated 6 September 1969

Above Unusually, this *Hornet* cover features a war story that is not related to either the Great War or the Second World War. In fact it concerns the Second Afghan War, issue dated 30 August 1969

Below The crew of HMS *Outcast* are in destructive mood when it comes to taking on Japanese warships, in the story of the same name. It appeared in *Hurricane*, issue dated 4 July 1964

Facing page "The Twin Terrors" was the cover story of "underwater charioteers" in *Rover and Wizard*, dated 21 December 1963

having lied to get him sacked from the Navy.

Other popular war stories in *Hornet* included "The Walkie-Talkie Warrior", which featured the adventures of Major Jock Brett, who used the eponymous technology to direct a crack squadron of Tempest pilots to enemy targets. The story was not new; it had appeared in *Hotspur* as a text story in 1945, when the technology was in its infancy.

"The Phantom Flyer" was another *Hotspur* tale of war in the air. Set during the early years of the war, it concerned 134 Squadron R.A.F., which was "helped by a mystery man known as the Phantom Flyer. Flying Officer Sam Fletcher… discovered that the Phantom Flyer was Hoodoo Hart, the former C.O. of 134 Squadron, who had been forced to leave the R.A.F. for health reasons" (issue dated 4 January 1969). In the same issue the story "The Yellow Sword", meanwhile, harked back to pre-Great War "invasion literature". Britain is invaded by the imaginary Oriental nation of Kushanti, whose emblem is a yellow sword. Despite fighting a guerilla war, the British are subjugated – until finally the oppressors are defeated in an uprising. Again, the story was not a new one. Originally called "Will O' the Whistle", it appeared in *Wizard* in 18 episodes in 1957 and 1958. First time around the "invasion" took place in 1993; in the

H.M.S. Outcast, ancient and rusty old destroyer, was ordered to the breakers' yard by the Admiralty, but her skipper, Lieutenant Wildeblood and his happy-go-lucky crew of misfits thought they could still play a vital part in helping to win World War II. The old warship blundered slap-bang into a powerful force of Japanese warships, causing them to collide in the mix-up! Outcast's quick-thinking skipper steered his ship under the tarpaulin-draped side of a damaged Jap aircraft carrier…!

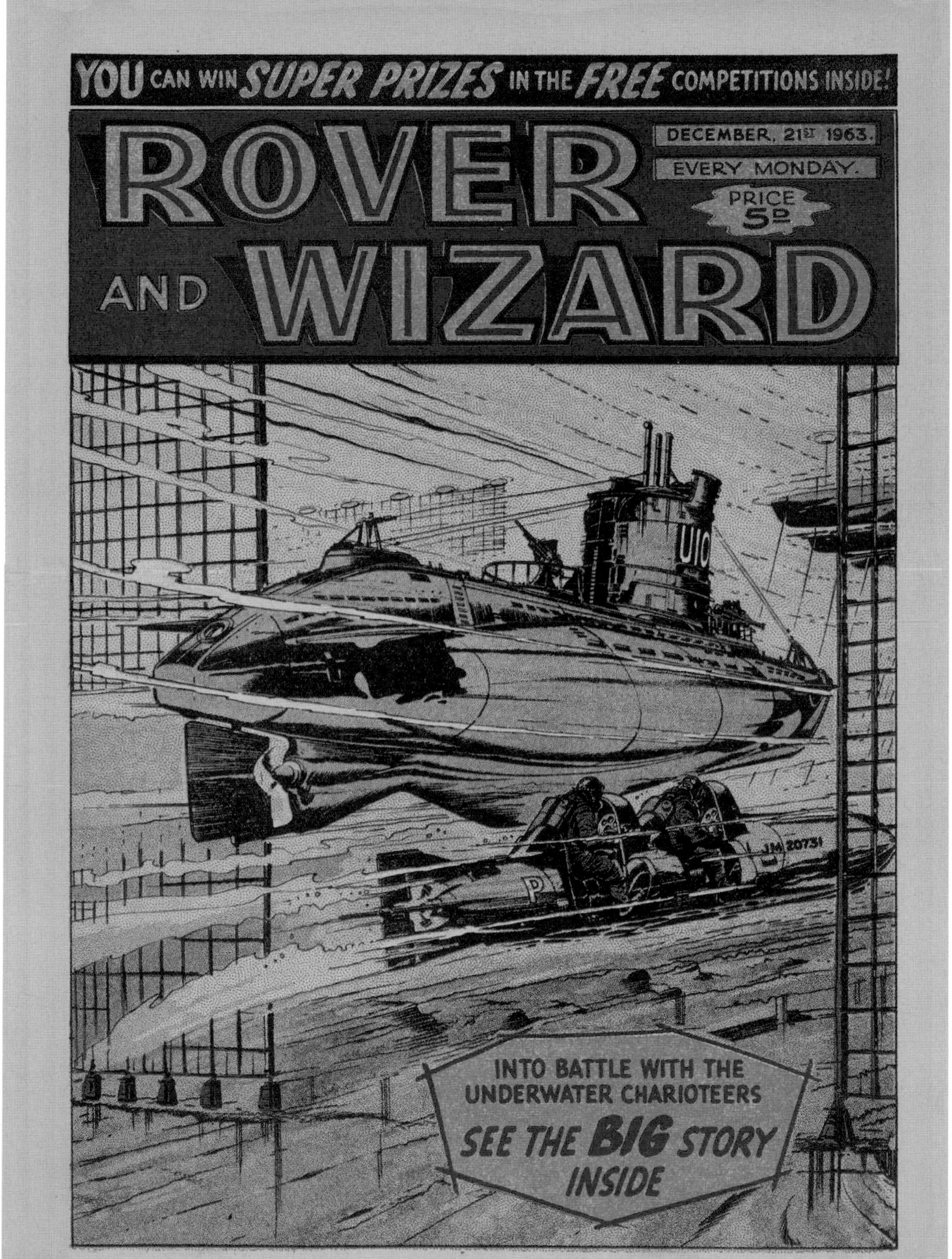
YOU CAN WIN SUPER PRIZES IN THE FREE COMPETITIONS INSIDE!
ROVER AND WIZARD
DECEMBER, 21ST 1963.
EVERY MONDAY.
PRICE 5D
U10
JM 20731
P
INTO BATTLE WITH THE UNDERWATER CHARIOTEERS
SEE THE BIG STORY INSIDE

IT TAKES OUTSTANDING COURAGE TO CLIMB OUT ON TO THE BLAZING WING OF A DAMAGED WELLINGTON BOMBER FLYING AT 90 M.P.H. IN PITCH DARKNESS. BUT THAT'S WHAT SERGEANT JAMES ALLEN WARD OF THE R.A.F DID IN THE LAST WAR TO STOP THE FIRE SPREADING TO THE FUSELAGE. HE WAS AWARDED THE VICTORIA CROSS FOR HIS BRAVERY.

Above A "true-life" story in *Hurricane*, issue dated 13 March 1965

Below "Paratrooper" was a popular story in *Hurricane*. Each tale was introduced by Sergeant Rock; this story of an explosives expert appeared on 18 July 1964

Hornet's reprint it was 1968 – a year before the story appeared in the comic.

The fourth of the new launches in the first half of the 1960s was **Hurricane**, with the first issue dated 29 February 1964. Billed as the "companion paper to **Valiant**", Fleetway's new publication stuck to the by-now tried-and-tested formula of action-adventure, sport and war. Among the stand-out war stories were "H.M.S. Outcast" and "Paratrooper!", with the former appearing in the launch issue. Lieutenant Wildeblood was in charge of the renegade HMS *Outcast*, a decrepit, battered old vessel that had been de-commissioned and condemned to the breakers' yard. Trouble was, she never quite made it back to Blighty; Wildeblood and his men stumbled across the Japanese and Germans en route, and got into many a close scrape. In one encounter HMS *Outcast* blundered slap-bang into a powerful force of Japanese warships, causing them to collide (issue dated 4 July 1964). In the confusion Wildeblood's men capture an enemy aircraft carrier, and proceed to "fire off" the ship's fighter aircraft, which are packed with explosives, into the enemy fleet. In no time the Japanese are routed – but there's no pleasing some folk. As the *Outcast*'s crew are mopping up a naval task-force arrives on the scene, primed and ready for action. But their work is already done, much to the chagrin of the commanding officer, who vows to get even with Wildeblood and his men for stealing his thunder.

170

The second war story in *Hurricane* was "Paratrooper!", a series of self-contained tales that were "exciting complete adventures with the Red Devils – tough fighting men of World War II. Each episode was introduced by "Sergeant Rock". A typical tale concerned explosives expert "Bango Brown", and how he accidentally blew up the wrong bridge on covert operations in Northern France shortly after the D-Day landings (issue dated 18 July 1964).

Another popular story was "Danger Island" – "A Thrilling Story of Naval Warfare in the South Pacific". The crew of HMS *Newley* have to abandon ship after being attacked by Japanese warplanes and are forced to seek sanctuary on "Danger Island" (story started 27 March 1965). Unfortunately for the story's leading characters, Steve Hazard, Dusty Miller and Buster Brown, the island is occupied by the Japanese. "Danger Island" was, in fact, not a new story – it ran in *Lion* in 1952 under the title "The Naval Castaways".

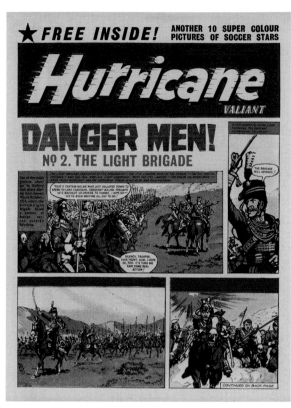

Above *Hurricane* turns back the clock with the legend that was the Charge of the Light Brigade, issue dated 10 October 1964

Below Corporal Tom Fox was "The Jungle Fox", who was parachuted into occupied Burma to spy on the Japanese. The story appeared in *Victor*, issue dated 10 October 1964

As well as fictional stories of the war *Hurricane* also carried tales of the heroes of the past. A cover series, called "Dangermen", featured military men from history – Roman charioteers, the Light Brigade – alongside racing drivers, test pilots and even lifeboatmen. But *Hurricane*'s was to be a shortlived existence.

WE HAVEN'T ANY MONEY, BUT THIS IS AN I.O.U. MY GOVERNMENT WILL PAY YOU FOR YOUR HELP WHEN OUR ARMIES FREE YOUR COUNTRY.

I WILL TAKE YOUR PAPER. I KNOW YOUR ARMIES WILL RETURN SOON, AND THEN I SHALL GET FAIR PAYMENT.

After just 63 issues it was incorporated into *Tiger*, on 15 May 1965.

Along with *Lion*, *Tiger* continued to fly the flag for the Fleetway stable. Roy Race's exploits in "Roy of the Rovers" were proving extremely popular and, backed by a strong supporting cast, *Tiger* continued to prosper. Its equivalent figure in the war stories was "Rockfist Rogan", who continued to dominate the skies over Europe. Other popular war characters included "Spike and Dusty", the naval frogmen, and the tough-as-teak "Commando One", aka Rex Royal. All three stories had first seen the light of day

Below No task was too tough for Rex Royal, *Tiger*'s "Commando One". This episode appeared in the *Tiger Annual* 1962

in the 1950s pages of *Tiger*, and all continued in the comic's pages throughout the 1960s. Another long-running story was "The Suicide Six", featuring the exploits of a know-no-fear six-man squad of troops from across the Empire. Fighting in North Africa during the Second World War, they were Captain Dan "Rocky" Rock, from England; Sergeant Rafferty; the Cockney "Sapper" Gunn; "Bluey" Doyle, an Australian and a crack shot; Dave Lawson; and "Sparks" Grant.

Tiger's sister paper, *Lion*, also prospered throughout the 1960s; like *Tiger*, its most popular war hero was a pilot of extraordinary bravery – "Paddy Payne – Warrior of the Skies". He was the comic's cover star and he had the honour to have his exploits in colour, for page one was the only one in colour. In the issue dated 6 July 1963, readers are told that "During World War II, Paddy Payne of the R.A.F. was given the task of smashing a special German battle unit known as the Double Eagles. He reached the island on which they had their headquarters, and saw an awe-inspiring experiment taking place. Lightning bolts were shot up from a blockhouse in the direction of the three target planes." For the Nazis had developed a weapon that made aircraft disintegrate in the skies, and Payne had to destroy the generator building controlling it. He manages to break into the building and sabotage the

equipment, and makes his escape by stealing a German Focke-Wulf 190 fighter, which he then uses to attack the enemy. The story comes to an end (issue dated 27 July 1964) when Payne bails out of the Focke-Wulf, with the runaway fighter ploughing into the camp's aviation fuel storage tank.

OPERATION MYSTERY ISLAND STARRING MAX MALONE BY TREVOR HUGH

Old favourite *Rover* continued throughout the 1960s, with *Rover* incorporating both *Adventure* and *Wizard* in the course of the decade, which also saw both *Rover* and sister-paper *Hotspur* gradually move away from text-based stories to embrace the comic-strip format.

Above War in the jungle was a popular subject in the comics. This tale appeared in the *Lion Annual* 1960

To start with, the combined *Rover and Adventure* continued pretty much as it was before the merger, with an all-action full-colour cover illustrating "The Big Story" inside. One example was "The Brake that Walked, Talked and Fought", a text-based story in which "The lives of thousands of British soldiers depend on the result of this strange tug-'o-war between Murdo McRae and the Lysander" (issue dated 12 January 1963).

Below Paddy Payne makes an electrifying discovery when he spies the enemy's new secret weapon, *Lion*, dated 21 December 1963

O ne of the most popular stories in the combined title was "The Secret War of H.M.S. Waddling Duck" (issue dated May 27 1961). It concerned the tale of Lieutenant-Commander Radstock, who at the start of the story is a prisoner of the Germans: "With his left arm in a blood-stained sling, Lieutenant-Commander Radstock, R.N.V.R., heard a cable catch the bows of the German submarine in which he had been a prisoner for ten days. From his seat in the tiny wardroom, Radstock could see the tense, listening figures of Kapitan Leutenant Premmer and other officers of the German submarine on the control platform." Readers are told that: "It was an autumn night in 1939, a few weeks after the start of the war. There was a rasping sound. It sounded as if the cable

Above Paddy Payne in a tight corner, *Lion*, 19 September 1964

fouled by the submarine was now dragging along the U-boat's jumping wires – wires that ran from bow to stern and over the top of the conning tower. No one spoke. There was not a whisper. The pale-faced German navigator and his assistant looked up from the charts that were spread out on the wardroom table. Something clanged outside the hull and then there was a thud. The scraping sound was resumed. The cable was sliding overhead. The U-boat, propelled by its batteries, continued to move ahead very slowly. Radstock did not expect to live more than a few minutes. He felt sure that the U-boat would soon be a battered wreck. Premmer had told him quite openly that the plan was to creep into Scapa Flow, the anchorage of the British Home Fleet, and torpedo a battleship. Radstock had told him, 'You haven't a chance'. The German had retorted arrogantly, 'I shall make it possible'. The rapping noise seemed to move faster. The cable slid away towards the stern and all at once the sound ceased. The navigator drew a deep breath and, losing his mesmerized look, peered down at the chart. The air was foul. Radstock's arm was terribly sore. A petty-officer, who acted as the U-Boat's doctor, had put thirty stitches in a deep gash received when the mine-sweeping trawler in which Radstock was serving had been sunk by gunfire. Radstock believed he was the only survivor. He had swum for his life

Below A grand old lady... the "Waddling Duck" is just the vessel to take on the German U-Boats, in the *Rover and Adventure* story "The Secret War of H.M.S. Waddling Duck", issue dated 27 May 1961

STARTING TODAY—Thrills at sea during the Royal Navy's desperate struggle to conquer the menace of German U-boats!

The **SECRET WAR** OF **H.M.S. WADDLING DUCK**

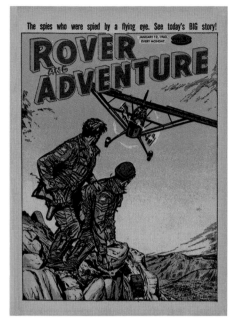

The spies who were spied by a flying eye. See today's BIG story!

ROVER
AND
ADVENTURE

JANUARY 12, 1963.
EVERY MONDAY.

for a long time, and then the Germans had pulled him aboard the submarine."

In the next instalment we read how: "The U-Boat glided on. The tension among the Germans was terrific. One of the hydroplane operators turned his head, and Radstock saw his face was glistening with sweat. The man was pounced on by a petty-officer for taking his gaze off the depth gauge. There was no tremendous explosion. Premmer lifted his eyes from the periscope abruptly. 'We're in,' he said. 'Down periscope!' There was a look of triumph on Premmer's face. Radstock sat there with his fists clenched. The U-boat had achieved what the British Navy had though was impossible. It had penetrated into Scapa Flow. Premmer had taken his submarine through the narrow gap between the block ships. Two or three minutes passed. 'Up periscope!' ordered Premmer. He again peered into the eyepiece. He snapped his fingers excitedly. 'Himmel, there is a battleship in our sights!' he exclaimed. He rapped out a series of orders, instantly obeyed by the helmsman and hydroplane operators. Radstock felt as if he were choking. He was so helpless; there was nothing he could do. Surely the presence of the prowling U-Boat would be detected at any moment, Radstock thought. Or had the Home Fleet been lulled into a sense of false security as it lay in an anchorage that was regarded as impregnable? No U-boat had ever crept into Scapa Flow during the Great War of 1914-18. Perhaps the belief that it was impossible had lasted over the years into 1939. Premmer turned to the voice pipe that linked the control platform with the torpedo compartment. 'Stand by to fire torpedoes,' he rapped. Radstock heard the German Captain give depth settings of eight feet and twelve feet. Evidently he was going to spread a salvo of

Left *Rover and Adventure*'s cover illustration for the story "The Brake that Walked, Talked and Fought", issue dated 12 January 1963

Below The Nazis strike back in the *Rover and Wizard* story, issue dated 4 December 1965

THE SPUD RUN

The men of H.M.S. Quartz have just hit the enemy hard. But now German planes arrive on the scene, and their pilots are determined to hit back—harder still!

> EASING HIS CONTROL COLUMN FORWARD, PADDY JABBED THE FIRING BUTTON

Above Paddy Payne in action, *Lion Annual* 1960

Right Man's best friend is especially helpful during times of war, as this *Rover and Wizard* story shows, in the issue dated 8 April 1965

Facing page The launch issue of *Jag* promises exciting war action stories, issue dated 4 May 1968

torpedoes. Beads of perspiration trickled down Radstock's face and he beat his free fist on his thigh. Wasn't the British Navy ever going to wake up? There was not a single propeller sound. 'Achtung!' rapped Premmer. 'Fire one!' As the torpedo was fired Radstock felt a sudden pressure on his ear drums and the U-boat gave a slight backwards lurch. 'Fire two! Fire three! Fire four!' There was a wait. The Germans tilted their heads and listened. Then a tremendous explosion rent the silence and the U-boat rolled in the shock waves carried through the water. A look of supreme exultation and excitement appeared on Premmer's face as he lifted his gaze from the periscope. 'A hit! Perhaps two hits! We have torpedoed a battleship of the Royal Oak class!' he exclaimed. 'Heil Hitler!' Hitler was the German leader. His portrait was on the wardroom bulkhead. 'Down periscope!' Premmer ordered. 'Dive!' As the U-boat glided down there was another tremendous explosion from the direction of the torpedoed battleship. The gloating faces of the Germans at their triumph was natural enough, but it riled Radstock to the depth of his being. It would have meant Radstock's death if the U-boat had been attacked by depth charges before it sneaked out of Scapa Flow, but he waited for them eagerly. There was no depth-charge attack and Premmer again performed a masterly feat of seamanship in avoiding all obstructions and taking his submarine out to sea. When there was no fear of attack Premmer summoned all his officers in the wardroom. Glasses were produced. Two bottles of champagne were opened. Premmer smirked at Radstock. 'We do not expect you to join in our toast,' he said, 'but take a glass of champagne just the

Newfoundland dogs were used as water and supply carriers in both world wars. One of them, Westerland Champion, became a hero at the siege of Hong Kong. A hand grenade landed in a British slit-trench and the dog seized it in its mouth and bounded over the parapet. Although it was killed, the dog saved 20 men from death or injury.

No1
WITH FREE GIFT INSIDE
BOBBY MOORE'S BOOK of the F.A. CUP
JAG
7D
4th MAY 1968
EVERY SATURDAY

same.' Radstock shook his head. Premmer faced the portrait of Hitler. 'Heil Hitler!' he exclaimed. 'We will drink to certain victory over Britain in which the submarines of the Leader's navy will take a leading part!' The glasses were emptied." But Radstock manages to escape, and sets about seeking revenge. He is assigned to a top-secret project; British boffins have created a hugely powerful depth charge with which to challenge the supremacy of the German U-boats. The trouble is, the devices are so powerful they can't be fired from any ordinary warships – in trials, the shockwaves from the super-explosives severely damaged the ships from which they were fired. That is until, during the testing, Radstock spots the *Thunderer*, also known as the "Waddling Duck". Radstock is told: "She's a monitor, of course. Monitors were used a lot in the First World War for coastal bombardments,

Above *Valiant* poses a "true-or-false" question to its readers in the issue dated 19 July 1969. In case you were wondering, the answer is no – this incident did not happen

Right MacTavish and O'Toole bickering on the battlefield once again, in *Jag*, issue dated 11 January 1969

Facing page "The Mouse Patrol" on a mission – to rescue their dads from the Nazis, *Jag*, issue dated 4 January 1969. The story continues on page 180

especially in shallow waters and I suppose the Admiralty thought we should need 'em again, but it hasn't worked out that way. I understand the Waddling Duck is to be broken up." But the vessel has a new role to play – she easily rides out the shock waves from the new depth charges and Radstock adopts her as his ship, to take on the U-Boats.

But the comic strips were taking over, with the text-based story format looking increasingly dated as the 1960s progressed. The established comics increasingly preferred comic-strip stories to text-based ones, although those still appeared. Fleetway Publications chanced its arm with the launch of two new titles: *Ranger* (launched 18 September 1965) and *Jag*

THE MOUSE PATROL

In the North African Desert, during the Second World War, three boys, named Cyril North, Blackie Knight and Ginger Nobb, steal a tank and set out in search of their fathers, who have been captured by the Germans. They find Blackie's father, but the other boys' parents are being held prisoner by Major Erwin Von Wolzen, the Mouse Patrol's arch-enemy. They discover Wolzen's secret base, a pyramid, and, disguised as Germans, Blackie and his father sneak into it. But then they are spotted by a Nazi guard . .

ACH! YOU DO NOT LOOK LIKE ONE OF OUR MEN! STAND WHERE YOU ARE..!

THIS IS IT! HE..HE'S COMING RIGHT UP TO TAKE A CLOSER LOOK AT ME!

THEN, AS THE CELL-GUARD PASSED THE MASSIVE SUPPORT PILLAR...

NICE WORK, BLACKIE! HE FELL RIGHT INTO THE TRAP!

I'LL GET HIS KEYS, DAD!

ZUNK!

GNNFFF!

SOON, THE STARTLED BRITISH PRISONERS WERE STUMBLING FROM THEIR CELLS...

STONE ME! WHAT'S HAPPENING? ONE OF THESE JERRIES IS JUST A KID!

DON'T LET THE UNIFORMS FOOL YOU, LADS! WE'RE BRITISH...AND WE'RE LOOKING FOR SERGEANT BILL NOBB, AND LIEUTENANT PETER NORTH!

I AM LIEUTENANT NORTH...AND THIS IS SERGEANT NOBB!

BUT 'OW DID YOU KNOW WE'D BE 'ERE?

IT'S QUITE A STORY, GENTLEMEN! YOU SEE, YOUR SONS HAVE BEEN LOOKING FOR YOU..!

AS CAPTAIN KNIGHT WENT ON TO EXPLAIN THE AMAZING QUEST OF THE MOUSE PATROL...

YOU...YOU MEAN GINGER AND YOUNG CYRIL ARE PLAYING HIDE-AND-SEEK WITH THE JERRIES?

BUT WE'VE GOT TO HELP THEM!

WE WILL, LIEUTENANT... AFTER WE'VE DEALT WITH VON WOLZEN'S LITTLE HIDE-OUT!

MOMENTS LATER, TO THE ASTONISHMENT OF THE GERMANS GUARDING THE PYRAMID ARMOURY...

HANDS HOCHE!

GROSSER HIMMEL! WAS—?

GET THEIR GUNS, MEN!

AS THE FORMER PRISONERS TOOK THEIR PICK OF WEAPONS AND AMMUNITION...

LOOK AT THOSE STACKS OF SHELLS, AND...AND EXPLOSIVES!

H'MM! YES, BLACKIE! MAKE QUITE A BIG BANG IF THEY ALL WENT OFF AT ONCE, WOULDN'T THEY?

FROM MATERIALS IN THE ARMOURY, DAVID KNIGHT RIGGED UP A MAKESHIFT TIME-BOMB...

I'VE SET IT TO GO OFF IN EXACTLY THREE MINUTES TIME!

THEN LET'S GET OUT OF HERE... MOVE!

THE HANDFUL OF GERMANS STILL GARRISONING THE PYRAMID HARDLY KNEW WHAT HAD HIT THEM.

THE PRISONERS! THEY... AAAAHHH!

KEEP GOING, LADS! BLAST YOUR WAY THROUGH!

THAKKA, THAKKA!

CONTINUED OVERLEAF...

WITH ONLY A FEW SECONDS LEFT, THEY REACHED THE MAIN DOORS...

CRE-EEK!

UUUU-UUUGH!

OKAY, THAT'S WIDE ENOUGH! EVERYONE RUN FOR THEIR LIVES!

AND EVEN AS THEY HURLED THEMSELVES FROM THE PYRAMID, AND INTO THE SHELTER OF NEARBY ROCKS...

WHRUUMPF!

EEEEEE!

TO VON WOLZEN AND HIS MEN IN THE HILLS THE NIGHT SEEMED TO EXPLODE...

BAA-OOOOM!

ZUM TEUFEL! THE PYRAMID... BLOWING ITSELF APART!

THOSE BRATS MUST HAVE SNEAKED PAST US AND SABOTAGED THE ARMOURY!

GET GOING, DRIVER! THEY SHALL PAY WITH THEIR LIVES FOR THIS FINAL INSULT!

BUT AS VON WOLZEN'S HALF-TRACK WENT THUNDERING BACK DOWN THE SLOPE...

FFFF-THAM!

EEEE YAAARGH!

CAPTAIN KNIGHT STEPPED INTO THE GLARE OF THE EXPLODING PYRAMID...

HIMMEL! THE PRISONERS! B-BUT, HOW—?

THAT WAS ONE OF YOUR OWN BAZOOKA-SHELLS, VON WOLZEN! NOW, TELL YOUR MEN TO SURRENDER!

THE NAZI COMMANDO-LEADER HAD NO ALTERNATIVE! AS HIS MEN WERE ROUNDED UP...

ROWWRR!

YIPPEEEE! HERE COMES THE HONEY!

DAD, DAD! IT'S ME... GINGER!

WHY, YOU LITTLE SON-OF-A...

GINGER ALMOST FELL INTO SERGEANT NOBB'S ARMS... AND THEN CYRIL NORTH WAS RE-UNITED WITH HIS FATHER...

THANK THE STARS YOU'RE ALL RIGHT, SON! BUT CAPTAIN KNIGHT TOLD US THAT CLEOPATRA WAS WITH YOU?

SHE IS, FATHER! LOOK OVER THERE...!

WHEEEF! AROOOGH!

AS THE MAJOR HAS CHASED US ALL OVER THE DESERT IN SEARCH OF HIS IRON CROSS, I THOUGHT IT ONLY POLITE THAT CLEO SHOULD RETURN IT!

DONNER UND BLITZEN! NO..!

VON WOLZEN DIDN'T SEEM VERY PLEASED TO RECOVER HIS CHERISHED DECORATION...

GNAAA-YEEEEGH!

WELL, THERE'S GRATITUDE FOR YOU!

POUND! STAMP!

HA, HA, HAWWWW!

THE TRIUMPHANT BRITISHERS SURVEYED THE DEVASTATION THEY HAD CAUSED...

THE WAR IS OVER FOR WOLZEN'S WOLVES, LIEUTENANT... AND I DON'T THINK THIS PYRAMID WILL BE MUCH USE TO THE JERRIES ANY MORE!

THANKS TO THREE BOYS, A TANK AND A CHIMPANZEE!

IT SEEMED ONLY FITTING THAT THE BOYS OF THE MOUSE PATROL, AND THEIR BATTERED LITTLE TANK, SHOULD LEAD THE WAY HOME...

TAKE IT EASY, CYRIL! WE'VE GOT SOME PASSENGERS, THIS TIME.. OUR DADS!

THE MORE THE MERRIER, EH, CLEO?

UFF! YAR-EEEEGH!

THE END

(launched 4 May 1968). There was also, sadly, one notable closure. Its first issue appeared on 18 January 1879, and the title became so popular and well-known that it became a generic term for all boys' story-papers. But *The Boy's Own Paper* finally closed down in 1967, the February issue of that year being the final one. The last few years of its existence had been troubled ones; it was bought by Lutterworth from Purnell, then quickly sold on to Haymarket Press, who closed it down. However, the *Boy's Own Annual* continued to be produced until that, too, was closed down, in 1979.

Ranger was a rival to the *The Boy's Own Paper* and similar in style to the very popular *Look and Learn*, describing itself as "The National Boys' Magazine". Lavishly illustrated and in a large format, *Ranger* was part-magazine and part-comic, and carried both fictional and factual stories about warfare. Like *The Boy's Own Paper*, it featured stories by big-name writers; the issue dated

Below International rescue… the six members of the "The Suicide Six" represented the far-flung corners of the Empire, to devastating effect. This story appeared in the *Tiger Annual* 1963

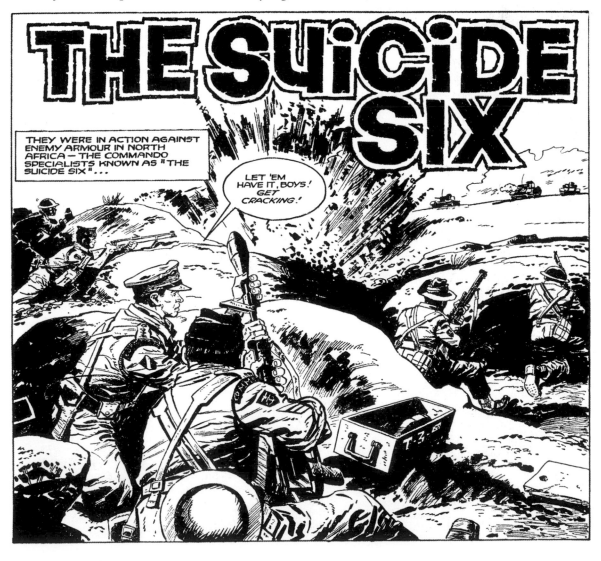

Above Action from the *Hotspur Annual* 1968 with "The Greatest Air War"

Below In The Gurkhas in action, in the pages of *Victor*, issue dated 12 July 1969

2 October 1965 contained a "New C.S. Forester story of World War II – Gold from Crete". Features included "Famous Fighting Aces" and "At First Hand" – "An on-the-spot account of a stirring event will appear every week". The issue dated 18 September 1965 carried the story "How I Rode and Fought with the 21st Lancers, by Sir Winston Churchill". Fleetway published just 40 issues of *Ranger* before it was sold to the *Look and Learn* stable, and it was incorporated into that title on 25 June 1966.

Fleetway had a little more luck with *Jag*. It started life as a large-format comic before changing to the traditional standard size on the 22 February 1969. Eye-catching with its vivid illustrations, *Jag* had high production values and was expensive to produce. Its war stories included the popular "The Mouse Patrol", which was set in North Africa during the Second World War. It concerned the adventures of three boys, Cyril North, Blackie Knight and Ginger Nobb – and a chimpanzee called Cleopatra – as they look for their fathers, who they believe have been made prisoners of war.

Other war stories included "MacTavish and O'Toole", one Scottish, one Irish, and both sergeants in the Number Three Commandos. The pair have a love-hate relationship – they are constantly at loggerheads, and frequently trade

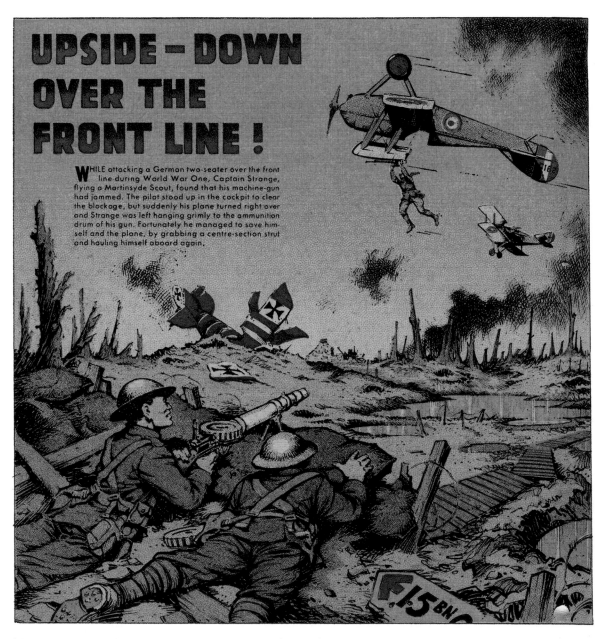

UPSIDE - DOWN OVER THE FRONT LINE !

WHILE attacking a German two-seater over the front line during World War One, Captain Strange, flying a Martinsyde Scout, found that his machine-gun had jammed. The pilot stood up in the cockpit to clear the blockage, but suddenly his plane turned right over and Strange was left hanging grimly to the ammunition drum of his gun. Fortunately he managed to save himself and the plane, by grabbing a centre-section strut and hauling himself aboard again.

Above A bizarre-but-true story of the Great War, in *Hotspur*, issue dated 22 March 1969

blows. But when the chips are down each puts his life on the line for the other. Another favourite war yarn was "The Daredevils", the men of the Long Range Desert Group who operated deep into enemy territory: "In the Lawrence of Arabia tradition, these daredevil raiders swooped out of the desert with guns blazing – creating havoc in the enemy's midst!" (issue dated 4 January 1969).

But *Jag* was not to last, and after its final issue, on 19 March 1969, it was swallowed up by *Tiger*, a fate that befell so many comics over the years.

But for lovers of the war stories in the comics, the best was yet to come, for the 1970s was to see a whole host of new launches dedicated entirely to the genre.

"WAR DOES NOT DETERMINE WHO IS RIGHT — ONLY WHO IS LEFT"

Bertrand Russell (1872-1970)

CHAPTER SEVEN

"FOR YOU, THE WAR IS OVER..."

IF THE 1960s HAD SEEN a huge shake-up in the comics market, then the next 15 years were to be even more tumultuous. The 1970s saw a revolution in comic publishing, with the first single-subject boys' comics being produced. I.P.C. (yet another name change for the Amalgamated Press/Fleetway Publications company) blazed the trail with the launch of not one but two dedicated football comics. *Scorcher* was the first, launched on 10 January 1970; it was followed by *Score 'n' Roar*, launched on 19 September 1970. Perhaps I.P.C. was being over-ambitious, for the two comics were quickly merged, to become *Scorcher and Score*, on 3 July 1971. But the blueprint had been drawn, and both I.P.C. and D.C. Thomson were to follow the football model with dedicated and ground-breaking war comics: namely *Warlord* (launched by D.C. Thomson on 28 September 1974) and I.P.C.'s *Battle* (launched 8 March 1975).

The decade also saw the disappearance of some famous names, which were either closed or amalgamated with other titles. So it was farewell to *Lion*, which was incorporated into *Valiant* on 25 May 1974; and to the long-running *Rover*, which after a staggering 2,481 issues, was merged with a re-launched *Wizard*, on 13 January 1973. *Wizard* "mark II" had hit the shelves on 14 February 1970, but was itself subsumed by *Victor*, in July 1978.

Before it disappeared, *Lion* was involved in one more takeover when it incorporated *Thunder*, on 20 March 1971. With it came an infusion of new characters; five *Thunder* stories made the grade in the new-look *Lion and Thunder*. One of them was "Steel Commando", a "Mark I Indestructible Robot" created by army bofffins and

Below Sergeant Trelawny – "Trelawny of the Guards" – is caught up in the British Expeditionary Force's retreat to Dunkirk in 1940. It appeared in the *Lion Annual* 1983

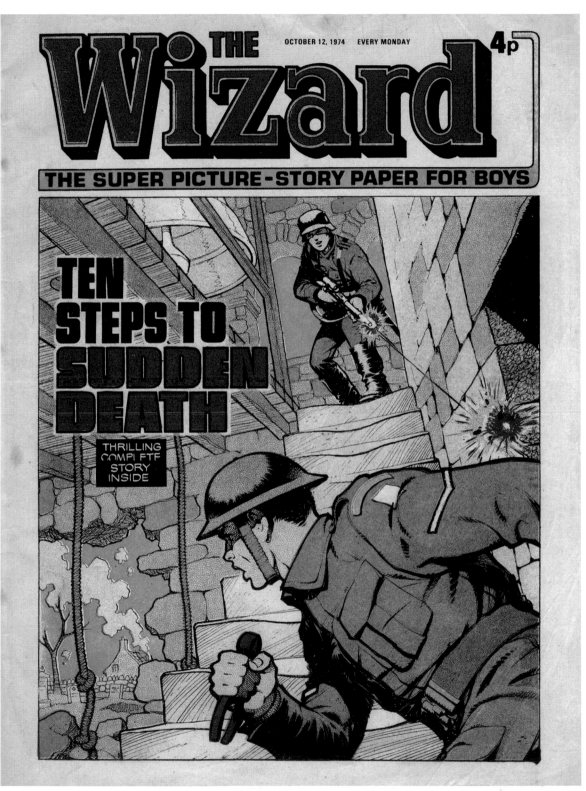

Above For whom the bell tolls… this cover story in *Wizard*, issue dated 12 October 1974, relates the story of how Signalman Bates flushed out a German sniper who was holed up in a shell-damaged bell-tower. Bates had no weapons and, armed with only a pair of pliers, sneaked up the the tower and cut the bell-ropes. The clanging of the heavy church bells was enough to bring the crumbling edifice down – and with it the German sniper!

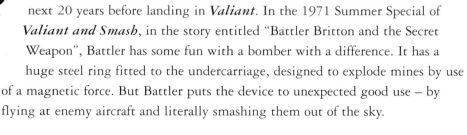

sent to the most dangerous troublespots in the war. His companion was Ernie "Excused Boots" Bates, the "laziest man in the British Army", but also the only one capable of controlling "Ironsides", as he was affectionately called. *Thunder* was an inventive I.P.C. title that ran for just 22 issues (launched 17 October 1970). Another notable *Thunder* war character was "Black Max", about a Great War flying ace called Baron Maximilien Von Klorr. His secret weapon was a giant bat, which on the Baron's orders ripped enemy aircraft apart!

Two popular titles launched in the early 1960s both met their demise in 1976 – *Hornet* and *Valiant*. Both entered the decade in rude health, with *Valiant* incorporating *Smash* on 10 April 1971. Captain Hurricane was still *Valiant*'s star attraction, his "ragin' furies" entertaining a new generation of comic readers.

But Captain Hercules Hurricane's was not the only war story in *Valiant*. Flying ace "Battler Britton" was a regular feature; he started life in the 1950s in the comic *Sun*, and featured in a number of titles over the next 20 years before landing in *Valiant*. In the 1971 Summer Special of *Valiant and Smash*, in the story entitled "Battler Britton and the Secret Weapon", Battler has some fun with a bomber with a difference. It has a huge steel ring fitted to the undercarriage, designed to explode mines by use of a magnetic force. But Battler puts the device to unexpected good use – by flying at enemy aircraft and literally smashing them out of the sky.

Above Good old Ironsides! "The Steel Commando" appeared in numerous *Thunder*, *Lion* and *Valiant* stories

Below It was an historic day when the Steel Commando and Captain Hurricane met for the first time. The story appeared in *Valiant and Lion*, issue dated 25 May 1974

Towards the end of its life, *Valiant* was chock-full of war stories. The strongest and most original were "The Black Crow", "Death Wish" and "Soldier Sharp – Rat of the Rifles" (Captain Hurricane was there, too, bashing up the Japanese). The tone of these new stories was much darker than the traditional *Valiant* ones; this was a concious decision on the part of I.P.C. to beef up the ailing comic's content. I.P.C. had earlier launched the dedicated war comic, *Battle* (on 8 March 1975), and John Wagner, co-creator of *Battle* with

THE SCHOOLBOY COMMANDER TACKLES A NAZI FIRING-SQUAD!

Above Johnny Quick was the schoolboy military genius who appeared in *Lion*. This story appeared on 24 October 1970

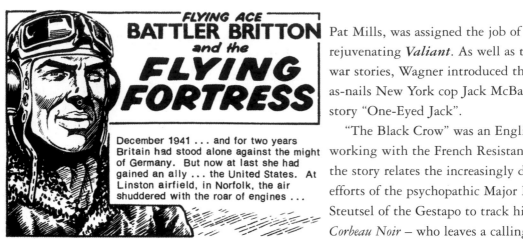

December 1941 ... and for two years Britain had stood alone against the might of Germany. But now at last she had gained an ally ... the United States. At Linston airfield, in Norfolk, the air shuddered with the roar of engines ...

Above "Battler Britton" thrilled comic readers with his aerial exploits over the best part of three decades. Here he is in the *Valiant Annual* 1973

Below "Black Max" was the story of Baron Maximilien von Klorr, a German air ace who trained giant killer bats to attack enemy aircraft. This story, in which British troops get the fright of their lives, appeared in the *Valiant Annual* 1980. Interestingly, the comic publishers continued to publish annuals long after comic titles had closed – *Valiant* ceased to exist as a stand-alone comic in 1976

Pat Mills, was assigned the job of rejuvenating *Valiant*. As well as the new war stories, Wagner introduced the hard-as-nails New York cop Jack McBane in the story "One-Eyed Jack".

"The Black Crow" was an Englishman working with the French Resistance, and the story relates the increasingly desperate efforts of the psychopathic Major Klaus Von Steutsel of the Gestapo to track him. But *Le Corbeau Noir* – who leaves a calling card of a symbol of a black crow on his victims – is not so easy to cage.

"Soldier Sharp – Rat of the Rifles" told the story of "Con-man and coward Arnie Sharp, a corporal with the Wessex Rifles and now a prisoner in Stalag 18... [he] had been taken for a hero and was much admired by the camp's senior British officer, Colonel Lambert" (issue dated 16 October 1976). Sharp is unusual in comic war stories in that he is a lying, traitorous, murderous thief, happy to rat on his comrades and collaborate with the enemy. But he has the luck of the devil – just when it seems he is about to be exposed fate intervenes, and he emerges with his dark secrets intact.

"Death Wish", too, is a war story with a difference: "Sergeant Joe Bannon was the sole survivor of his section in the opening stages of the battle to drive the Germans out of Italy during the Second World War, and he now no longer cared if he lived or died..." (issue dated 3 July 1976). Haunted by thoughts of his

dead compadres, Bannon takes suicidal risks in order to avenge them. By the final instalment the tortured sergeant is seeing visions of his fallen friends – "My lads! The boys who died in Sicily! All, right, I'm coming!" – and Bannon's final act of storming a machine-gun nest at Monte Cassino in Italy leads to the death he craves (issue dated 18 September 1976).

But the end was nigh for *Valiant*; efforts to toughen up the comic left it in "no-man's-land"; the tough and gritty war stories did not sit comfortably with the gentler stories from a previous era. "The Black Crow" and the schoolboy high-jinx of "Billy Bunter – The Heavyweight Chump of Greyfriars" made uneasy bedfellows, and so the decision was made to join the old and the new. So on 16 October 1976 *Valiant* readers – having dropped *Vulcan* from its title on 9 October 1976 – were told that there was "Important news for all readers – in this issue!" This "important news" was that "Next week *Valiant* joins *Battle* to bring you the most exciting action stories ever!" Promising a "super full-colour pull-out poster", readers learn that "From next week, you'll be getting the best of both worlds… the best of *Valiant*, with Arnie Sharp, The Black Crow and, of course, One-Eyed Jack in a thrilling new up-to-the-minute setting; plus the best of *Battle Picture Weekly*'s tough exciting war stories… the hard-fighting Darkie's Mob, do-or-die D-Day Dawson, super-cool soldier, Major Eazy and the tough Marine fighter, Bootneck Boy."

So on 23 October 1976 *Valiant* was finally incorporated into new-kid-on-the-block *Battle Picture Weekly* (more of which later); there were 730 issues of *Valiant* over its 14-year lifespan.

Another esteemed title also produced its last issue in 1976 – D.C Thomson's *Hornet*. The title always had a strong war bias, carrying both fictional and war-related fact-based tales. One example was the story "The Hero on the Hook", one of the comic's cover series called "The *Hornet* Gallery of Courage" (issue dated 16 January 1971). It concerned one William Fisher, whose story was told inside: "William Fisher was not a soldier, but when the German bombers raided Southampton during

the last war, the gallant dock worker found himself on the front line. One night, as the planes roared over the city, dropping their loads of death, one of the first casualties was an anti-aircraft gunner, on a roof fifty feet above the dockside. The gunner was badly wounded about the head and face. Fire quickly broke out on the gunsite and the gun crew was ordered to abandon its position. It was found impossible to lower the wounded man over the parapet of the roof and he had to be left behind. On hearing of the young soldier's fate, William Fisher got the help of a crane driver. Making a sling with a rope, he fixed it to the hook of the crane, and had himself hoisted up to the roof. By this time, the fire had spread alarmingly and the anti-aircraft's gun's ammunition was exploding in the heat. Nevertheless, Fisher slipped the soldier into the sling and watched him lowered to safety. With shells exploding all around and the flames creeping ever nearer, Fisher had to wait above on the roof until the hook and sling returned once more, enabling him to make his escape. For his magnificent courage in such a dangerous situation, William Fisher was awarded the George Medal." That issue of **Hornet** also carried the war stories "Volts of Vengeance", "The Raiders from Wreck 16" and "The Grenadier".

"The Raiders from Wreck 16" concerned the adventures of the "Special

Above William Fisher was a real-life hero of the Second World War. His story appeared in *Hornet*, dated 16 January 1971

Below Something was close to Sergeant Joe Bannon's heart – a bullet he copped on D-Day, and that could kill him at any time. The story appeared in *Valiant*

Above The "Rat of the Rifles" proves why he got his nickname, in the final issue of *Valiant* before it merged with *Battle*

Liaison Detachment: "During World War II, *H.M.S. Scorpion* was sunk and lay on the bed of the English Channel. Although listed as Number 16 on the Admiralty chart of wrecked vessels, it was the base of the Special Liaison Detachment – an underwater group which undertook all sorts of dangerous missions." In this episode, the Germans are also trying to form a rival

THE BEASTS OF BRAXEN

IN 1940, a British patrol passing through the Belgian town of Braxen came face to face with a strange enemy!

WHAT ARE THEY? MEN OR BEASTS?

THEY'RE FIRING AT US, SO THEY'RE THE ENEMY! CHARGE!

A CASE FOR SERGEANT MORGAN

Above "The Beasts of Braxen" acquired mythical status in *Hornet*, dated 6 July 1974

underwater squad – efforts foiled by the Raiders of Wreck 16.

"The Coonskin Grenadier" was a long-running saga of when "that plush English regiment, the Royal Grenadiers (King George's Own), was jolted by the arrival of Zebadiah Flood, an American hill-billy. Under a Royal Warrant granted by George III in 1760, Zeb became an Honorary Sergeant in the Regiment." "The Coonskin Grenadier" is played for laughs, as was another *Hornet* story based on the premise of an American misfit joining the ranks. "Hank the Yank" is "the clumsiest cowboy to come out of the West – but, if it's laughter you're after, he's one of the best!" (issue dated 1 December 1973). Hank is always stumbling into tight situations where he makes matters worse – but the cowboy from Wyoming always comes out on top in the end.

"The Beasts of Braxen" was an unusual and interesting story, the first in a series called "A Case for Sergeant Morgan". Sergeant Morgan was "the battlefield detective, for whom no mystery is too obscure – or too dangerous!" (issue dated 6 July 1974). Set in Belgium in 1940, a British patrol passing through the Belgium town of Braxen comes face-to-face with a strange enemy ("What are they? Men or beasts?"). These strange foe were seemingly indestructable, and "the story of the 'Beasts of Braxen' spread like wildfire through the British troops being forced back to Dunkirk. As it spread, it grew wilder, until men were being told that the Beasts had wiped out two whole battalions." In fact, the Beasts of Braxen were crack German troops wearing masks and heavy body armour, which deflected bullets and so gave them their air of invincibility.

Another unusual story was "The Spy in the Suitcase" (first appeared in the issue dated 16 August 1975). It was "the gripping tale of a cripple and a midget

THE RAIDERS FROM WRECK 16

DURING World War II, H.M.S. Scorpion was sunk and lay on the bed of the English Channel. Although listed as Number 16 on the Admiralty chart of wrecked vessels, it was the base of the Special Liaison Detachment—an underwater group which undertook all sorts of dangerous missions.

The Germans were also trying to form an underwater squad and a German General came to see what progress they had made.

WELCOME TO THE UNTERWASSER GRUPPEN, HERR GENERAL. OUR GALLANT SWIMMERS ARE READY TO PUT ON A DEMONSTRATION FOR YOU.

GOOD! IF THEY ARE EFFICIENT, I AM AUTHORISED TO GIVE YOU AN OPERATIONAL MISSION!

who formed the most deadly sabotage team of the Second World War". After being wounded in action, Sergeant Mike Halsey is left with a permanent limp. He meets Monty Cass, a circus midget keen to do his bit, and frustrated at being unable to join the forces. Cass's circus skills come in handy for sabotage attacks in occupied Europe, so Halsey becomes Cass's "bag" man, carrying the circus performer to missions in a large suitcase. The story ends with Cass destroying the German fleet sent to invade Britain in 1940 (issue dated 8 November 1975).

T he story "12 Days to Save Britain" has a similar theme (issue dated 6 April 1973) – it is also a race against time, for "a deadly new terror weapon is soon to be loosed on Britain – and only one man knows the antidote!". The Second World War had been raging for three years, and in a rundown building in Serbia the Nazis are testing a new killer gas on the underground fighters they have captured. Only one man survives; he is Professor Posen, who had been forced to administer the gas, and who realises there is an antidote. Posen is in fact British Secret Agent, John Fenwick. He has just 12 days to get back to Britain with the antidote before the Germans release the gas on the British population.

Interestingly, *Hornet* turned back the clock to put one of D.C Thomson's best-loved non-combatant characters into a war setting. William Wilson was a mysterious athlete who, while sporting an all-in-one black leotard, smashed numerous world records. Wilson started life in the pages of *Wizard*, when he helped boost the morale of war-weary readers with his incredible feats. "Wilson of the Wizard", as he came to be known, broke the

Above and below "The Raiders from Wreck 16" were a crack group of frogmen who undertook dangerous wartime missions. This *Hornet* story is dated 16 January 1971

four-minute mile 140 years before Roger Bannister's famous run; for Wilson was no mere mortal. He was born in 1795, and in his youth had been told of a secret elixir of life, a unique herbal potion, that slowed the heart down to just 30 beats a minute from the regular 70 or 80. This gives him superhuman powers; as well as a host of athletic records, Wilson also ran 20 miles cross-country in two hours to warn the Duke of Wellington of Napoleon's advance at Quatre Bras in 1815, so he was just the man to be fighting for Britain against Hitler. On 20 July 1974 **Hornet** trumpeted: "Now it can be told! The amazing war-time secret mission of Britain's wonder athlete!" In the story "Wilson at War", which ran until 28 December 1974, Wilson is sent on a secret mission to South America, where is dropped in the Amazon jungle with orders to find Colonel Cedric Fawkes, who has been lost for seven years. Fawkes is a skilled codebreaker and he is needed to break the German's cyphers. Wilson befriends a native tribe and is required to undertake a serious of trials of strength and athleticism. But a group of fanatical Nazis are aware of Wilson's presence and try to sabotage his mission. But Wilson is too good for them; he finds Fawkes in the Temple of the Sun, where he had gone to decipher the inscribed sacred stones.

Above and below "Wilson of the Wizard" also appeared in the pages of *Hornet*, where he joined the war effort and became a crack Battle of Britain pilot. The images below come from a story that appeared on 20 July 1974

Above Killer Kennedy is out to help the Partisans, in the *Victor* story dated 23 October 1971

But, by now, *Hornet* had pretty much run its course – on 13 February 1976, it was incorporated into *Hotspur*, the pair becoming *Hotspur and Hornet*.

In that issue was the story "Wilson's Wonders" – "The exciting war exploits of the most amazing athlete the world has ever known". With echoes of the story of Jesse Owens, the black athlete who humiliated Hitler and the Nazis in the 1936 Berlin Olympic Games by winning four gold medals in track and field events, it relates how, in 1939, Wilson is in Germany taking part in the Stuttgart International Steeplechase. He beats a world-class field, including the best the Nazis can offer. But the race's organisers are less than happy, and try to kill him. Wilson escapes, although he is believed to be dead. Wilson turns up again at the outset of war wishing to join the RAF, although he has doubts that they will have him: "Come off it! It's only public schoolboys, university types and geezers who've done some private flying who get to be pilots." Naturally, Wilson passes the rigorous fitness test and joins the RAF, where he chalks up 24 kills while flying Spitfires in the Battle of Britain.

Of D.C. Thomson's famous "Big Five" comics, the last survivor was *Hotspur*. It lasted into the 1980s, but eventually it was incorporated into *Victor*, on 31 January 1981. *Victor* continued to go from strength to strength during the 1970s and 1980s, with war stories an important part of the mix. Much of its output was based on "real-life" stories of the war, ranging from straightforward re-tellings of some of the key battles in British history to tales

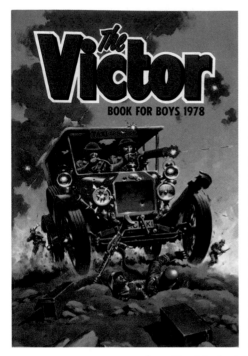

of the "weird-and-wonderful" variety. But there was no shortage of fiction in the pages of *Victor*. The ever-popular Matt Braddock made a welcome return in the tale "Braddock and the Secret Weapon" (issue dated 23 January 1971). It was "A Great New Story about Matt Braddock and his fight against a devastating new German Rocket" – but it was far from plain sailing, or rather flying, for our hero. Braddock is court-martialled for striking a fellow officer, who Braddock believed had endangered the lives of his men. Proceedings are interrupted when an American officer enters the court to pass on the thanks of his commanding officer for Braddock's assistance in identifying and capturing a German spy ring. Braddock is found not guilty, and leads the specially formed "Force H" in a raid on the factory producing Germany's deadly rocket, Braddock delivering his payload down the factory chimney.

Above Taxi! Privates Powers and Purdy failed to hook up with their regiment in the Western Desert when their truck was stolen – so the only way they could avoid being accused of desertion was to purloin this ancient London cab for the journey. The story, called "The Taxi Went to War" appeared in the *Victor Book for Boys* 1978

Below "Faraday's Phantoms" cause more damage to the Japanese war effort, in this *Victor* story dated 16 October 1971

Facing page The Gestapo are on the trail of "The Black Crow"

"The Men from the Black Volcano" was "the story of Jeff Armstrong and his pal, Huang Lee, and how they fight their own private war against the Japanese!" (issue dated 10 July 1971). They sabotage factories, destroy food and weapon supply lines from their secret base – the black volcano of the title. The story ends with the atomic bombings of Hiroshima and Nagasaki, with the Japanese surrendering to Armstrong. Just in time, too – the volcano erupts and Armstrong and Lee return to England, heroes.

"Faraday's Phantoms" was also set in the Far East; it was "the story of how Sergeant Bill Faraday and his men gave the Japs the fright of their lives" (issue dated 16 October 1971). During the Second World War, Sergeant Faraday and

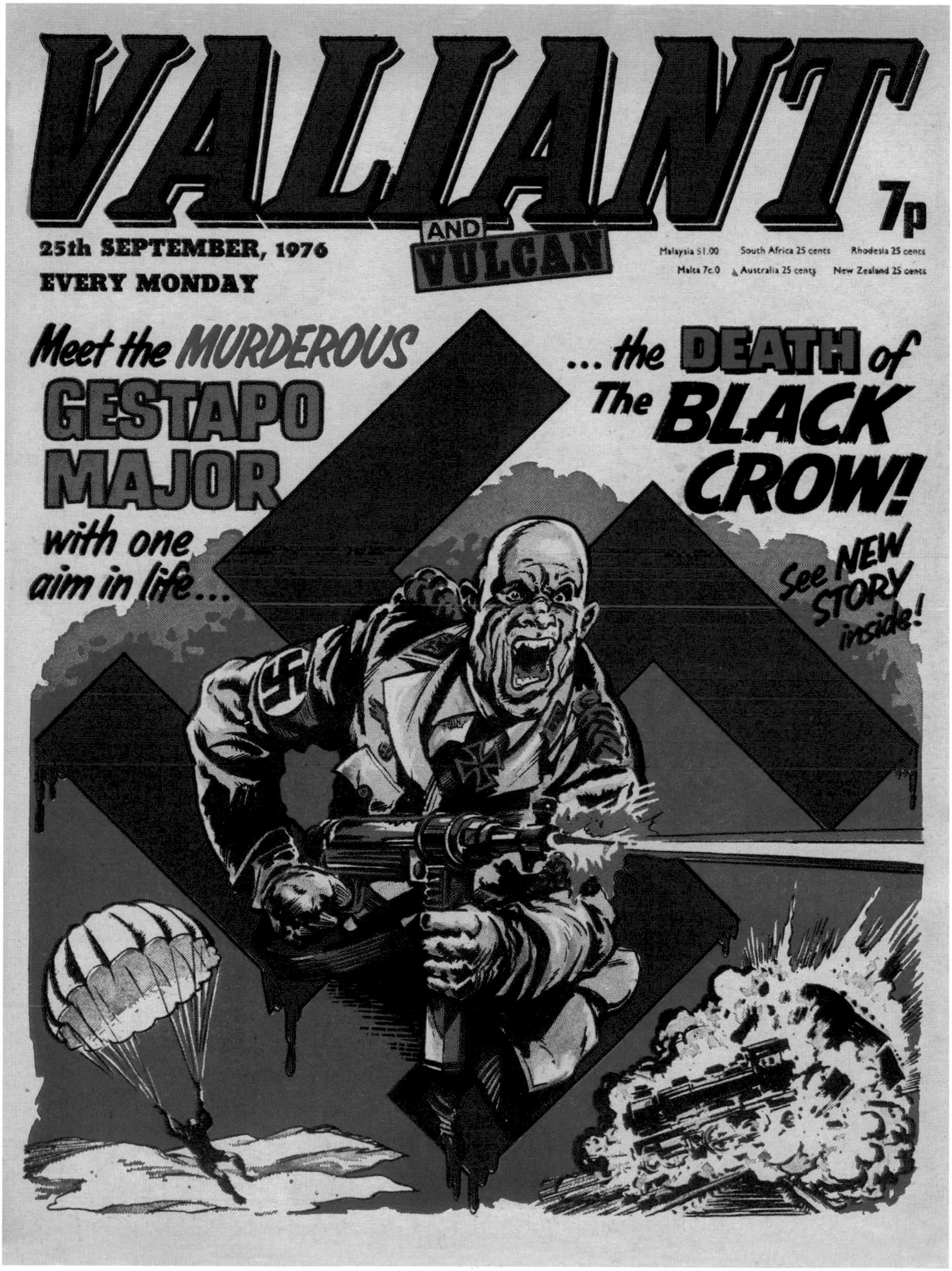
VALIANT
7p
AND VULCAN
25th SEPTEMBER, 1976
EVERY MONDAY
Malaysia $1.00 South Africa 25 cents Rhodesia 25 cents
Malta 7c.0 Australia 25 cents New Zealand 25 cents
Meet the MURDEROUS GESTAPO MAJOR with one aim in life...
...the DEATH of The BLACK CROW!
See NEW STORY inside!

Above "The Men from the Black Volcano" – Jeff Armstrong and Huang Lee – are in trouble. The story is from *Victor*, dated 10 July 1971

Below There is no trusting the enemy… this true-life tale of a German ship disguised as a merchantman appeared in *Victor* on 2 January 1971

his men were cut off behind the Japanese lines in Burma. Chu Li, an old Burmese tribal leader, showed them a huge cave which the retreating Allied army had used as a supply store, and Faraday decides to use it as a base. From here the British soldiers struck at the unsuspecting Japanese when and where they least expected it. So swiftly and silently did they strike that the Japanese began to believe they were phantoms or evil spirits. After sabotaging the supply lines and weaponry, Faraday and his men assist in the landing of Allied troops and defeat the Japanese invaders.

Two popular characters appeared in a number of stories throughout the 1970s. "Killer" Kennedy and Bill Doyle featured in "Strike First, Strike Hard" (issued dated 16 January 1971), which was set in the North Sea in 1943. Sub-Lieutenant Bill Doyle was second-in-command of a motor torpedo boat serving under Lieutenant-Commander "Killer" Kennedy; the pair were part of a disastrous raid on the German port of Bremerhaven in an attempt to torpedo the enemy battleship *Mannheim* that was docked there. They returned in the story "Killer

On April 9, 1940, a harmless-looking Russian supply ship steamed into the North Atlantic. But behind the disguise lurked the German raider "Atlantis," commanded by Captain Bernhard Rogge. Her deadly mission was to seek and destroy unsuspecting Allied merchant shipping.

Kennedy's Rag Tag Navy" (issue dated
23 October 1971). Kennedy and Doyle
are dropped into Yugoslavia to help the
Partisans – Yugoslav resistance fighters
– create a navy. They manage to capture
a German E-Boat and use an abandoned
enemy base to carry out raids on
German shipping.

The Lieutenant-Commander appeared
again in "The Strange War of Killer Kennedy"
(issue dated 26 February 1972). A "prequel" to the earlier stories, it
relates how Killer Kennedy declared war on the Germans long before the rest of
Britain. During the uneasy peace before the outbreak of war in 1939, Kennedy
was a lorry driver. On one occasion he made a trip to Hamburg to deliver spare
parts for a British yacht which had broken down. Kennedy happens upon
German officer Lieutenant Ritter, who is beating a political prisoner, and strikes
the Nazi. Ritter is about to exact revenge when a German admiral comes to
Kennedy's aid, saying: "Not all Germans are like Ritter." Ritter swears revenge,
but Kennedy escapes from Germany – and Ritter – by crashing his lorry
through a border checkpoint. Back in England Kennedy joins the Royal Naval
Volunteer Reserve, and he crosses swords with Ritter again when he visits the

Above and below "Cadman"
had the reputaion of being a
hero, but he was in fact "the
spy with the yellow streak".
Sent undercover to infiltrate the
Nazi movement, he was
eventually made an officer in
the SS. The images are from a
story that appeared in *Victor* in
the issue dated 7 October 1978

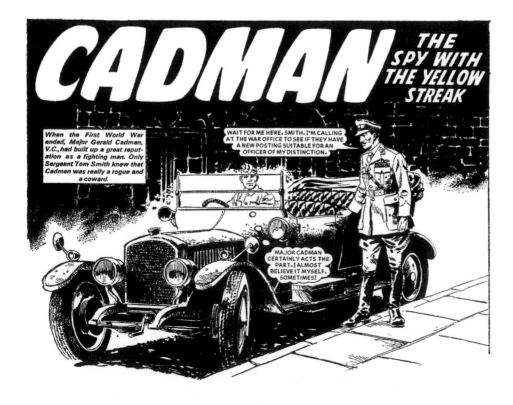

Above "Killer Kennedy" in action, in the *Victor Book for Boys* 1977

Facing page "Jungle Joe" Jenner came from Kenya, and he used all his hunting experience to bring the Nazis to book in this story which appeared in *Victor* in the issue dated 13 January 1972

RNVR training base, HMS *Grenville*. Kennedy allows his temper to get the better of him on several occasions, and is thrown out of the RNVR, deciding to fight the war as a civilian. Kennedy assists in the evacuation from Dunkirk, and his heroics earn him a commission in the Royal Navy MTB squadron.

A more unusual story was "Bird Boy" (issue dated 1 July 1972) – it was "the super story of how a young British boy takes vengeance on the Germans with his strange allies – the birds of the air". Stunned in a car crash that killed his parents during a German bombing raid, Tim Randolph is found by a mysterious stranger – "The Birdman". But The Birdman is shot by the Germans, and on his deathbed gives Tim his collection of bird callers, through which he "talks" to his feathered friends. Tim swears vengeance for the death of The Birdman and the loss of his parents. The young lad is able to communicate with the birds and they with him, and he sets about helping the Maquis – French Resistance – in their fight. With the help of the Maquis, Tim discovers his parents are still alive but being held in Internment Camp 417. But all ends happily; the family are reunited and escape to England.

Victor stuck to the tried-and-tested formula that had served it so well throughout the 1970s, and the incorporation of *Wizard*, on 1 July 1978, did little to upset the equilibrium. "Zeppelin Safari" (started issue dated

The men of number 3 platoon are fearfully awaiting two German tanks—but Jungle Joe means to make sure the tanks never arrive!

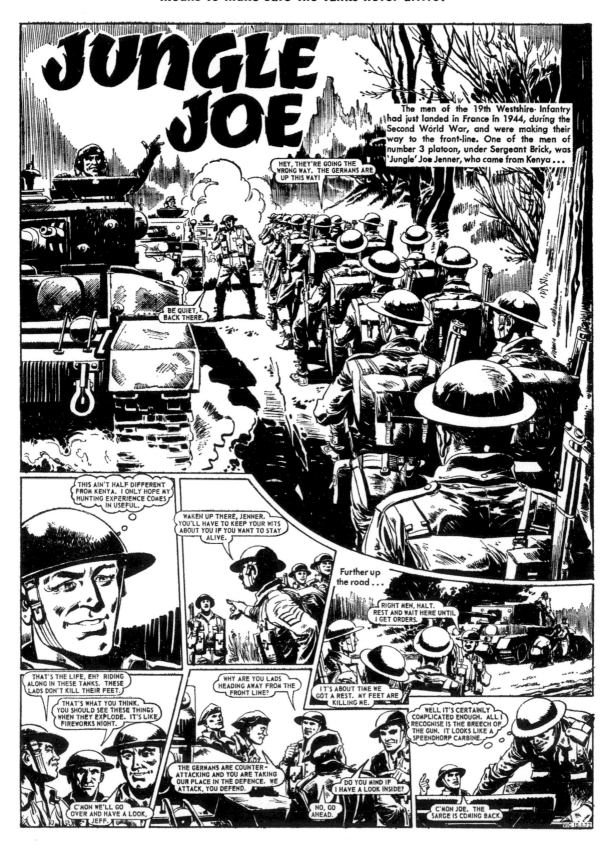

7 January 1978) was set in the Great War. Lieutenant Ken Irons of the Royal Naval Air Service was posted to Alexandria after a Court of Enquiry had found him guilty of failing to protect a Zeppelin from damaging British property. With the Mediterranean port and its airfield being bombed by a Zeppelin, a message lands on the airfield from Kapitanleutnant Ludwig Bockholt, the German responsible for bombing British cities, the action which led to Irons' disciplinary and posting to Alexandria. Irons, with his mechanic, Scruffy, decide to attack the Zeppelin, and this turns into an extended chase across Africa. Eventually the British duo succeed in destroying the Zeppelin, gaining revenge on Bockholt for the raids on Britain.

Above Cadman meets the Führer in *Victor*, issue dated 9 December 1978

Facing page Lord Peter Flint goes undercover in *Warlord*, issue dated 19 March 1977

Below Tim Randolph is "Bird Boy", *Victor*, 1 July 1972

While the remnants of the "old guard" soldiered on into the 1980s – *Victor*, *Tiger* and the second coming of *Eagle* – it was the new upstarts who really grabbed the attention of the war-story devotee.

Two dedicated war comics and two cutting-edge general interest comics broke the mould of British comics, and, predictably, all four came from the D.C Thomson/I.P.C. axis. The quartet were *Warlord*, launched in September 1974 by

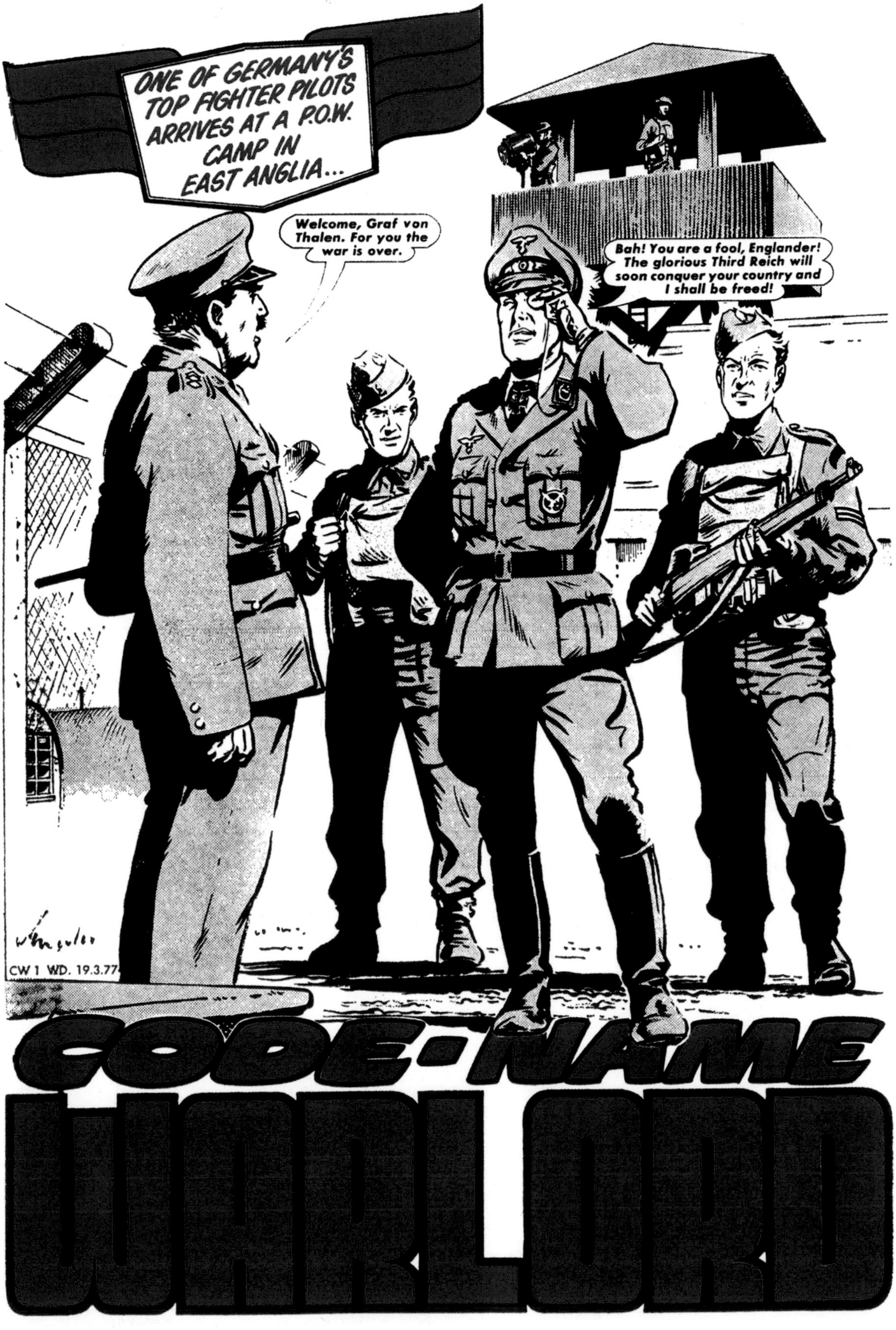
ONE OF GERMANY'S TOP FIGHTER PILOTS ARRIVES AT A P.O.W. CAMP IN EAST ANGLIA...
Welcome, Graf von Thalen. For you the war is over.
Bah! You are a fool, Englander! The glorious Third Reich will soon conquer your country and I shall be freed!
CW 1 WD. 19.3.77
CODE-NAME
WARLORD

Above and below Ken Irons of the Royal Naval Air Service stalks his prey in the story "Zeppelin Safari", which appeared in *Victor* throughout 1978. They finally nailed the L59 and her skipper, Ludwig Bockholt, in the issue dated 1 April 1978

Facing page "D-Day Dawson" knows no fear as he swings into action to save a strategically important river crossing

D.C. Thomson; *Battle*, an I.P.C. title launched in March 1975; *Bullet* (D.C. Thomson); and *Action* (I.P.C.); *Battle* and *Action* were launched on the same day – Valentine's Day, 1976.

Warlord was Britain's first dedicated war comic, and it set the bar very high. The launch issue – which came with a free gift of eight replica war medals – introduced the world to Lord Peter Flint, who was "Code-name Warlord". Like many war heroes in the comics before him, Lord Peter led a double life. While appearing to be a titled gentleman of leisure, he was in fact a crack spy, operating covertly behind enemy lines, stealing valuable secrets from under the noses of the enemy. Occasionally, Lord Peter went undercover behind his own lines. In the issue dated 19 March 1977, he is sent to a prisoner-of-war camp for Germans in England, where camp staff are suspected of foul play ("I suspect treachery among the camp staff, Smith. Even the Commander is under suspicion. There are five hundred Nazis in that camp. They're up to something – and we've got to find out what it is!"). Flint is "Graf von Thalen", supposedly a decorated German air ace. But he is invited to escape on his first night in the camp – the Nazi prisoners have plans to steal a bomber fitted with revolutionary bomb-sighting equipment from a nearby American Air Force base. Once on the outside, Flint decides it is time to quit the escape party,

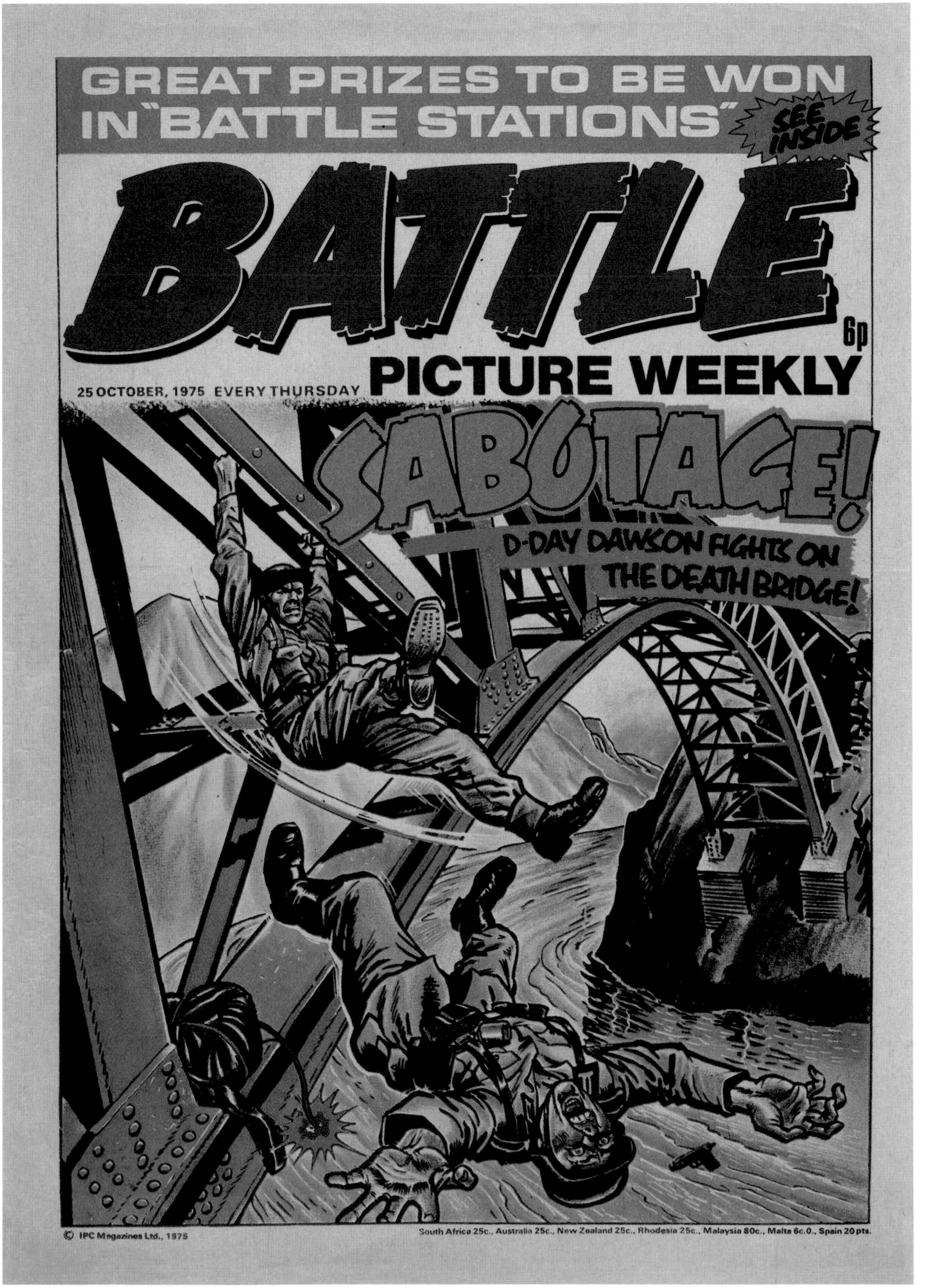
GREAT PRIZES TO BE WON
IN "BATTLE STATIONS"
SEE INSIDE
BATTLE
6p
PICTURE WEEKLY
25 OCTOBER, 1975 EVERY THURSDAY
SABOTAGE!
D-DAY DAWSON FIGHTS ON THE DEATH BRIDGE!
© IPC Magazines Ltd., 1975
South Africa 25c., Australia 25c., New Zealand 25c., Rhodesia 25c., Malaysia 80c., Malta 6c.0., Spain 20 pts.

and makes off to see his handler, the aforementioned Smith. But Smith is a double agent, and he exposes Flint to the escapees, who plan to force him onto the U.S. bomber and fly him back to Germany. But our hero escapes once more, and as the Germans take-off is forced to shoot the bomber down. Now he has just one task – and the traitor Smith is felled by a single punch, before being dragged off to face the music. The story is unusual in that Flint is operating in England; a more typical story appeared in *Warlord* in the issue dated 23 June 1979. It is 1940 and "resistance in France is rapidly collapsing as the Allies retreat before the advancing German armies. Heading towards the Germans is Warlord, Britain's top secret agent...". Flint's task was to organise the underground resistance units, and under his direction they set about destroying a German ammunition dump. But that is only half the action – no sooner has this been achieved than Flint and the Resistance are ordered to hijack a German train carrying prisoners-of-war, including the important figure of General Matrand. This they succeed in doing – but only after they've set the forest on fire in making their escape, frying Fritz in the process.

While undoubtedly the leader of the pack, Lord Peter Flint had an excellent supporting cast. They included "Union Jack Jackson", "Killer Kane", "Spider Wells", "Parker's Private Army", "The Shark", "Cassidy" and "Sergeant Rayker" to name but a few – even perennial favourite Matt Braddock made a re-appearance. *Warlord* also carried real war stories and features, and each issue carried a "Calling Warlord" page. This featured readers' letters, competitions, and a special message from Lord Peter Flint himself, in which he passes on snippets of information for the benefit of members of the "Warlord Secret Agent Club". For a small fee readers could join in the fun; for their money they received a secret agents' kit including a "Top Secret" agent code book, an identity card and a badge, by which they could identify fellow agents. The pack came with a letter from Lord Peter Flint himself, which new agents had to "memorise and destroy". Lord Flint's message read: "To whom it may concern. Being a Warlord secret agent can be great fun, sending coded messages which only Warlord Agents can understand. It's your special task to find out other Agents to communicate with in your

Above "Union Jack Jackson" was a British Royal Marine serving with the American forces. He displayed his patriotism by painting a Union Jack on his helmet. The story appeared in *Warlord*

school or area. They will be identified by the Winged 'W' Badge. Special features for Agents only will appear in Warlord each week along with competitions in which only Warlord Agents can take part. Good luck. Peter Flint."

As *Warlord*'s letters page showed, readers were desperate to be a part of it – here's a typical missive: "Hello Lord Peter, old fruit, I'd just like to inform you what whilst out skiing in Glenshee, my colleagues and I saw a man behaving very suspiciously. We kept him under surveillance until he began to suspect us. He sped down the slope with us trailing after him! When we reached the bottom, he met up with another two men. Together they drove off in a car with foreign markings. These men looked dangerous and could have been enemy agents! 5.3.16.25.16.2." Obviously impressed, Lord Peter replied: "Well spotted 5.3.16.25.16.2., old boy. However, I have had no other reports of any enemy agent activity in the Glenshee area. I, therefore, feel the situation does not warrant a Red Alert. I have sent an Agent to investigate, though! – Lord Peter Flint" (issue dated 2 April 1977).

As well as the chance to experience the thrills and intrigue of being a secret agent, *Warlord* readers also had a smorgasbord of great war stories on which to feast. "Union Jack Jackson" related the adventures of the eponymous British

Above "The Barbed-Wire XI" were a team of prisoners who were formed into a commando unit to tackle dangerous missions. This story appeared in the *Tiger Annual* 1986

Below Major Heinz Falken was "Kampfgruppe Falken", the man who led the German equivilent of "The Barbed-Wire XI". Falken's band of renegades came from military penal battalions; Falken's crime was disobeying orders when he refused to carry out atrocities. He appeared in the pages of *Warlord*; this image is from the *Warlord Annual* 1981

Royal Marine, and his American buddies Sergeant Lonnighan and Sean O'Bannion, as they wage war in both the European and Asia-Pacific theatres. In one episode, after the boys cross the Rhine in the push to Berlin after D-Day, the trio are separated from their unit (issue dated 23 February 1980). Stalking the streets of a bombed out and seemigly abandoned town, Jackson and cohorts meet four American infantrymen. Fired at by a sniper, the men take cover, and spot a strange fighting force approaching: "Blimey, look at this lot! The Volkssturm – the German Home Guard! Old men and boys! We can't shoot them!". The Home Guard surrender meekly, but demand to be treated as prisoners-of-war – which give the men a headache: "Suffering sweetcorn! We can't take this mob with us to Berlin! Move out, fellas!" Looking for a place to incarcerate their prisoners, Jackson stumbles across a cellar packed with explosives. For on the edge of town the Nazis are plotting: "Firing reported from the town, Herr Oberst! The Volkssturm must be engaging the forward units of the enemy." "Good. Prepare to detonate the explosives we hid. The Volkssturm will be destroyed as well as the enemy, but they are expendable. They are not real soldiers." But Jackson disconnects the fuse and it is the German officers who have trouble in store, when the marine buddies track them down and open fire: "That was a nice surprise you laid on, Krauts! Here's one for you!"

"Killer Kane" is an ace pilot of the Second World War, a man of action who doesn't suffer fools gladly. In fact, exhausted after one prolonged bout of flying, he loses his cool and lashes out at an officer (issue dated 23 February 1980). Facing a court martial, he is transferred to Australia, and becomes attached to an American squadron. There he is taken under the wing of Captain Lynx

Below "Killer Kane" in typical fighting mode. The story appeared in *Warlord*, with this image from the issue dated 5 May 1980

Facing page "Major Eazy" saves the day once again. This story appeared in the *Warlord Annual* 1981

IT WAS 6th, JUNE 1945 – EXACTLY ONE YEAR AFTER ALLIED TROOPS HAD MADE THEIR FIRST ASSAULT ON HITLER'S "FORTRESS EUROPE". HITLER WAS DEAD AND HIS REDOUBT, BERLIN, IN THE HANDS OF THE ALLIES. THERE WAS A LOT OF CLEARING UP TO BE DONE – THE SORT OF CLEARING UP THAT COULD ONLY BE ACHIEVED BY MEN LIKE THE UNCONVENTIONAL MAJOR EAZY...

THIS IS THE LIFE, EH, DALY? ALL THE WAY FROM THE BRENNER PASS TO BERLIN BY CAR, AND WE DIDN'T USE MORE'N HALF A PINT OF PETROL!

YESSIR!

MAJOR EAZY

THE WHOLE OF GERMANY'S IN A MESS! IT'S GOING TO BE A HELL OF A JOB TO SET IT RIGHT AGAIN, BUT . . .

WHO'S YOUR FRIEND, GENERAL?

YOU MUST BE MAJOR EAZY! WHAT THE DEVIL D'YOU MEAN BY BRINGING THAT SCRUFFY CAR TO BERLIN? IT'S NOT INCLUDED ON THESE MOVEMENT ORDERS!

I'M COLONEL CRISPIN AND I DEMAND THAT YOU COME TO ATTENTION!

AAAGH!

ME – ATTENTION? . . . I'VE GOT BETTER THINGS TO DO!

AAAARRH!

YOU WANT ME TO GET OUT OF THE CAR? SURE!

EAZY! WHAT IN THUNDER . . ?

A KRAUT SNIPER, GENERAL! I SPOTTED HIM LURKING IN THE RAFTERS THROUGH MY WING MIRROR!

Above "Darkie's Mob" pulled no punches in its depiction of Japanese brutality. This story appeared in *Battle*, issue dated 11 September 1976

Facing page "Sergeant Rayker" fought prejudice and the enemy in the pages of *Warlord*

Newtown, and the pair form a formidable partnership: "After dropping bombs near an American supply base and stealing machine guns to upgun their planes, an American Mitchell squadron flies to New Guinea to escape arrest. Leading them is Flight Lieutenant Killer Kane… Known as the 'Barracudas', they fly as an independent unit from the Australian Air Force Base, causing havoc amongst the Japs" (issue dated 5 April 1980). The "Barracudas" are sent to blow up a Japanese supply base, Lynx Newton is hit by a stray bullet and killed, and Killer is voted the new Squadron Commander: "Thanks, boys, I don't know if I'll be as good as Lynx Newton was, but I'll do my best."

"Sergeant Rayker" was another of *Warlord*'s renegade heroes, but his was a more unusual story than most – for Rayker is black. Rayker is not only fighting the Germans, he has to fight prejudice from his own side, too: "That black punk used us. He scared the livin' daylights out of us just to prove himself to the rest of the men. He made a laughin' stock of us southern boys. We can't let him get away with it, guys. We gotta do somethin' about that sergeant" (issue dated 23 June 1979).

Not all stories were written from the Allies' perspective. "Iron Annie" was the story of Germany's fight with Russia on the Eastern Front. The aircraft of the title is a supply plane, but her crew manages to get involved in all manner of scrapes. "The Shark" was "high-speed action in the Mediterranean" with Leutnant Paul von Lief, the commander of "Germany's top-scoring E-Boat, The Shark".

I.P.C.'s response to the success of *Warlord* was to launch *Battle*. Following the same blueprint, *Battle* was a hard-as-nails, no-holds-barred feast of fighting action. Like its rival, its characters and storylines were many and varied, but as with the D.C. Thomson title certain characters stood out. In *Battle* – or *Battle Picture Weekly*, to give it its full title – "D-Day Dawson" was one character who inspired devotion among the comic's readers. Sergeant Steve Dawson took a bullet in the chest at the D-Day landings, meaning that he is living on borrowed time. With death imminent, Dawson is prepared to take the sort of risks normal soldiers shy away from; he is first in and last out when it comes to fighting the enemy. In the issue dated 25 October 1975, Dawson's unit has to storm a bridge, while making sure it is not destroyed by

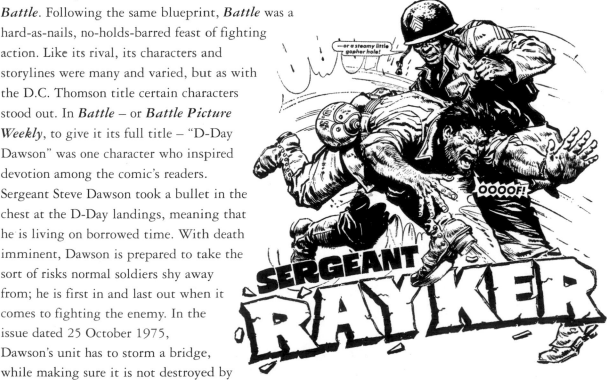

Above "Only One Came Back" told the true story of the RAF's attempts to blow up the bridges at Maastrict in May 1940, to hold up the Germans' advance. The mission was a succes, but of the five Battle aircraft that set out only one returned. Flying Officer Donald Garland and Sergeant Thomas Gray were posthumously awarded the Victoria Cross for their part in the action. The story appeared in the *Victor Annual* 1978

Above Aerial action with "The Coonskin Grenadier", the adventures of Zebadiah Flood fighting with the British in *Hotspur*, issue dated 13 October 1979

Below "3 Men in a Jeep" was a story in *Bullet* concerning the wartime adventures of three pals – Joe, Moose and Arnie. This image is from the issue dated 20 March 1976

the Germans. As the men engage the enemy on the bridge itself, Dawson spots a German planting explosives underneath it: "He's planted explosives. The Jerries are going to bring the bridge down sooner than let us capture it." Dawson swings into action – literally – knocking the German into the river below, before grabbing the explosives and jumping into the river himself. A comrade asks about Dawson's plight and is told: "He's okay! The water put the explosives out of action! Hang on sarge, we'll get a rope! You've taken enough chances for one night." The story closes with Dawson's thoughts: "Another second and I'd have been dead. But chances don't matter when you're living on borrowed time."

Another standout *Battle* character was "Major Eazy" who, in terms of character and attitude, was the polar opposite of D-Day Dawson. A laid-back, long-haired, scruffy, cigar-smoking Clint Eastwood lookalike, Eazy knew no rules and had only one motivation – to win. If that meant stealing a brigadier's car or hijacking a train, so be it. Eazy first appeared in *Battle* in the issue dated 10 January 1976, with a story set in Sicily in 1943. When he introduces himself to his sergeant, Bert Daly, the shocked Daly thinks: "New commander! Blimey, he looks more like a refugee from Hollywood." In that first episode Eazy single-handedly takes on a German King Tiger tank and the bedazzled Daly admits: "Eazy, you're crazy. You're the toughest, coolest bloke I ever fought with and that's a fact."

Another hugely popular *Battle* story was "Rat Pack". A four-man team lead by Major Taggart, the Rat Pack are Kabul Hasan, aka "Turk", Ronald Weasel, Ian "Scarface" Rogan and Matthew Dancer. All had one thing in common – they were convicted criminals, who were sprung from prison by the mysterious Major Taggart: "You men are rats – nasty, crooked rats! But rats with special skills the army desperately needs... Because of this, I'm offering you a chance of freedom." And so "Major Taggart

explains that he had been given the job of striking at difficult and dangerous targets behind enemy lines. He has chosen these four men for their special abilities. The prison break-out had been a test for them" (issue dated 8 March 1975). Each week the Rat Pack get the opportunity to demonstrate their special skills in defeating the enemy. While "Rat Pack" pulled no punches, it was easy reading compared with the dark, uncompromising brutality of another popular story, the bleak "Darkie's Mob". First appearing in the issue dated 14 August 1976, readers are told that "in 1946, after the defeat of the Japanese, a small, blood-stained notebook was found at the scene of a brutal jungle battle. In it was one of the strangest stories ever to come out of World War 2..." The notebook belonged to Private Richard Shortland, and started: "This is the story of a madman, a hard, cruel son of Satan who led us into the very pit of hell – and laughed about it. Then he began to turn us into animals – the most savage fighting force the Japs had ever known...". But Captain Joe Darkie is no ordinary soldier. In fact, he is not a real soldier at all. His father was Japanese and his mother English, and his real name was Joseph Daakee. The family is oppressed by the Japanese, and eventually flee to Burma to escape persecution. Eventually, Joe falls in with a band of cut-throats, becoming their leader. When the Japanese invade Burma, all Joe's old hatred is rekindled, doubly so when he finds his mother and father murdered by the invaders. At that point Joe swears he will gain vengeance. He figures the best way to do this is to pose as a

British soldier, and thus he ends up "recruiting" Darkie's Mob. But as the story unfolds, Darkie's Mob are gradually killed off – the final episode ends with Darkie's death (issue dated 18 June 1977). Along the way there's some blood-curdling stuff, including one episode where Joe is nailed to a roof in a scene reminiscent of the crucifixion.

Above Captain Jake Cassidy was the eponymous hero of the *Warlord* story "Cassidy". This story was in the issue dated 10 March 1979

Below "Death Squad" followed the adventures of a German punishment squad – "Wehrmacht rejects and no-gooders" – fighting Russia on the Eastern Front. This story appeared in the *Battle Annual* 1982

Above Aerial action with "Johnny Red" in the pages of *Battle*. It told the story of 19-year-old R.A.F. pilot John Redburn, who after being unfairly discharged ends up flying with the renegade Russian "Falcon Squadron". His daredevil exploits lead to Johnny being nicknamed "Djavol" – the Red Devil. This image is from the comic dated 22 July 1978. "Johnny Red" eventually became *Battle*'s longest-running strip

Harrowing stuff indeed, and there was more of the same in possibly *Battle*'s most famous story, "Charley's War". A Great War story, it used a narrative device similar to the one in "Darkie's Mob", only this time in the form of correspondence between Charley in the trenches and various members of his family (*"Dear Dad, I hope you are well. I am verey well. I shared Ma's treacle pud with me chums. It was verey tasty. The tin was useful too as it kept the rats out. When this is over i will take you all on holliday down to MarGate"*).

At the start of the story, Charley is a naïve 16-year-old desperate to join in the "fun" in the trenches, and beguiled by the patriotic propaganda assailing him from all sides. Charley lies about his age to get enlisted, and is sent to France in the build up to the Battle of the Somme, in July 1916 (issued dated 6 January 1979). Once the action starts, Charley grows up very quickly indeed, as he grasps the reality of the horrors of trench warfare. Charley is, in many ways, a comic anti-hero – he has no special skills, is not imbued with superhuman strength or boundless courage – he is an uneducated, although not stupid, ordinary Tommy. As the war grinds on Charley toughens up, and finds solace and support from his mates, a motley crew of characters including "Old Bill" Tozer, Ginger Jones and "Weeper" Watkins, so called because the effects of poison gas means he is constantly crying. Shockingly for a comic story, Charley's best mate, Ginger, is killed off – and he is not the only one of the story's characters to suffer death or injury (issue dated 13 October 1979). Charley is more fortunate – he survives the war and, later, is rushed into service at the start of the Second World War when the story finally ends, in October 1985.

Both D.C. Thomson and I.P.C. were eager to exploit the success of their dedicated war comics, and each launched a new title on the back of the

EVERY SATURDAY 7p

16th OCTOBER, 1976

Australia 25c: New Zealand 25c: South Africa 25c: Rhodesia 25c: Malaysia $1.00: Malta 7c.

ACTION

It's cold-blooded murder on the Russian Front... and HELLMAN is the coldest of all

successes of **Warlord** and **Battle**. D.C. Thomson's new comic was **Bullet**, launched in February 1976. **Bullet** was packed with "Action stories – fast and furious" and was most notable for the appearance of "Fireball", who happened to be the nephew of Lord Peter Flint of **Warlord** fame. **Bullet** ran for almost three years – some 147 issues – before it was incorporated into **Warlord**, on 9 December 1978.

Above "Hellman of Hammer Force" was one of *Action*'s most popular stories. This iconic cover appeared in the issue dated 16 October 1976

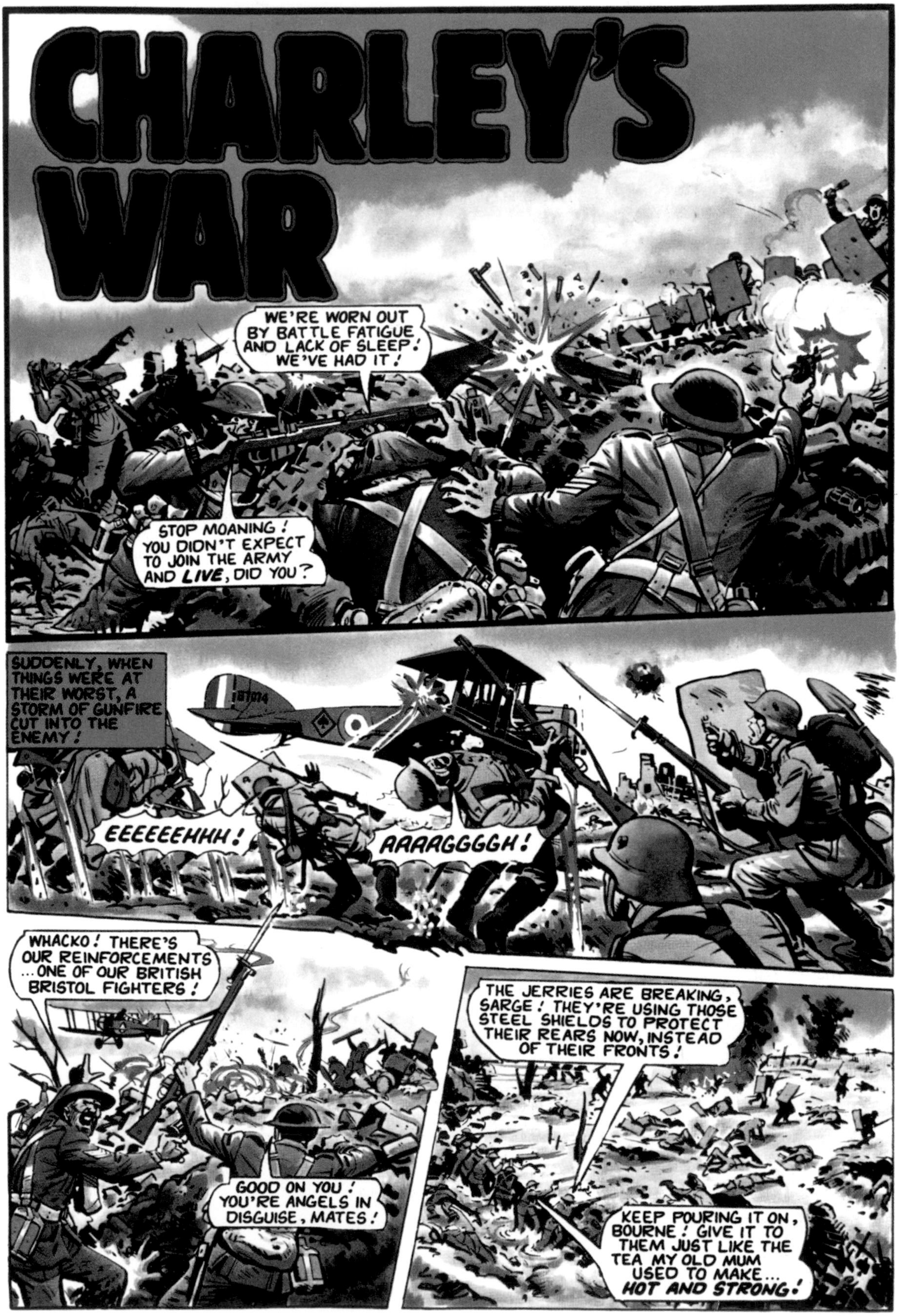
CHARLEY'S WAR
WE'RE WORN OUT BY BATTLE FATIGUE AND LACK OF SLEEP! WE'VE HAD IT!
STOP MOANING! YOU DIDN'T EXPECT TO JOIN THE ARMY AND LIVE, DID YOU?
SUDDENLY, WHEN THINGS WERE AT THEIR WORST, A STORM OF GUNFIRE CUT INTO THE ENEMY!
EEEEEEHHH!
AAAAGGGGH!
WHACKO! THERE'S OUR REINFORCEMENTS ...ONE OF OUR BRITISH BRISTOL FIGHTERS!
GOOD ON YOU! YOU'RE ANGELS IN DISGUISE, MATES!
THE JERRIES ARE BREAKING, SARGE! THEY'RE USING THOSE STEEL SHIELDS TO PROTECT THEIR REARS NOW, INSTEAD OF THEIR FRONTS!
KEEP POURING IT ON, BOURNE! GIVE IT TO THEM JUST LIKE THE TEA MY OLD MUM USED TO MAKE... HOT AND STRONG!

I.P.C.'s *Action* comic was launched on the same day as *Bullet* but did not last as long as that title. It did, however, garner a lot more headlines in its short life. *Action* was, without doubt, the most controversial comic since the heyday of the "penny dreadfuls" a century earlier. *Action* featured sports, war, adventure and action stories – with attitude. So much attitude, in fact, that *Action* provoked the ire of the tabloid press, prompted questions to be asked in Parliament, and even got the gander of that moral guardian of the nation, Mary Whitehouse. The *Sun* newspaper described it as the "sevenpenny nightmare", and while the controversy stoked sales and stirred even greater interest in *Action*, it was also the comic's undoing. When the publicity became too much, W.H. Smith, the country's biggest newsagent, threatened to ban it, a move that prompted much soul-searching at I.P.C. – in fact, the comic was pulled, with the issue dated 23 October 1976 withdrawn from wholesalers and some 200,000 copies of pulped. The decision was made to tone down the language and content of the stories, and after a hiatus the comic reappeared on 4 December 1976.

On the war front, notable *Action* war stories were "Hellmann of Hammer Force" and "Green's Grudge War". In the former, Kurt Hellmann was the commander of a German Panzer tank. He was no Nazi; in fact, he was a soldier of honour who, unlike so many Germans in the boys' comic stories, did not revel in the death and cruelty inherent in warfare. Hellman hated Hitler, but as a professional soldier made a formidable enemy. "Green's Grudge War" was also a story with a

Above *Action* was eventually incorporated into *Battle* to create *Battle Action*, on 19 November 1977

Below and facing page Images from "Charley's War", widely considered to be the finest war story ever to appear in a comic. These images are from the *Battle* annuals of 1981 (below) and 1982 (facing page)

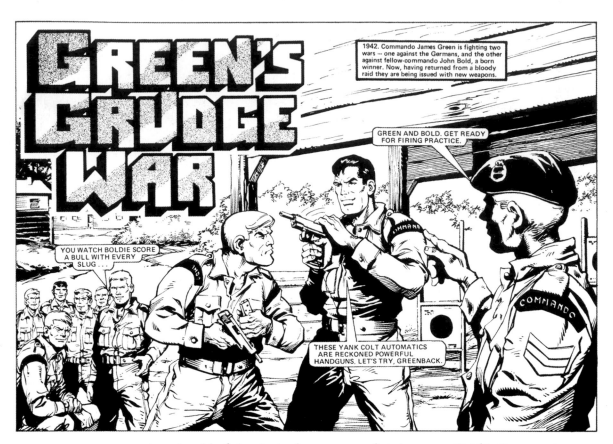

Above James Green just had to beat John Bold in whatever challenges the pair faced in the story "Green's Grudge War", which appeared in *Action*. This image is from the issue dated 12 June 1976

twist – it told of the rivalry between two fighting men: "1942. Commando James Green is fighting two wars – one against the Germans, the other against fellow-commando John Bold, a born winner" (issue dated 12 June 1976). But after the much-publicised problems of October 1976, the new-look, emasculated *Action* was never the same again. Eventually it merged with *Battle* to become *Battle Action* (first issue dated 19 November 1977). It was a bitter blow to the fans of the comic, but for all fans of the genre the writing was on the wall as the 1980s approached. Many comics had already disappeared, and only two major titles managed to make it into the 1990s. One of them was *Victor*; the D.C. Thomson title finally shutting up shop on 21 November 1992 (it had incorporated *Warlord* on 4 October 1986). *Eagle* was the other; by the time of its close in January 1994 it had incorporated five other titles: *Scream* (7 July 1984), *Tiger* (6 April 1985), *Battle* (30 January 1988), *Mask* (29 October 1988) and *Wildcat* (8 April 1989). And so, with *Eagle*'s closure came the end of an era. Well, not quite. The War Library and Commando Library series continue to be popular, and vendors of second-hand comics continue to do a roaring trade, both in shops and online. Popular stories, notably "Charley's War", have been packaged in book form and have sold very well. They take older readers on a welcome journey down memory lane and offer the young a glimpse into the magical world of the comics.

WAR HEROES

FROM THE 'BOY'S OWN' PAPER TO 'THE SHARK'

THE ULTIMATE WAR COMIC

WE HAVE PUT TOGETHER A COMIC FROM THE ARCHIVES, COVERING
THE PERIOD FROM 1910 TO THE 1970s. IT INCLUDES:

STONE ME, IT'S RIMFIRE!

A SERIALISED STORY OF WAR AND EMPIRE, WRITTEN BY REVEREND R. MARTIN. THIS FIRST EPISODE APPEARED ON 6TH JULY 1889

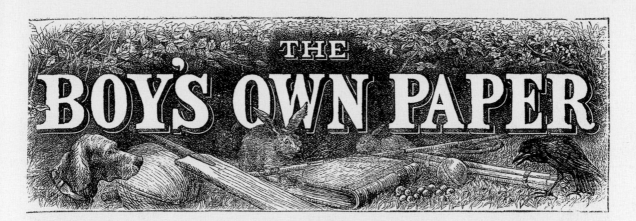

THE BOY'S OWN PAPER

No. 547.—Vol. XI.   SATURDAY, JULY 6, 1889.   Price One Penny.
[ALL RIGHTS RESERVED.]

Gulab Singh

"Ride for your lives!"

GULAB SINGH:

A STORY OF PERIL AND HEROISM.

By REV. R. D'O. MARTIN, M.A.

CHAPTER I.—A RIDE FOR LIFE.

"THIS is really jolly!" said Jack Pentland to his companion, Alick Seymour, as they cantered along a sandy road with a clear, starry sky over their heads.

"Yes; but we must not go so fast, or we'll get so hot that we shall never cool again!" replied his companion, laughing.

Jack Pentland, the son of an officer quartered in Delhi, was at the time of our story—in the month of May, 1857, A.D.—in the eighteenth year of his age. He was tall and active, but his frame was slightly built, and it was evident that he had somewhat overgrown his strength, and that for some years his body could not endure much fatigue.

Alick Seymour was two years older, and very different from Jack. Slightly below average height, he was strongly, almost heavily, built, and yet with such perfect symmetry that few were his equal in manly sports. He was especially noted for his speed and endurance, and had won all before him in long-distance races at the large public school at which he had been educated. He was also famous for his skill with single-stick and the gloves, his quickness and activity enabling him to hold his own even with those whose weight and height gave them an advantage.

He had joined, six months before, the native cavalry regiment of which Jack's father was the colonel, and a warm friendship had sprung up between him and the colonel's son, cemented by the fact that they were both keen sportsmen. Many a long day had they spent together stalking the black buck in the country round Delhi, or pig-sticking in the scrub along the river's banks. This latter was their favourite amusement, and they were now riding out to the great tomb of the Emperor Humaiun, about three miles from the city of Delhi, where they had made arrangements to sleep the night, so that the next morning as soon as it was light they might enter a large piece of low-lying ground close to the river, and just beside the tomb, where they felt sure that they would find sport.

They had started after mess, but as they were mounting their ponies an unusual thing had taken place. One of the troopers of the regiment had come forward and entreated Alick not to leave cantonments that night. Gulab Singh, for so the trooper was called, had been acting in a very mysterious manner for several days. He was the colonel's orderly, and on several occasions, when in private, he had been dropping mysterious hints as to the need of caution and of danger being near, which had greatly irritated the colonel. Ever since he heard of the projected pig-sticking expedition his manner had become even more mysterious than before, and now, when he ventured to address Alick after Jack had mounted, the colonel got into quite a passion, and reprimanded him severely for daring to interfere in matters which in no way

concerned him. The trooper retired respectfully, evidently much pained at the way in which he had been received, and Alick, mounting his pony, followed Jack, who had set off as soon as he heard his father's burst of wrath descend on the trooper's head.

The cantonments lay two miles from the city. The road led the rider along the top of a ridge of ground which was soon to become famous in the history of the siege; and here, though it was the night time, they could still feel the heat coming out of the great red sandstone blocks of which the ridge was composed. Then for another two miles they skirted the walls of the great old city, which had been once the capital of an empire of an extent and importance which has rarely been surpassed in the history of the world. The great King-Shah Jehan, two hundred years before, had sat in his marble palace on the famous Peacock Throne, so-called because behind the throne there was the most beautiful representation of a peacock's tail, the sole materials being the most costly and magnificent precious stones. Now in the same palace —but not on the Peacock Throne, for it had been broken up and taken away by a former conqueror—there lived a descendant of the founder of the Great Mogul dynasty, who still held a nominal court, but whose power did not extend beyond the limits of his palace.

After passing the city they rode in silence through a flat country, covered with the ruins of former cities, past the great walls of the fort built by Humaiun, at whose tomb they meant to sleep that night—a fort which drew forth Bishop Heber's admiration and the words, "These men built like giants and finished like jewellers."

But Alick and Jack thought little of these ruins of bygone years, each engrossed in his own thoughts, till at last Jack said, "I don't like Gulab Singh."

"Is that fair?" replied Alick. "Till to-day you have always done so, and we can hardly change our opinion of him in so short a time. I have always thought him the most frank and manly trooper in our regiment."

"I dare say," replied Jack; "but why should he do his best to stop our sport? He confessed to father that there was no reason, but said something silly about it's not being a good time of year for pig. I must say, though, that I am sorry father pitched into him so warmly for interfering."

"So am I," responded Alick. "We English people use our tongues much too freely on these natives. It's true that many of them are liars and cowards, but still they are men, and it's a disgrace to our manhood to treat them as we do." Then, after a pause, he added, "I wish I could understand what that fellow was driving at. He came to me as mysteriously as possible this morning, and said, 'Don't go to Humaiun's Tomb. Stay here.' But there's no good troubling ourselves.

Here is the tomb. I hope that Hosein has everything comfortable for us."

Hosein, Alick's servant, had everything comfortable, and it was not long before the two friends climbed up the steep steps leading to the flat roof of the tomb, where their beds were laid. In the middle of the great flat roof there rose a massive dome of white marble, and in the shadow of this, so as to be protected from the moon's rays, their beds had been prepared. In a few minutes they were sound asleep.

Early next morning they were roused by Hosein, a very small, wiry Mohammedan, between whom and Alick a closer feeling of friendship had already sprung than that which generally exists between a young officer and his bearer.

After an early breakfast they mounted their ponies, and as the sun was rising they entered the scrub in the river-bed. The River Jumna in the rainy season rushes along in a swollen torrent nearly a mile in width; but in the month of May it was, though still a quarter of a mile wide, a shallow, sluggish stream, across which in many places men could easily wade. That part of the bed of the river which it covers in the rainy season alone at other times of the year is in many places covered with tangled tufts of long grass. Into this dry river-bed Alick and Jack entered on their ponies in search of pig.

Jack had a mount which was the envy of the station. No pony could gallop as Micky could. Full of spirit and life, he had not a particle of vice, and if he was only allowed to go his own pace he could be managed with a silken rein. But there was one thing that Micky would not allow—another pony or horse to pass him, and the sound of a galloping steed behind him was always the sign for Micky to run away.

Pig-sticking is considered great sport in India. Each rider is armed with a stout, sharp pig-spear, and, owing to the rough nature of the ground and the sharp turns and twists round clumps of grass when following a pig, it needs a tight grip and a steady balance to keep a good seat.

They entered the scrub about thirty yards apart, and almost immediately there was a snort and rustle.

"Pig!" shouted Jack. "Look out, Alick!" And off started Micky, Alick closely following; but on coming to an open space Jack saw that it was not a boar, and the rules of sport forbade a further chase.

Five minutes later another pig was raised, and this time it was a large boar with enormous tusks. Twice Jack thought he had the tusker, and was within a foot of him when round a clump with a sharp turn the pig disappeared, and then the chase began again. Alick then got a chance, but his pony stumbled when he was close up, and the pig again escaped. At last the pig burst out into the open, and Jack with a whoop followed, sure of him now, and close on his heels. The pig seemed to know his danger, and swerved across Micky so unexpectedly that he shied violently and Jack was thrown heavily to the ground. Before he could stir the boar had turned. It glared a moment, and then dashed straight for him.

A wild pig is a fearful animal when it turns enraged on a defenceless foe, and it was lucky for Jack that Alick had been following close behind. Just as the pig was commencing its rush Alick charged. Straight through the chest and heart passed the spear, which was wrenched from Alick's grasp. But the boar lay dead, and Jack, as he gazed at its quivering limbs, felt thankful that the ugly tusks had not ripped open his side.

He was little the worse for the fall, though very dusty and a trifle shaken, but he soon was able to remount his pony; and as the sun was already uncomfortably hot, he and Alick returned to the tomb.

After they had taken a cold bath and dressed themselves in clean white suits, they sat down to breakfast, for which their morning's ride had given them an excellent appetite.

They had not quite finished when they were startled—in the midst of a merry peal of laughter at a remark of Jack's—by the sound of musketry firing followed by a discharge of cannon.

"What is that?" Jack quickly asked. Alick was puzzled. For a few moments he sat silent, listening. Again there came the rattle of musketry.

"There is a riot of some sort in Delhi, Jack. That is not blank cartridge being fired, but ball!"

"What can have happened Alick?" replied Jack. "Could it be from some suspicion of this that Gulab Singh warned us to stay in cantonments?"

"We must not delay here, that is plain."

Turning to Hosein, his servant, Alick gave him directions to have the horses saddled immediately for a return to Delhi.

Then hastily finishing breakfast they moved to the clump of trees at the entrance of the large garden in the centre of which the tomb stood. They found two grooms leading the ponies, on which they had hunted that morning, up and down the road, for they were not yet cool, while other men were hastily putting saddles upon Alick's Arab charger and a small pony which belonged to the Colonel and on which Jack had ridden out the evening before.

"Be as quick as you can," said Jack to the grooms.

The words were not out of his mouth when they noticed a sawar (as a native cavalry soldier is called) galloping towards them.

"It's father's charger Monarch," said Jack, surprised.

"Yes, and Gulab Singh is riding," added Alick.

Gulab Singh was waving his lance excitedly as he came towards them full speed.

"Mount! mount!" they heard him shout.

Jack mounted his father's pony, and Alick ran to his charger. The girth of his saddle was not yet tightened when Gulab Singh reached them.

"A massacre of the English," he said, hurriedly. "A party of sawars are on my heels. You must ride for your lives!"

As he spoke a party of twenty horsemen swept round the turn of the road a few hundred yards away. And when they saw the Englishmen they shouted loudly and waved their lances.

A wrench at the girth, and Alick vaulted into his saddle, and he and Gulab Singh followed Jack.

The tomb of the Emperor Humaiun lies off the main road between Delhi and Muttra, but there is a road leading to it from the side nearest Delhi, and this road, passing the entrance of the tomb, takes a turn back to the main road, which it rejoins a mile from the point from where it diverged.

It was down this old road, which was very rough and steep, that Jack had dashed, leading as it did in a direction opposite to that from which the sepoys were coming.

Before Alick and Gulab Singh had gone more than a few yards, Hosein, Alick's Mohammedan servant, seized the rein by which the groom had been leading Jack's pony Micky, and though it was not saddled, he jumped on its back and fled after the others.

The grooms ran through the gateway into the tomb and escaped, for the pursuers did not heed them, but with loud exulting shouts followed the riders.

As long as they were on the old rough road it was impossible for the horses to go fast, but as soon as they reached the high road leading to the great Hindoo city of Muttra they seemed to fly.

A hundred yards alone separated the pursuers and pursued. It was a race. Time would show which had the better horses.

Fighting was out of the question. Not only were they four to the troopers' twenty, but also Jack and Hosein were unarmed, while Alick had only his pig-spear in his hand. Gulab Singh alone was fully armed, having his sword at his side and his lance in his right hand.

Over the old bridge built by Akbar the Great, round the curve to the left, and along the flat road they galloped. Gulab Singh, on Monarch, the colonel's splendid charger, and Alick on his beautiful Arab, which was perfectly fresh, had to restrain their horses to keep on the same level as Jack, who was worst mounted of all, for though Micky, on which Hosein was riding, had hunted all that morning, he was a much better pony than that which Jack rode, and seemed to enjoy the rapid pace at which they were going.

Soon they had increased their lead from the main body of horsemen, but three of their pursuers, better mounted, kept close behind them.

Not a yard on that first hundred had they gained, and only that the troopers had already ridden seven miles from cantonments to the tomb their fate would have been quickly sealed.

Already it was getting desperate, and after they had passed the temple of Kalka, nestling amidst the trees on their right, and as they swept round a turn over some rising ground Alick saw over his shoulder that the three sawars who were leading the others were gaining on them, while their comrades were close together three hundred yards behind them.

Jack had to force his mount, and it was evident that if this terrible pace had to be kept up, in another mile his pony would be thoroughly exhausted, and they must fall into the hands of their pursuers.

Noting all this, Alick made up his mind to try and check the three leading troopers. Speaking a few hurried words to Gulab Singh, who rode on his right, he turned to Jack and explained his intentions to him.

"You and Hosein keep on at this pace; Gulab and I, who are better mounted, will gallop forward so as to increase our distance. We will then turn and charge the leading sepoys. You and Hosein keep to the sides of the road and leave us the centre."

It was necessary for them to gain a long lead, otherwise when they turned the pursuers would be on them before they could get up speed in the opposite direction.

As soon as they gave their horses their heads the two gallant chargers raced away from the ponies, and Alick and Gulab soon made a wide gap between themselves and their comrades.

The troopers behind them, thinking that fear had prompted the two, who were better mounted, to desert their comrades, spurred on their horses with a loud cheer.

When Alick saw that his lead was sufficient he gave the word to Gulab. They reined in quickly, and charged back over the ground they had travelled.

It was but a short distance, and the horses could not get up full speed. This tells enormously in a cavalry charge, and the troopers were going faster than they were. But the move was a complete surprise, and, losing the advantage that they would have had, the pursuers stopped their horses. It was fatal to them. Before their horses could recover, Alick and Gulab were upon them. One of the troopers turned and fled, the two others were ridden down. But the spear of one as he fell pierced Alick's charger, and Alick and his horse rolled over and over.

Gulab Singh could not rein in quickly, and was almost into the main body before he could turn Monarch. They, too, had halted to see the result of the charge. This gave Gulab a moment. He rode back to Alick, who was standing in the centre of the road, dazed from his fall and with his face and hands cut and bleeding.

"Quick, quick, sahib!" shouted Gulab, seizing him.

With an effort Alick swung up behind him. It was not a moment too soon. Already the spears of the lances were within a few yards of them.

Could Monarch carry the two riders? He was a grand English horse, big-boned and full of power, accustomed to carrying weight, for the colonel was a heavy man. He did not seem to feel the difference, and galloped right away from the troopers.

"But he can't keep it up long," thought Alick; and he was right, for weight must tell in a long run.

(To be continued.)

GULAB SINGH:

A STORY OF PERIL AND HEROISM.

By Rev. R. D'O. MARTIN, M.A.

CHAPTER II.—THE RUINED CITY.

THE check that the troopers had received from the courageous charge made by Gulab Singh and Alick allowed Jack and Hosein to get half a mile ahead, and Hosein suggested a change of horses, for Micky had much more lasting power than the other pony. They made the change as quickly as possible, and though they lost a few

moments, Hosein's light weight made a great difference to the pony. They were, moreover, approaching a walled village, through the centre of which the road lay, and if necessary Hosein could slip off the pony he was riding, and escape down a narrow street unnoticed.

But the pony now went as well as the other, and when Monarch overtook them they were far ahead of their pursuers.

But they were not yet out of danger, for the troopers were still following them.

The horses flew through the great gateway of the walled village, clattered madly down its central street and out at the other gate, and before the people ceased wondering their amazement was increased by the arrival of the sawars, who, without halting, dashed along at full gallop in pursuit.

The fast ride through the air revived Alick, who had almost lost consciousness from the shock of his fall on the hard road.

Their steeds were now covered with white foam, and the heat of the sun, which was high in the heavens, was trying both to horses and riders. But it was apparent that the extra seven miles to the tomb was telling on the horses of the troopers, and the fugitives rapidly increased their lead.

"This can't go on much longer," said Alick, as he noticed that Hosein was forced to use every means to urge on his pony, while both Micky and Monarch were labouring heavily.

"What are we to do, Gulab?" he added.

"I have a plan, sahib. We are now two miles from the village; in another mile we shall have reached a great nullah, which in the rains is a rushing, unfordable river, but is now perfectly dry. Let us gallop there as fast as possible, and then dismount, all except Hosein. He will lead our horses, and, deceived by their tracks, the troopers will follow him, while we on foot rush up the nullah."

"But they will see us in the nullah," objected Jack.

"No, sahib, for there is a turn, round which we will have time to disappear."

"And where will we go then?" inquired Alick.

"To the ruins of that great city that you see to the right, sahib. It is five miles away, and if we can reach it we may hide in safety till nightfall."

Then calling to Hosein and riding close to him, he said,

"Hosein, do you try and lead the troopers astray, and return to Delhi; we will try and reach your house before daybreak to-morrow."

"Bismillah! I am ready," said Hosein. "The plan will succeed, Insha Allah-ta'ala" (God willing).

"But why to Delhi?" asked Jack, after a moment's pause.

"He is right, Jack," replied Alick. "Delhi itself is the last place where we will be looked for."

"Ay! and perhaps we may hear of father," said Jack.

They had been spurring on their horses during this conversation, and the noble animals had responded gallantly, as if they understood that it was their efforts alone which could save their riders. The explanations had only been completed when the nullah came in view.

Quickly dismounting and handing their reins to Hosein, Gulab Singh, Jack, and Alick, turned to the right and rushed over the rough stones and gravel that formed the dry bed of the nullah. Hosein, meanwhile, galloped straight across it and continued along the road, going at full speed to be out of sight before the pursuers arrived at the nullah.

The three others had to run two hundred yards, and then a sharp turn in the bed hid them from those who might look up the nullah at the point where it was crossed by the road.

They had only just reached this turn when they heard the rush of horses as the sawars galloped up.

They had suspected some plan at the nullah and reined up a moment; but, seeing that the three horses leading across it and up the other side, their leader shouted,

"Forward! They are still before us."

It was a moment of breathless suspense to the fugitives, for, had the horsemen looked carefully, they could not have failed to notice their tracks in the nullah's bed. As soon as they heard the soldiers in full gallop following Hosein, they went quickly along the nullah which wound back towards the road they had travelled. After a short distance it approached to within fifty yards of the road, and then Gulab begged the youths to ascend the bank and follow him to the road, making as plain marks as possible.

"Why should we do this, Gulab?" asked Alick. "The ruins lie in the other direction. Should we not hasten to them?"

"The troopers will return and find our tracks, sahib. I wish them to think that we have taken the road as if returning direct to Delhi."

Alick and Jack saw the wisdom of the course suggested, and, following Gulab, they went to the road; but after walking along it a few hundred yards they came to a place where very dry rocky ground enabled them again to leave the road, without leaving any traces that they had done so, and re-enter the nullah at a point half a mile away from the place where they had ascended the bank and gone to the road.

From this point the nullah led almost directly to the ruins for which they were aiming.

Till now excitement had kept them from being tired, but the rough stones of the nullah tried their feet terribly, while the sun shone down fiercely upon them. At last, wearied out they reached the ruins, into which they entered, and choosing a place where they could command a view of the nullah and road, they threw themselves down to rest.

They were hiding in a great deserted city. Nearly five hundred years ago, this city had been built to satisfy the whim of an emperor, but was deserted a few years later by his grandson.

Its walls are probably the most massive in all India, and are most extensive; but now this great city is unpeopled, save only that a small village nestles in one corner, but so completely hidden as not to be seen from the greater part of the ruins. Great walls, massive buttresses, and strong towers stand as a monument of former greatness; but the walls are in places falling down, the buttresses are crumbling away, and the strength of the towers is gone, while the silence and sense of desolation that pervades the place tells but too plainly that the greatness is departed—the pride and the magnificence all passed away.

The place in which the fugitives lay was a ruined upper-chamber from which they could see all around, and easily make their escape if danger threatened.

Here they determined to wait till nightfall.

(To be continued.)

SO-CALLED 'INVASION LITERATURE' WAS HUGELY POPULAR. THIS STORY, IN CHUMS, WAS DATED 4TH JANUARY 1913

NOTICE.—This story is not intended to stir up race hatred, but is written as a true picture of what would happen if a great Continental nation attacked our country.—*Your Editor.*

THE SWOOP OF THE EAGLE

A Great Story of the Motherland's Dire Peril

By CAPTAIN FRANK SHAW

If You are a New Reader You can Begin Here

THE long-threatened German invasion comes at last. Thousands and thousands of the soldiers of the Eagle land on the east coast of Britain during a fog. The first to discover them is Sergeant Dick Reynolds, of the O.T.C., who is returning from range practice with a few of his men. They rout a small scouting party, and thereafter Dick is forced into the thick of affairs by force of circumstances. He helps to rouse the country, and after many adventures is sent by General Cook with dispatches to the army advancing from London. He hides the dispatches in a Mauser pistol, and in escaping from some Germans who are after him he loses the pistol. Going back for it, he is captured and is thrust into the corner of a barn, but is rescued when the Suffolks arrive and beat back the Germans after a tremendous engagement. He delivers his dispatches, and is detained for service with Captain Latham, of the Flying Corps. He goes up with him and they suddenly see a vast army of Germans beneath them. The aeroplane comes down and they are captured, but Dick gets away by leaping over a bridge into a river. Two German soldiers are told to shoot him.

The Escape by Water

SO he stuck it out, watching the German soldier clinging frantically to the pontoon, with the bullets zip-zipping about his head. But the German shooting was not good, and so the man survived. On the bank, immediately above Dick Reynolds' head, a couple of infantrymen discussed the situation.

"He cannot last long there," one said. "Leave him; he will drown fast enough."

"The order was that he was not to escape alive," said the other.

"Then let us go on and say that we have shot him and that he sank," said the first. "No one will know; and if he does escape he will not be such a fool as to show his nose amongst us again." Dick complimented the man voicelessly on the sound common sense he was displaying. But the other still had a word to say:

"We must make another attempt, Karl; if the prisoner escapes and is recaptured, we shall be flogged."

"Well, here goes for another shot." The rifle cracked, and Dick looked towards the pontoon. He saw the man disappear; a second passed, another—several—and the agony-distorted face did not reappear. Evidently that last shot had settled the matter finally.

This was the opinion of the two men on the bank. "We've done for him," said one. "He won't try to escape again. Serve him right." They waited for another few seconds and then moved away; Dick could hear the squelching of their feet in the trampled mud above him. He drew in the first deep breath since his dive.

It occurred to him that it might be as well now to study his exact position. Fortune had smiled upon him so far, although it was at best a frosty smile; but he could not hope for such good luck to attend his every movement. He could not see what was happening on the bridge, but the rumble of wagon wheels had ceased; evidently the corps had either passed over or had halted on the other side. He itched with desire to know the exact state of affairs; and gradually, curiosity overpowering every other sensation, he began to draw himself upwards a little. He sank back swiftly; only just in time. The force had crossed, but it had left details behind to guard the bridge, as was only natural. This military bridge formed one of the enemy's lines of communication with its base, and possessed almost incalculable value. Over it supplies of every description would be forwarded from the base depot near the coast in order that the mighty force might be sustained in its manœuvrings. Dick found himself possessed by a monstrous desire to destroy that bridge. Such an action would hamper the movements of the army greatly, for the bridging train would be compelled to return to repair damages.

But he had to relinquish this hope; it was entirely out of the question. Better a live dog than a dead lion, thought the lad; and he had news of moment to communicate. It was up to him therefore to escape as swiftly as he could and leave all such quixotic ideas severely alone.

But crouching there, with only his head above water, would not help England. He must do something, if only to rid himself of his growing numbness. He decided on taking a risk. In all probability the enemy would take it for granted that he was out of harm's way, and would not trouble to scan the river's surface. He therefore drew in several big breaths, finding they warmed him considerably; and then, without so much as a splash, sank under water and struck out down-stream, swimming like an otter. He had practised swimming under water a lot in more peaceful days; and when he was forced to come to the surface for fresh air, he discovered that he had made fair headway down-stream. There was also a cluster of bushes abreast of him; a couple of strokes placed him under their shelter. From his new point he could see the bridge more clearly, as also the men who guarded it. They had rigged up a rough shelter out of brushwood and fragments of the wrecked bridge; only one man now mounted guard. Dick remained where he was for a few minutes, recovering his breath, and then swam on again, not taking such particular pains to conceal himself as he had done before.

So, alternately swimming and resting, he placed a distance of a clear half-mile between himself and the enemy, and at long last drew himself out of the water and crouched down on the chill earth to take a clear observation.

There was not much to be seen. It was a comparatively bare tract of country just here—long, low-lying stretches of agricultural land, with clumps of pollard willows here and there. But something like half a mile away was a house of considerable size—a wealthy man's residence in all seeming. Dick made up his mind to reach this haven. He was very weary from his long immersion, and he thought that here might be a chance to obtain dry clothing, warmth and the like.

He moved forward boldly, making a bee line for the chimneys, and noticed as he went that no smoke showed from them. He scaled a hedge, climbed out of the ditch, and ran as nimbly as he could across the open field. The exercise did him good, made a fresh man of him; but the discomfort of his sodden clothing and squelching boots depressed him again as he crouched behind the next hedge, surveying the outlook before venturing farther.

A hundred yards farther on he found signs of the invasion. A detached cottage had been destroyed; it lay there roofless and gaunt. The ground about was trampled into thick mud. By dint of using his scoutcraft—Dick had been a scout before he was found old enough to join the O.T.C.—he discovered that a mounted patrol had visited the place. A moment or two later he discovered the reason for its destruction. There was a hastily dug grave at the roadside. Quite evidently the occupants of the cottage had resisted the demands of the patrol, and had been punished according to the orders issued by the German commander-in-chief, by which all civilians in arms were condemned to extermination. But of the original occupants of the cottage there were no signs; Dick hoped they had made their escape, but feared the worst. If they had been burnt in the cottage there would be no trace remaining of them, and there was no time to make an exhaustive search. He passed on, found a small lodge beside an open gate, saw the door was open, and entered cautiously, ready to turn and fly if it were in the occupation of the enemy. But it was deserted; it bore traces of a hasty flight.

He went up the drive, and discovered the house was of considerable size. Like the lodge, it was empty, or apparently so. The patrol had raided it to some effect, there were traces of their work everywhere. Furniture had been destroyed, hangings had been torn down, the remains of a rough meal were on the table in the big hall. By the muddy prints leading through to the rear Dick decided that the foraging party had looted the cellars completely; a broken wine-bottle at a stair-head gave further proof of this. But the tide of war had flowed on after it had done its work. The lad moved very cautiously, because he knew the place might still be occupied; but, though he examined room after room, he found no living thing.

He was descending to the hall again, with the idea of kindling a fire to dry himself, when he thought he heard a sound. Very silently he crept round the turn of the stairs.

He heard the click of a rifle-bolt; a voice spoke, bidding him surrender on penalty of instant destruction. Looking, he saw a figure below with a rifle to its shoulder.

"Caught again," he thought.

A German 'Plane

"COME down here, you beggar," said the man below. "Come on; don't stop staring there—I'll shoot if you don't." The threat was spoken in English, and Dick's heart gave a great leap of thankfulness; the position was infinitely better than it had appeared at first sight. He walked down the stairs, the rifle muzzle still covering him unwaveringly.

"I'm English, too," he said. "Don't shoot!" The rifle dropped to the floor with a clatter.

"Dick Reynolds! Well, I'm hanged! Dick, what on earth are you doing here?"

"Why"—the lad could not believe the evidence of his senses—"it isn't you, Fairburn? I thought—I believed——" The sudden relief was too great; he burst into hysterical laughter, hiccupping savagely.

"Steady, Dick. It is you! I recognised your voice, but that's all. What have you been doing to yourself?"

"Swimming," laughed Dick, although there was no merriment in his laughter. "Swimming, running away, everything! Are you really Fairburn?"

"Looks like it. Where've you been? We heard you were killed. I say, old chap, I am glad to see you. Here, sit down."

He pushed a half-ruined chair forward. Dick threw himself into it, and it collapsed unconditionally, precipitating the soaked lad to the ground. At the sight Fairburn dissolved into choking laughter also, and for a clear two minutes the pair screamed and squirmed.

It was Dick who recovered his calm first. He extricated himself from the ruins of the chair and caught at Fairburn's shoulder, shaking him strongly.

"Steady, lad; no time for fooling now. What's happened? Why are you here? You're in uniform, too."

"I've been sent home. School was broken up, so I came home. Got here only an hour ago, and found—this." He indicated the devastation about. "We broke up in such an almighty hurry that I hadn't time to get my civilian gear together, so I cleared out in this kit. Stayed with some friends at Reedham; they said it was dangerous to try to get home—Germans everywhere. But I wanted to know what had happened, so I came on. Railways all smashed up, no chance of getting that way—German treachery at work there. But I snaffled a bike from my cousin, and sprinted along like the wind. Found our old gardener—I live here, you know; it's my pater's place—Lowland Lodge. He told me the pater'd cleared out on the first alarm. He's retired from the Army, but went to offer his services. Plucky old thing, my pater. My mother's dead, you know."

Dick tried to take it all in. It seemed like centuries since he had last seen Fairburn, one of his chums at school, one who had helped gallantly in the first escapade with the invading Germans. He had sent him off to convey a warning—long, long ago, although it was actually but a very few days. Fairburn still wore a bandage on his forehead, to show where he had been wounded in the brisk little action—the first of the war.

"But where've you been, Dick? I'm awfully glad to see you. Jove! but you're in no end of a mess."

"I'll tell you all that some other time. Look here, I must be moving on now. I've got information to take to General Calder; it's urgently necessary. Do you know where I can get a horse?" Fairburn shook his head.

"Every living thing's been cleared out of this part of the country, my son—every horse, every cow. They killed the cattle and stole the horses, and they seem to have shot a tidy few people who resisted. That's why I got this rifle; didn't intend to be shot without shooting back. I tried to get taken on with the troops, but everything was upside down. No one seemed to want me—said I was only a boy. Be hanged if a boy can't do his whack! We showed 'em that the other day, didn't we?'

"Rather! Look here, if we can only get away from here I might get you some work to do, old man. They've taken me on; I've been having the very mischief of a time. I'll tell you about it later; but I must get away and join General Calder's army."

"Where's that? Is there a British army? Where I've been everything seems to be German. They've cut a clean swathe across this part of the country; they've burnt no end of houses, raided villages; goodness only knows what they haven't done! It makes a man sick when he thinks of it. And I'm too young to volunteer, they tell me; I'm only sixteen years old. As if I couldn't shoot as well as many a man of thirty! If you hadn't spoken when you did, old son, you'd have been potted clean."

Dick was awakened to his need for dry clothing by chill shivers shaking him, and put a question at once.

"I don't know. Let's hunt about and see what we can find, if these beggars have left anything." They commenced to explore, and found plenty of clothing; but just as Dick was stripping off his soaking khaki, he paused.

"If I get into plain clothes I can't go on as a combatant," he said. "I've seen men shot down like dogs for taking up arms when they weren't in uniform. Think I'll stick to what I'm wearing." But Fairburn insisted on his donning a change of underclothing, and as there was plenty lying about, overlooked by the marauders, the lad donned a couple of suits of thick woollen clothing, which bred up immediate warmth in his veins. Over these garments he pulled on his damp khaki, which Fairburn had wrung out as well as he could.

The man swung about as Dick leaped at him, the club lifted high. The man snatched at his revolver; but before he could draw and cock the weapon the blow fell squarely on his head.

"I feel better now," said Dick. "But there's still the difficulty about getting away. One thing's certain: I've got to make a shot for it, even if I go on foot."

"You could take my bicycle," began Fairburn dubiously. "It isn't up to much, but it might serve. Only, if the enemy are between you and General Calder, how are you going to get through?" Dick scratched his head, which he had just finished towelling briskly.

"That's a bit of a problem. But I'll have to do my best." And as he spoke he heard from outside a loud throbbing whir. He ran to the window and peered out; these last few days had made him a boy of quick action and quicker thought.

"That's an aeroplane," he said. "Hope it's British; we can send on word by it. There it is!" The aircraft was showing above a belt of trees less than half a mile away. The lads watched it eagerly, saw it swoop downwards and alight within two hundred feet of the main doorway of the house. There was an open stretch of ground there, an admirable place for a descent. A begoggled man stepped out of the craft, tripped, and fell, and—the window where the boys stood was partially open—they heard him give an exclamation.

"No good!" said Dick in a low voice. "He's German; and there's another man with him. He's coming up to the house."

"Well, there's your chance to take your dispatches," said Fairburn. "You can't ride through the German lines, but you could fly over them." He said it jestingly, but Dick took it in earnest. "That's an idea," he said. "There are only two men in it—one of them's out of it, come to think of it. But I don't think I know enough about handling the thing. No; it's too big a risk. You don't understand them, do you?"

"No, not a bit. But I'll tell you what, Dick: we understand enough to smash the thing up and prevent these people from going any farther. Hist! That man's coming in." He crept to the door and heard a man's footstep in the hall. Fairburn had left his rifle downstairs; it was an old Martini which he had procured from his relatives overnight. He railed at his neglect.

"We could have potted him, made him surrender," he said. But Dick added nothing to the discourse; he was thinking hard. In war-time men must take great risks; their lives were of very small account when weighed in the balance with the welfare of their country. He had escaped death miraculously many times, and it is not to be wondered at that he had come to consider himself the possessor of a charmed life. He had picked up one or two hints from Captain Latham about the handling of an aeroplane; and whilst recognising that a little knowledge is a dangerous thing, had confidence in his lucky star. And the risk was worth running, because if he were successful in his desperate venture all his problems would be solved.

"Can we get out of here without going through the hall?" he asked swiftly.

"Yes; but you'll have to move quietly. Quick, if you're going, before that man comes upstairs!" They were in Fairburn's bedroom all this time. Now they went to the door, which they had fortunately left open, and on tiptoe, hardly daring to breathe, crept along a corridor, away from the stair-head. Dick would have given a good deal to know what the airman was doing, but had to allow his curiosity to remain unsatisfied; there were more urgent matters afoot. Fairburn piloted him to the head of a narrow secondary staircase, evidently used by servants. They descended and reached the open air, at the side of the big house. Creeping forward, they found themselves at the corner, whence they could observe the motionless aeroplane. The second man was walking about the machine, examining it expertly. Twenty yards from the 'plane was a clump of rhododendron bushes, and Dick, using all his eyes, saw that it would be possible to reach their shelter undetected if he moved cautiously.

"Don't come if you'd rather not," he said to Fairburn. "It's a risky job. I'm going to sneak up behind those bushes and watch my chance of snaffling that chap there."

"Here's something to club him with," said Fairburn, snatching up a heavy piece of wood from the ground. "And here's something else—I'll have this." He possessed himself of a serviceable weapon—a garden stake, as was shown by the mud on its point. "I'm going too; you don't get rid of me so easily as all that, Dicky boy. Sing out when you're ready." Dick watched until the man's back was turned, and then slipped away to fresh cover, remembering everything he had learnt about skirmishing. They reached the protection of a belt of shrubs without discovery, sneaked softly along until they were behind the rhododendrons, and then took fresh council together. They were now within easy striking distance of the aeroplane, and its custodian, a non-commissioned officer, was examining the engine carefully, blind and deaf to all outward happenings.

"If we can't snaffle it we can smash it up," said Dick, gripping his club firmly. "Remember that; we'll take a shot at the stays. Hit them hard, and they ought to snap. But try to get it whole." They waited another tense minute, and all the time the under-officer examined the machinery.

"Now," said Dick; and they ran out of cover together. On the sodden turf their feet made no sound of moment. They were side by side, crouched low. They were within ten yards of the bending man, five yards—they were gathering themselves for a spring when there came a warning shout from the front of the house The officer was returning. The man swung about as Dick leaped at him, the club lifted high. The man snatched at his revolver; but before he could draw and cock the weapon the blow fell squarely on his head. But for his padded cap it must have split his head open; as it was it dropped him inert and lifeless to the ground.

A pistol-shot rang out, but the distance was too great from the hall door to permit of effective shooting with an uncertain weapon. The officer was running towards them across the turf, firing as he came.

"Coming?" panted Dick, who had seen the spare seat behind the driver's. Fairburn merely nodded.

"In you get, then—look alive!" Fairburn leaped upwards, gripping at the stays. He struggled into the seat, and Dick followed him. A bullet whizzed past his head as he did so; another followed it. The officer still came on, but he had ceased firing; evidently he had expended the cartridges in his pistol. Dick realised how narrow his margin was. If he failed to start the 'plane they might both be shot down. The officer had halted for an instant, and was cramming a fresh clip of cartridges into his pistol. The lad seized the starting-crank and turned it desperately; the propeller whirred, grew slower, stopped. He cranked away again like a madman; the propeller re-started, it commenced to roar. The officer threw up his pistol, and the bullet drew blood; Fairburn yelped with sudden pain.

But the aeroplane had started; it was running briskly down the slight slope. A belt of trees showed ahead; if the craft did not lift now it was heading direct for destruction. In a frenzy Dick juggled with levers, pulling this and pulling that, trying to apply his powers of reasoning to the work. But this aeroplane was not built on the same lines as the other one; and all the time he strove to discover its peculiarities it was driving with considerable velocity towards the trees. The German officer, meanwhile, having recovered from his astonishment, had stopped running, had taken from his pocket a wooden stock which fitted his pistol, and now, using the weapon as a rifle, was taking close aim as he fired. It was well for the pair in the 'plane that the machine's progress was more than erratic, otherwise they must have been dropped like scurrying partridges. As it was the bullets clipped and hissed about them, and the trees grew alarmingly near. So near, that the officer apparently decided the end could not long be postponed. He ceased firing and ran afresh in pursuit.

"Hold tight!" Dick flung over his shoulder. The 'plane made a weak attempt to rise, sank down again, plunged sickeningly. It surged from side to side like a small boat beam-on to a heavy sea; it was a wonder both the lads were not hurled out. Fairburn, who had never experienced such an adventure in all his life, clung to the struts of his seat like a monkey at the end of a fishing-rod; but Dick had no thought for himself. The trees seemed to rush down on the 'plane; he tugged at another lever. There was a sensation as though he were shooting up on a rocket. Up and up towered the ungainly craft; it lurched again, more sickeningly than ever, as the uppermost branches of the trees caught at the wheel. One wheel was wrenched clean off; but with a bucketting lift and a swoop the obstacle was cleared, and the momentary danger was past.

Dick kept that ever-blessed lever hauled back so long that Fairburn deemed it necessary to protest.

"We're miles up," he said weakly, gripping Dick's shoulder. "Hadn't you better get her steadied?" The amateur pilot looked down; the country lay like an unrolled map beneath his feet. In a series of almost vertical leaps the machine had ascended to a height of over a thousand feet!

"Don't know how to steady her," he grunted, feeling the effect of the various levers. "This might bring her down." He jerked a lever that corresponded with the one Captain Latham had used for descending; its effect was to make the 'plane sway sideways, rocking like a cradle. Dick replaced that lever in its original position just in time to prevent them both being hurled out to death.

"Think we'd better stop her?" was Fairburn's next question. But Dick was beginning to understand a little more about his capture now; he had had time to trace the rods to their destinations. He moved a couple of handles and the 'plane shot away on an even keel, going magnificently. The fierce rush of air past their temples had an intoxicating effect on the lads; their fears fled away as on wings. This wonderful gliding through space, hardly perceptible yet amazingly swift, was exhilarating to a degree. To be sure the swift rush caused Dick's blood almost to freeze in his veins; but one effect was that the outer clothing dried rapidly.

"What are you going to do with her now?" asked Fairburn. Dick sent the 'plane surging downwards on a long slant, caught her in mid-air, steadied, and shot up afresh.

"I'm getting the hang of things; I'll try to steer here now," he replied. His young heart was full of joy; once more had good fortune been on his side. He had taken almost incredible risks, but he had won out in safety. The conviction came to him at that moment that he was destined to play a part of no small importance in this devastating war. He experimented carefully, always remembering that in the event of accident he had only one way to fall; he spun the 'plane round in a circle, which he gradually diminished. All the time the engine beat powerfully; whatever had been the reason for the real owner's descent, it had not been a breakdown.

"I'll head along for the army now," Dick said, when he recognised how completely he could control his capture. "Let's see—we'll have to reckon up the course." There was a large scale map of that part of the country mounted on a sheet of aluminium, placed in front of the pilot's seat, and beside it was a spirit compass, a beautiful instrument. Lowland Lodge, the place they had left—Fairburn's home—was plainly marked on the map, and Dick studied the many radiating lines. Finally he found one that passed through the village where he had seen General Calder; the course lay about west-south-west. He worked the levers as well as he could, and after a struggle managed to get the 'plane's head pointed towards that point of the compass. But it was by no means an easy matter to keep a straight course, the machine swayed and swooped so erratically. However, it remained aloft, and that was the main consideration.

In a surprisingly short time the army that had crossed the river appeared in sight; it looked like a great writhing snake. Having no wish to invite inquiries, Dick lifted the 'plane upwards. They shot across the rear-guard of the force like a homing pigeon, and something whistled suggestively about their ears. But their distance from the ground was so great that they could not hear the reports of the rifles discharged at them.

On they went, Dick, from some whim, keeping poised above the moving mass of humanity. He was committing its disposition to memory; noting its independent cavalry in the distance, hovering ahead as protection; on either flank of the columns were other parties of horsemen—a formidable force. He stooped to the engine and its beat quickened, just as a sharp explosion sounded behind. He thought at first it was a burst in the engine; but Fairburn caught at his shoulder and explained.

"Looked like a shell," he said. "It burst two hundred yards away. Mighty poor shooting, I call it!" The Germans had unlimbered a small, powerful gun carried on a motor-car, and fired repeatedly, but did no damage. And seeing the car beneath, scudding swiftly along a road, Dick altered course so that the 'plane took across open country, where the car could not follow. They went on and on, and as Dick's experience increased, so did the motion of the 'plane grow steadier. They left the German army in the rear; they passed over the advance guard, some twelve miles ahead of the main body; they sped forward like the wind. And then, after an hour of magnificent going, Dick felt a little glow of satisfaction permeate him. He lifted one hand and pointed away to the left, bringing the 'plane round in that direction.

"Calder's army," he said. "We've arrived in time."

Fairburn joins Dick

THE alighting of the captured aeroplane was ludicrous in the extreme; and it was miraculous both members of its crew were not killed outright. If the 'plane had not lifted miraculously and cleared a high wall like a hunter, it must have been smashed to fragments; but it did rise, and its remaining wheels plunged so deeply into thick plough on the other side as to arrest the craft's motion at once. Dick was shot out like a sack, and, taking the fall on his shoulder, was half buried; Fairburn, thrown clean up into the air, descended feet first, and remained up to his knees in clinging mud.

"Well, we're down, anyway," said Dick. A small force of cavalry came towards them, leaping the intervening hedges beautifully. The subaltern in charge reined in, looked at the pair, and incontinently burst out laughing.

"I suppose you're British?" he said. "The general's orders are that you shall be brought to him at once." Dick contrived to clean off some of the thickest of the mud, and expressed himself as ready to obey.

It was a matter of some time to reach General Calder's position, but eventually this was done. Dick was brought straight to the general, who had halted the column in anticipation of hearing a report.

"Who are you?" was his first question. Dick identified himself.

"Oh, you were detailed to accompany Captain Latham, yes. Well, where is he? Why doesn't he report himself?"

"He's a prisoner in the enemy's hands, sir. We were captured. I made my escape, found a German aeroplane, and came along, sir. The enemy is advancing in force over there." He pointed the way he had come. And then, without pausing, he set to work to recite everything he had observed. It was a somewhat lengthy process, because Dick's memory was a retentive one. He gave his estimates concisely; told, too, of the dispositions of the hostile force.

"An entire army corps, eh? That's a pretty big order," said General Calder to his staff. "It seems to me, gentlemen, that but for this lad's reports we might have thrown the entire force away. But if we wait here for the supports to come up, as promised, and then go on, we ought to strike this man somewhere near Dickleburgh. We shall halt here until the reconnoitring force brings us in clearer detail."

The force under Calder's control was accordingly ordered to rest on its arms, and a meal was prepared forthwith. The division occupied a road space of some fourteen miles from van to rear, and the head of the main body was now at a point some three-quarters of a mile from a small village. Dick was ordered to accompany the general and staff to this village; and he jerked his head to Fairburn to accompany him as Calder moved on.

"Dick, get him to give me a job; never mind what it is, so long as I'm with you," pleaded Fairburn.

"Righto! I'll do my best. I say, old man, there's going to be a beautiful dust-up just now. I'm going to ask permission to take that 'plane back with explosives and cut the communications of this army."

"Now, Reynolds, detail exactly everything that happened from the moment of your leaving here," said the general when he had established himself in the study of the Vicarage. The vicar, a nervous old man, was almost beside himself with horror at thought of a possibility of his parish being made a battlefield; but his wife, a capable woman, supplied the staff with a hastily prepared meal.

Dick proceeded to do as he was told, from the commencement to the finish. Calder snorted with indignation when he heard the particulars of their capture by the enemy.

"My best airman—my only airman, if it comes to that! Well, how comes it that you escaped when he didn't?" Dick told him of his plunge into the river, of the long waiting before he could make his escape; of his arrival at Lowlands Lodge.

"I found Fairburn there, sir."

"Fairburn, Fairburn; who the deuce is Fairburn?"

"A schoolfellow of mine, sir, in the O.T.C. He was in that first engagement with me, sir. But for Fairburn I shouldn't have been able to get through with this report."

"Um! You boys seem to be all alive and kicking, I must say. How did Fairburn help you to get the reports through?" Dick told of the capturing of the aeroplane, and some of the staff, who listened, laughed at the sheer devilry of the scheme. "And, if you please, sir, Fairburn wants to have a shot at the enemy—another shot," said Dick anxiously. He asked nothing better than to have his old school-chum beside him in his succeeding adventures.

"You bloodthirsty boys amaze me, amaze me," said the general. "Well, well, it's a good sign. How old is this other boy? Your age?"

"About that, sir. He's outside; I'll call him in, if I may."

"No; no need yet. You've done very well, Reynolds—very well, indeed. Major Malone, are there any combatant officers who understand the handling of an aeroplane?"

"I hardly think so, sir; all flying officers were ordered to their hangars as soon as we mobilised."

"Make inquiries throughout the division; order all flying men to report to me." Dick started forward eagerly, and his action did not escape unobserved.

"Well, what is it, youngster?"

"I was thinking, sir, that if you'd allow me, Fairburn and I could take the aeroplane back, with some explosives, and damage their lines of communication badly. You see, sir, the bridges were blown up, and they've only their military bridges now—round about here, at least."

"It's a good idea, lad; but I can't give you permission to do a thing like that. We'll see what happens later on. I wish I had a couple of dozen aeroplanes, though—I wish I had them. Meanwhile, you attach yourself to my bodyguard here, and—yes, your chum can count himself enrolled also. Distinctly against regulations; and the whole war is against regulations, if it comes to that. Now, gentlemen——" Dick was dismissed forthwith. He found Fairburn anxiously awaiting events outside, and to him he communicated the result of his interview.

"We're going to be together, eh?" said the delighted lad. "That's good; we'll have some mighty hefty times, one way and another. But what are you going to do just now?"

A staff-officer came out and beckoned to Dick—it was that same gunner with whom he had spoken before.

"I'm just appointed. Captain Fyldes, was thrown from his horse this morning and broke his collar-bone; he's no end sick. You youngsters come with me; I've got orders to look after you. Reynolds, my son, you seem to have all the luck."

"What's going to happen, sir?" inquired both boys in a breath.

"You'll see soon enough. We're going to tackle this army, although we're only a division and some patches. And when we meet them there's going to be the very mischief of a fight!" He was right. Before dawn next morning the battle of Dickleburgh had commenced.

(Another fine instalment next week.)

A bit mixed

A LADY went into a confectioner's shop and, pointing to some buns, asked the girl: "Are these buns to-day's? Because those I bought yesterday weren't."

Teacher's Rights

"MOTHER," said a small boy, "ought teacher to cane me for something I did not do?"

"Certainly not," answered his mother.

"Well," said the boy, "he did to-day when I didn't do my sum."

Brave Boy

JINKS: "Yes, sir. I gave it to the rascal, straight, I can tell you. He's twice as big as me, a regular giant, in fact, but I told him exactly what I thought of his rascally conduct. I wasn't afraid of him."

Binks: "And didn't he hit you?"

Jinks: "No, sir, not he, and when he went to answer back I just hung up the receiver and walked out of the telephone box."

"SENTENCES" COMPETITION RESULT.

First Prize .. .. £2.

HARRY SNOWDON,
191 London Road, Highfield, Sheffield.

Second Prize .. .. £1.

M. HOLMES,
Combe Martin, nr. Ilfracombe, Devon.

Third Prize .. .. 10/-.

ESMOND B. PERRY,
8 Radnor Park Crescent, Folkestone.

Fourth Prize .. .. 5/-.

E. V. LLOYD,
31 Hillside, Neath, S. Wales.

Twenty Prizes of "Chums" Solid Silver Pencil Cases.

A. E. Parlow, 12 High Lane, Ch./Hardy, Manchester; G. Chappell, 88 Everton Road, Endcliffe, Sheffield; C. R. Clarke, Station House, Surfleet, nr. Spalding, Lincs; W. Crathem, 27 Bewell Head, Bromsgrove, Worcester; Arthur Evans, Parkgate Road, Longhall, Chester; H. G. Flacks, 17 Week Street, Maidstone, Kent; R. B. Greig, 21 Ravenscourt Park, W.; Dorothy Gundry, St. Ann's Cottage, Staines, Middlesex; May Haythornthwaite, Agra Lodge, Northwood, Middlesex; W. Hockings, 25 South Luton Place, Adamsdown, Cardiff; F. R. Martin, 14 Kimbolton Avenue, Bedford; Ladybird Patton, St. Anthony's, Vicarage Road, Eastbourne; Noel Richardson, 175 Barth Road, Totterdown, Bristol; C. Shaw, Mount Westcott, Dorking; H. V. Smith, 198 Elms Road, Clapham, S.W.; F. B. Snelling, The Grove, Chepstow Road, Newport, Mon.; Ritchie Soutar, 2 Roseangle Terrace, Dundee; R. W. Wayne, Cottage Homes, Erdington Birmingham; R. W. Webb, 15 Market Square, Stafford; P. Wood, Lawrence House, St. Anne's-on-Sea, Lancashire.

The Result of the "Clues" Competition will appear next week.

A BATTLEPIECE OLD STYLE

by F. BRITTEN AUSTIN

Here is a vivid story of the Great War, of a big advance and what it met with.

"THAT, gentlemen, will conclude the first phase of the attack. The brigade will then press on, at all costs——"

The officers of four battalions filled the large barn. It was illumined, through the wide-open great doors in its flank, in a cool reflection of the blaze of hot summer sunshine outside. At the farther end, on chairs brought from the farmhouse, sat the red-tabbed Brigadier, the red-tabbed Brigade-Major, the four Colonels and their four Seconds-in-Command. Among them, erect, stood another red-tabbed staff officer, middle-aged, tall, precise-mannered, with an air of authority and the rank of Lieutenant-Colonel. In front of him, a table supported a large relief-model of a section of country scriggled over with red and blue lines. Behind him, on the wall of the barn, was a large map similarly reticulated. As he talked, he emphasized his points with a thrust of his cane to various features of the map and the relief-model "which he hoped all would presently come forward and study with the utmost care."

The infantry officers, in a curious mixture of ages that did not at all tally with their ranks, stood closely grouped or found precarious seats on such agricultural implements as had been left in the barn. There was a curious nervous tension in the silence with which they listened. And not without cause. They were listening to what, for an unknown percentage of them, was a sentence of certain death. No one voiced that aspect of the matter. A psychological X-ray would have revealed each one resolutely suppressing any personal thought, focussing his attention on the technicalities being expounded to them, and attuning himself stoically to the unemotional professionalism of the tall, neatly-uniformed, awkwardly-spoken staff officer. There was going to be another "push." Here, in this peaceful back area of ancient farmhouses embosomed in full-grown summer verdure where the Divisions had, in cynical mess-parlance, been "fattened for the slaughter," the high gods of the "Army" staff, having duly impressed upon the Corps Staffs and the Divisional Staffs what was expected of them, had condescended to explain their requirements, in a series of "Brigade Conferences," to the people who would actually do the work. That humble, lowest-paid arm of the service which throughout the army had succinctly become known as the P.B.I.—translatable for delicate ears as "Poor Blooming Infantry"—should in consequence go forth to battle inspired to Berserk-ecstasy in that welter of close-quarter killing and dying which was its interesting prerogative.

Bitterly although every infantry officer in that barn hated the Staff—with a hatred far transcending any they felt for the enemy—they nevertheless listened with an instinctive awe. It was an awe for which every infantry subaltern in the army kicked himself and yet to which he could not but succumb. That symbol of red-tabs on the lapels and a red band round the cap was so manifestly the symbol of a superior race. On those who wore it the gods had conferred immortality as well as authority. None of them would be killed, except by accident. Few of them had spent a night in the open since the war began. It was rumoured that some of them even

A Long Complete Story of the Great War

dressed for dinner every evening. And on the intermittent occasions when they were seen in the squalor of the trenches, for sojourns of the briefest possible duration, they had—awkward in rarely-worn steel helmets and concerned about the mud on their nicely-polished leggings—irresistibly the air of aristocratic philanthropists visiting the slums. Even hard-faced infantry colonels of long and arduous service became soft-spoken and polite when addressed by some second lieutenant A.D.C. wearing that mystic colour. The prestige of it was irresistible. It betokened membership of the sacred caste to whom war was a matter of poring over maps or signing endless floods of paper—who could, and did, release with a word (written cigarette in mouth in a quiet office) a fury of annihilating forces from whose destructiveness they themselves were happily exempt. They listened, therefore, to the staff officer at the table—he was G.S.O. 2 at Army Headquarters and had a reputation for being uncommonly efficient—almost as pariahs might listen to a Brahmin, with a sense of being in the Presence. He concluded his remarks.

" . . . Co-operation with the other arms—tanks, artillery and aircraft—will be as nearly perfect as we can get it. I need not tell you that. But I need not tell you either that it is on the infantry that all finally depends—it must advance with unflinching determination, regardless of its losses—— "

"Poor wretched infantry again!" murmured a disillusioned youthful subaltern in the throng. "All the kicks—and no blinkin' ha'pence!"

The staff officer picked up his gloves from the table. He would have scorned to be an orator, and winding up a speech was even more difficult to him than commencing one. He coughed and hesitated over his last sentence, forbore to meet

the disturbingly experienced eyes concentrated on him, sought refuge in a platitude that camouflaged ugly but distant realities.

" . . . And I'm sure, gentlemen, we're going to put up a really good show this time."

He sat down.

The brigade-major rose to explain the details of the relief-model. The battalion officers crowded up to the table.

The grey dawn had already broken, revealing a landscape beyond imagining in its utter desolation. Its few trees had been splintered to short jagged points and the whole of it might have been stamped on by brutal giants. From unseen origins, a violence of rolling, throbbing thunder, of ear-splitting crashes, of rending disruptions repeated in savage little groups, interwove itself with the whining, wailing, cascade-like rush of projectiles in the air, ceaselessly renewed. Founts of black smoke, of flying mud and debris, leaped by thousands from the tortured earth. From under the low rain-swollen clouds, handfuls of dark smoke-puffs sprang from nothingness with quick, sharp cracks and a prolonged menacing drone. On all the battlefield not a human figure was to be seen. It wanted ten minutes of zero-hour. The preliminary bombardment—swelled by partial counter-bombardment—was at its height.

Behind a wrecked trench parapet, an infantry subaltern, faceless and grotesque in a gas-mask, crouched with his eyes upon the dial of his wrist-watch. In the semi-fluid mud of the depression between one crumbled traverse and another, crouched some of his platoon, similarly anonymous and grotesque in their masks—weird figures divorced from humanity in a demoniac world divorced from normality. Each had a hand upon the weapon of his job—bayonet-tipped rifle, the divided paraphernalia of Lewis guns, bags of bombs. Among them, rolled on to his face, was the body of a man half-covered with a remnant of sack. The mud under him was red, and very fluid. A shell had landed in the trench just before. Two other men had completely vanished in its flash and smoke and stunning detonation. Nevertheless the others crouched patiently in the slush, their only horizon that broken trench parapet beyond which the noise of their own bombardment of the enemy position was one vast paralysing roar—the men they were about to kill, or by whom they would be killed, quite invisible to them.

The subaltern wondered what they were feeling. His own heart was thudding violently. His chest was gripped in a curiously stifling constriction; there was an emptiness in his abdomen, an internal sinking of his viscera that seemed to deprive him of physical strength. Their stolidity was odd, fantastic. In half an hour, how many of them would be alive? He himself? He shut off the thought, reverted to remembrance of his objective, repeated it doggedly to himself. "N 25 c," "N 25 c." It was the map reference to an infinitesimal section of the enemy second line. He was to press on to it, hang on, consolidate, wait for the second wave of the attack to pass over him, proceed "mopping up" behind that second wave. He visualized that objective as he had seen it in miniature on

A BATTLEPIECE
OLD STYLE
by
F. BRITTEN
AUSTIN

the relief-model, prayed inwardly that he would recognize it. The chances of it not being blasted out of original semblance by that pulverizing rain of shells were remote. "N 25 c"—he must get there, hang on. At all costs.

He looked again to his watch. Six minutes. Quite a time yet. Curse these gas-masks! One could not breathe in them. The nose-clip already hurt him. He shivered with a cold that soaked into his bones. That was a nice comfortable billet, that last one. Duck your head!—*down!* CRASH! Fragments all gone over?—Yes. Sickening sound, that hissing rush as it arrives. Brutes! We must be giving 'em hell, though. Wonder how many of their machine-guns are escaping? Don't think—no use wondering. Know presently. Five minutes. Still five minutes. He had a sudden vision of that nice clean staff officer at the Brigade Conference in the barn, heard his diffident cultured voice—"You will advance from here to there, and thence to somewhere else." Easy enough for him! He was sitting now, cool and neat in a quiet office somewhere far back, waiting for reports, a cigarette in his mouth. (If only one could smoke in a gas-mask!) He wondered if the war would come to a sudden end if all the staffs who ordered attacks had personally to participate in them. The ironic imagination of it gave him a grim amusement. Four minutes. He willed his heart to beat normally, refused to let himself wonder what death was really like. (By Jove! That was a near one! Anyone hit? No. Good! Curse these shells!) Staff officers—yes—supposing they had to attack, too—they wouldn't be so glib then with their "at all costs"—or would they? Good chaps, really, no doubt. Brave as anyone else, probably. Part of a system, that's all. Doing their jobs—ordering other people to wounds and death. Nice job. Wish he hadn't been such an enthusiastic ass. His father could have wangled it—nothing refused to really big contractors. His father—he'd be still in bed now, asleep—snoring—his mother—he saw his mother lying awake in the dawn—stop it, you silly fool! Three minutes. How the hand crawled! Was his watch stopping? Couldn't be—wound it when he synchronized last night. He would not think of anything—keep his brain a blank—blank—blank. Politicians at home, sleeping also in nice white beds, getting up to shout "Win the war at all costs." His uncle. Shut up—*shut—up!* Don't think. An eternity. Could one keep one's mind from thinking? God, this noise! Could understand chaps going mad. Two minutes. Only two minutes now. What's that? Three fellows blown up—best sergeant, too. Keep down, you idiots! One minute? It couldn't be really only one minute! It was. Less than one minute. He rose automatically, still crouching, eyes on that watch. Half a minute. A fraction—— *Now!* He sprang for the parapet, waved his arm to the figures jerking up out of the trench. To right and left of him, hordes of other faceless figures had emerged as by magic, were all going one way.

What followed was a dream—a phantasmagoria that had no reality. Those faceless men who dropped around him were not killed—or were phantoms who had never lived. The little group of tanks that lurched and plunged like ships in a rough sea were prehistoric creatures of a nightmare. The earth leaped up, almost at his feet, in quick red flash, black smoke and studding concussion—leaped up all around him, in front, behind, on either side. The enemy counter-barrage. He wasn't killed. A vaguely apprehended miracle. Worst of it was these confounded shell-holes—couldn't hurry—up to his waist in water that time—nice job for his servant cleaning off the mud. What was that insistent hissing, like an engine letting off steam, audible through the infernal din? Must get on—at all costs—N 25 c. Look at all those fellows throwing themselves down, taking cover! They weren't going to move. Kick 'em forward? Silly ass! Casualties. Hissing was machine-gun bullets. Marvel he wasn't hit. Charmed life. Thank God, enemy wire blown to bits. Enemy trench just beyond—hell erupting in it—no one visible. Anyone following? Yes. Scattered figures emerging through the smoke. Good chaps. He waved to them.

In their trenches. Ghastly mess. What a lot of blood a man has—never believe it—running down in a stream like that. That faceless snouted figure who had popped up from a hole. His revolver had gone off automatically at it. Figure had dropped. Wonderful how quick it was—fellow was alive then, dead now. What's that coming over? Bombs! Down in the mud—face down—can't help what it is. Ugh! *Bang-bang-bang!* Close call, that! Bombers! Bombers this way! Here they come—round the traverse—throw—dodge back—*bang-bang-bang-bang!* All quiet behind there? Yes. Only groans. Get on! Come on, all of you—don't matter what regiment you are—*come on!* Curse these gas-masks! Can't shout in 'em! Necessary, though. See that fellow whose mask has been perforated? Pretty ghastly, getting killed like that—just one gasp of air—poison. Place must be saturated with it. Ours or theirs? Ours first; theirs now. Half these shells gas-shells. Muffled bursts. Plenty of H.E., all the same. Shrapnel like rain. Enemy gunners enjoying themselves. My God! Down! Down quick! Devilish machine-gun nest! How many hit? The whole bunch? No. Four. Keep down. Into the mud. Tanks!—where in Heaven's name are the tanks? That's what they're for. Here comes one. Wonderful things. It's seen the nest—slewed round—shouldn't like it coming for me. Uncanny great brute. There it goes—clatter of its track like an agricultural machine—letting 'em have it all round with all its guns—what's it like in there—cooped up? There she goes. Over that damned nest like an ant-heap. Up we get! Come on, lads! On! They can't hear in this infernal row. Can't shout properly either. *On!* That's right. Along here. Bombers first. Bombers and bayonet-men.

Farther on. An aeroplane nose-diving—all but at the earth—in flames. Is this it? Must be second-line. Nothing looks like anything. All right for those fellows sitting behind with their nice maps and models. N 25 c—junction of trench with switch. That must be it, over there. Where that dead tank is—looks very dead, head foremost and still, great wound in its back. Smoke issuing from it. What happened to the crew? Not your business. Come on, boys! How many of 'em? Six—eight—nine. Is that all? Yes. No more. Must barricade the junction quick. Where's the rest of the attack? Can't see anything in this smoke. There's some of 'em. Digging in. Barricade—barricade—anything—yes—dead men—better than nothing—they don't know—shove 'em along—that one, too. Push that arm down out of the way. No. He's dead all right. Thought he wasn't. Not the time to be squeamish. . . .

An eternity. All sorts of things had happened. Things he could not remember. But the shelling had never stopped. The enemy's shelling—and then their own, when the counter-attacks had developed—little groups of snout-faced men emerging suddenly from the mud, machine-gunning, throwing bombs, stabbing with bayonets when they got the chance—there had been incidents like individual murders. It was incredible that he was still alive. He still had men around him—anonymous in their gas-masks—but they were not the same men. These had adhered to him, he could not remember when or how. They crouched now in the mud of the shell-crater along with him. Together they had been driven back—had fought forward again in some sort of new attack that had caught them up and melted away—that was the time those snout-faced fellows had been trapped in a corner of a blocked trench—had been butchered redly, sickeningly—their bare hands trying to push away the bayonets. He remembered he had glanced at his watch. That must have been soon after one-thirty. A long time ago. Eternity. Was it the same day? There had been no victorious second wave behind which to "proceed." Some low-flying aeroplanes had circled over suddenly appearing through the drenching rain that had lashed them for hours—had dropped boxes of ammunition that fell with a heavy splash in the liquid mud—most of them out of reach. The shelling was vindictive in its persistence. He could only hang on—hang on.

A counter-attack had sprung up from nowhere, been blotted out—mysteriously, from that apparently untenanted earth. There was a temporary lull. He was desperately hungry—his stomach gnawing at him—fevered with a maddening thirst. There was an "iron-ration" in his haversack; he still had his water-bottle. But he could neither eat nor drink in his gas-mask. It was death to remove it. Two men had died like that before he could stop them. The air was thick with gas, the ground splashed with chemical compound. The leaden sky was still raining in torrents. Little streams of yellow fluid ran down from the mud, mingled with water that was red. Mustard stuff. He was burned with it—it ate into them like corrosive acid—he had been careful, but it had come through his boots. He could not walk—none of those five recently-acquired men with him could walk. But they could still work the machine-gun whose tripod sank into the mud of the crater, brass-studded belt running through the breech—would use it, if, in the failing light, there were another counter-attack. That was improbable. Enemy wouldn't use mustard stuff if he meant to come back. But their job was to hang on. They were hanging on—hanging on, masked, soaked to the skin, like those other wretched little groups here and there whose presence he could divine rather than see. He had heard them "loosing-off" a few minutes back, through that demoniac persistence of eternally-leaping shell-

RAMBLING

WITH the numerous guide-books that railway companies and clubs are continually bringing out there should be no difficulty in fixing on a spot for a country ramble.

Much depends on individual taste, whether one goes with a crowd of about twenty or confines the number to a few intimate friends. There are special advantages attaching to each, and on such outings it is generally agreed "the more the merrier."

It is well to have a leader who will make himself responsible for the route to be followed, the halting places and refreshments on the road. This is especially necessary if the party is a large one. Assuming one is going for the day, and remembering that distance is not the aim of rambling, it is well to pick a spot about twelve miles from the starting point and plan your route on a circular basis, so that the return journey does not cover the same ground.

A golden rule for all ramblers is: Travel light. It is only the novice who sets out encumbered with numerous packages, coat, umbrella, oil stove, bottles of lemonade, and enough paraphernalia to run a camp for a week. Assuming you are taking your food for the day, you can eliminate those heavy bottles of liquid refreshment by choosing items that will quench your thirst just as well. Cucumber, tomatoes, and lettuce make ideal sandwiches, especially made with brown bread. On the road a green apple or an orange are tried thirst-quenchers, though some folks declare the much-condemned chewing-gum can't be beaten.

It is essential to have comfortable footwear, which means that they should be on the heavy rather than the light side. A light "mac" which can be rolled up and stowed away in the pocket is always advisable in face of the vagaries of the British climate. Clothing should be of the "knock-about" kind, roomy and light. If you are in any way on the road to becoming an expert rambler you will not venture far without your "thumb-stick," which is best cut from a sapling with a fork at the top to take the thumb on a level with one's elbow. Such a stick will be of far more aid than the ordinary walking-stick.

With intimate friends conversation on the road will never flag, especially if one of them can translate into interesting and everyday language the many wonders of our country lanes. With a large party where there is bound to be a few who want to have a good rest half-way it is a good idea to have a short open-air discussion, say, on the country traversed. For lighter mood, seek out the raconteur of the party and prevail upon him to enliven the halt. As a rule, it will be found that spirits and conversation run high enough.

With that love of the open road that grows upon one after a few rambles it will be found that miles can slip by with not a word said, the keen pleasure of the countryside and its quiet calling forth thoughts that make chatter difficult. Especially is this so at night. That brings us to that most exciting of adventures, a midnight ramble. To go striding along some leafy lane at dead of night, noting the strange noises of the after-dark, halting at some watchman's ruddy fire, catching the first glimpse of dawn from some lonely hill . . . this is an experience well worth having.

Rambling has so many advantages: it is cheap, it is healthy, instructive, and inspiring. Try it!

bursts whose red cores became ever more lurid in the gathering dusk.

It was black night—would have been black night if the opposing horizons had not flamed and flared incessantly from end to end. The thunder of massed guns, scarcely diminishing all day, had leaped to a new and frantic pitch of vehemence. The mile-wide belt of churned mud where their shells fell was an inferno of blinding flashes, of shattering detonations. Both artilleries were "taking it out of little brother"—each viciously destructive on the other's "little brother," the infantry scattered sparsely in a myriad shell-holes, denying to them further attack or counter-attack. Presently, the staffs behind would issue a communique, stating that the new front was "stabilized." He thought this as he lay on his back, head below his boots, in another shell-hole. He did not know how he came to be there. He remembered only the vivid red flash of an explosion in among them. There had been, oddly, no sound to it. When he had opened his eyes again the sky over his head had got quite dark, and he was in this position. He had found that he had no strength to alter it. He believed he had slept—once or twice. Thank God, anyway, the cries of that wounded wretch—out of sight somewhere—had ceased. The man had screamed that he was sinking into the mud. Suffocated? Very likely. He could not bother about it. Wounded himself, of course. Must be—or he would be able to change his position. God! how that mustard stuff burned! When would they pick up the wounded? Not till this shelling died down. Madness to try it now, of course. Sheer madness. . . . It was all madness . . . a riot of madness . . . Must remember to keep this mask on.

He was in that barn, with peaceful summer sunshine hot outside. The staff officer was speaking. "We have done our best to make it easy for you—co-operation perfect—push on—at all costs—never mind your losses—attrition—we can afford to lose men—he can't—millions more at home—millions—millions—millions—they'll all go forward into hell and die as we order 'em—we know what we're doing—we run the war, you see—it's *our* war—*our* war—good old war!" He half-woke from the delirium. Had the staff officer said that, really? He could not remember. Something like that Poor wretched infantry! The voice came again, over the heads of the crowd of infantry officers, grains of chaff dancing in the broad band of sunlight from the barn doors, a diffident, gentlemanly voice. "I'm quite sure, gentlemen, we're going to put up a really good show this time." My God, what a burst of shelling! Surely they couldn't have so mad as to attack again? All very well for them—*they* didn't attack—and then went to bye-bye in nice clean sheets. For God's sake, stop this infernal shelling! Each crash came inside his head. He would go mad with it. Mad. He was at home, lying in his own bed, his mother bending over him—he was ill, of course—home from school. Dreadful headache. Tortured with thirst—tortured. Why couldn't he drink? There was something over his face, preventing him—was it a cat, a cat lying over his mouth? Something like that had happened—once—beyond remembrance—a baby horror that revived in him in an automatic swift paroxysm. He wrenched at it—wrenched off his gas-mask—had a last stare at lightning-lit sky as he choked.

Back at Divisional Headquarters that day—in one of a neat row of semi-circular corrugated-iron Nissen huts, with gravel paths and flower-beds picked out with whitewashed stones in front of them—the Divisional Commander stood by a staff officer who sat near a telephone.

The staff officer answered into the instrument. His tone was aggrieved.

"My dear fellow, it's no use cursing us. We're doing our best. Better get on to the Heavy Group. They brought their barrage right back on to our men—spoiled the show. What? Well, that's the reports I get——" He changed his tone suddenly to one of profound respect. "Yes, sir. Speaking, sir. Very good, sir. Yes, sir—we'll order it at once, sir. What time, sir? Half an hour, sir? You're arranging with the gunners? Very good. Good-bye, sir." He put back the receiver, looked up to his superior. "That's Corps strafing, sir—General himself—very angry we haven't gone farther ahead—says we've left the flank of the 101st in the air. Wants another attack immediately—in half an hour."

The Divisional General tugged at his ragged white moustache.

"All very well for them!" he growled, in exasperation. "These fellows behind never seem to realize what we're up against. What's the latest?"

The staff officer rose from his chair, went towards the wall where a large map, stuck with coloured pins was hanging. The Divisional General followed him with a heavy tread, beat his cane irritably against his brilliantly polished brown leggings.

"We've got some odd men hanging out here and here and here, sir," he indicated the spots on the map—"in the enemy second line—about all that's left of that brigade—the brigade on their right seems to have got completely smashed up by the enemy barrage and their confounded machine-guns—what's left of 'em are with what's left of the third brigade. We can send 'em forward again, sir, of course," he concluded hopefully, with a glance at the Divisional Commander.

The Divisional Commander grunted. He listened for a moment to the unceasing thunder of the guns. The hut vibrated with their concussions.

"We must. Tell the brigades. They've got to get on at all costs." He glanced at his subordinate. "We're going to get unstuck for this, you and I, my friend—if they don't." He sighed, staring at the map. A terrible number of Generals had "come unstuck" lately. He pulled himself together, grinned sardonically at

"Wonderful how quick it was—fellow was alive then, dead now."

his subordinate. "That'll mean the P.B.I. again for *you*, my lad—and some dull training depot for me. But not yet! Not without a fight for it. Is Corps warning the Heavies?"

"Yes, sir."

"Right. Get on to 'em yourself. And get on to the brigades. And for God's sake, see they co-ordinate this time." He looked at his watch. "Half an hour. One-thirty. Objectives as before. —And they've *got* to reach and hold the third line Got to—mind! No excuses."

The staff officer sat down, picked up the telephone again. It wasn't their fault if the Division hadn't got on. They had done all they could. He began to hate this war. He rattled viciously at the instrument. Weren't they ever going to put him through? Lunch-time, too. The General was watching him. Should he "straf"—or be encouraging? "Hallo—brigade!——"

"Corps" lived in a *chateau*—a long pretentious building, with box-of-bricks pinnacle towers on each wing in the gimcrack manner of the Second Empire. Save for the numerous telephone wires, supported on the thin black-and-white posts of Army "Signals," which crossed its small and formal park, its exterior appearance had not appreciably altered from peace-time. Even the flower-beds had been kept in something like order by the successive Corps Headquarters which had occupied it, each for months on end. The rooks were undisturbed in the patch of tall elms which formed its background. Swans preened themselves in the rain that lashed its ornamental water. Within, however, evidences of military occupancy at once met the eye. The hall and the broad stairs leading from it were without carpet and muddied with the tread of many boots. The white paint of the tall double-doors was dirtied and defaced. What had been the drawing-room was labelled "Q—Clerks' Office." An overpowering clickety-click of feverishly worked typewriters issued from it whenever the door opened for the ingress or egress of some harassed little man in a private's uniform, glasses on his nose, and a pen behind his ear. On other doors were the labels of a surprising number of other special departments. Behind nearly all of them typewriters clicked furiously. A great many people were desperately busy at their share of the war.

The Corps Commander saw himself in a mirror at the angle as he went up those broad, echoing, dirty stairs. He was a big, heavy man—ex-cavalry, with pouched eyes and a regulation-clipped grey moustache, a stubbornly pugnacious face that was now sullen with bad temper. The sight of himself in his steel helmet kept him in his mood of highly serious happenings. He had just been in his car to "see for himself"—had been to the Divisions—had even been to the various Brigade Headquarters or at least to those he could conveniently reach on the edge of the battle-field—there had been plenty of shelling and much mud—"damned unpleasant"—and things were going badly over there on the ridge spouting from end to end with a double barrage. Confoundedly badly, things were going—his Divisions could not seem to get on at all. The next and rival Corps apparently had done much better. He had expressed himself with some vehemence—scared a lot of those fellows stiff. They'd come unstuck if they weren't careful. He reached the upper corridor, opened the door.

Within, seated at his desk, pipe in mouth, tranquil, undisturbed, pince-nez on the nose of a thin, studious face, poring over a batch of message-forms that had just come in, was the G.S.O. 1 left in charge during his absence. The staff officer looked up at him, smiled.

"Well, sir, how's the war looking?" he asked, in his quiet pleasant voice. The war had lasted three years now and he had seen too many "pushes" to be ruffled. He had the reputation of being a tower of strength to every staff he had been on—and it was a reputation he cherished.

"Rotten. A rotten bad show," answered the General gruffly. "That half-past-one attack broken down almost as soon as it started."

"I know," concurred the staff officer, equably. "There's been another since then—fizzled out also. And three counter-attacks. Speaking generally, we're hanging on to their second line. Fortieth Corps makes us look a bit poor—they're through to beyond the third—screaming about their flanks."

"H'm!" The General strode across to where the big operations-map hung on the wall, stared at its heavy reticulations of red and blue lines, its massed groups of coloured flags. There—that ragged bunch beyond the others—was where the Fortieth Corps, comparatively speaking, had done its job. The position of the flags marking his own Corps exasperated him to a dull anger—not unmixed with personal trepidation. He swung round to his staff officer.

"Anything from Army?" he jerked out.

"Yes, sir. They've been ringing up, off and on, all the time. In a distinctly bad temper. We can consider ourselves 'strafed.' The General himself was on just now—wanted to speak to you personally."

"H'm!" The Corps Commander grunted. "You told him I'd gone up to the forward area, I suppose?"

"Yes, sir. Seemed to mollify him a bit. Said he wished every general would see for himself—we might get on better then. Hoped you'd really tackle the situation." This was a highly diplomatic rendering of what the formidable Army Commander had really said.

The Corps Commander glared at his subordinate.

"Doesn't expect me to lead an infantry platoon myself, does he?" he snapped.

G.S.O. 1 shrugged his shoulders.

"He's feeling a bit chippy, sir," he said, soothingly. "He's been 'strafed' himself by G.H.Q. G.H.Q.'s annoyed about the losses—they've got some politician or other with them—makes 'em a bit sensitive."

"Losses?" snapped the Corps Commander. "What do they expect? This isn't a beanfeast. Of course there are losses. Must be. Can't make omelettes without breaking eggs."

G.S.O. 1 smiled.

"The trouble is that this time we haven't made the omelette," he murmured.

"Well, whose fault is it?" The Corps Commander glowered at him. "It isn't ours. We've done our best. Haven't been to bed properly for four nights. It's theirs—all their Army interference—they run the transport themselves—can't go over a road without their permission—run the Heavy Artillery themselves—send us contradictory orders every five minutes—and then expect us to fight the battle! Our fault if it goes wrong—their cleverness if it goes right!"

The staff officer relit his pipe, while the Corps Commander made a movement to doff his steel helmet, then, catching sight of himself in one of the mirrors left in the room, decided to leave it on. That politician might take a fancy to tour round Corps Headquarters—it would look well to be wearing it. He flung himself heavily into a chair.

"Well, what's the next move?" he asked. "Any orders from Army?"

"Yes, sir—they're pulling out two of our Divisions to-morrow—sending us two more from reserve. I don't yet know which."

"Up to strength, I hope?" growled the General. "Not the slightest use if they're not."

"I believe so, sir. Two *good* Divisions, they told me. And they expect us to get forward with them. Giving us a second chance to earn some thing in the next Honours List, sir." He smiled.

"H'm! That confounded 110th—don't know what they were playing at—they simply didn't go forward at all—scarcely reached even the second line—left the 101st absolutely in the air. Hope these are better than that. We want fighting troops—fellows who'll go through anything."

"So many new drafts lately," murmured the staff officer. "The troops aren't what they were."

"All right if we had enough of 'em. These wretched politicians! Ought to put the whole nation into uniform. They don't seem to realize. What we want is a million more men—and we'll have to have 'em, too, before we finish. It's the only way. Keep up this killing game. Man for man, we can afford 'em better than he can. Only way to win." The General absent-mindedly took off his steel helmet. It was uncomfortable, slipped sideways on his head.

The staff officer puffed at his pipe in silence. Privately, he held altogether heretical and revolutionary views on the conduct of warfare—on the absurdity of first churning up vast areas into a quagmire by massed bombardment, for example, and then sending masses of troops to be stuck in the impassable swamp as a target for the enemy—but it was no part of his job as a tactful staff officer to make himself unpopular by expressing them. He'd put in a good word for the General, he thought, with a pal of his on the Army Staff. The Corps Commander had the brains of a child, and about as much imagination as a bull, but he had undeniable character and driving-power with the troops. Pity if he came unstuck. He'd only be replaced by someone as like him as two peas—more difficult to get on with, perhaps. Yes. He'd drop a word in the right quarter. Over the 'phone, privately, later on, to a man with whom he, the staff officer, had been at school. He glanced at the General sitting gloomily in his chair, the steel helmet on his knees. Yes—decent old chap, really—he'd be sorry to see him go.

He shifted the pipe along his mouth, rose from his seat.

"What about a spot of tea, sir? It's ready in the Mess."

The General rose also, with a sigh.

"I think so. I'm dying for a cup." He sighed again. "This interminable war—I'm getting tired of it." But at the back of his mind he knew that without "this interminable war" he would still be only a cavalry colonel, about to retire on the age-limit, and felt guilty almost of a disloyalty to this magnificent world event.

The staff officer smiled at him.

"Cheer up, sir. It isn't so bad. And we've got those two new Divisions coming to-morrow. I'll give 'em a good talking to. Perhaps they'll do better. And we'll soon fatten up again the Divisions that we're pulling out. I've been talking to the A.G. about drafts."

They descended to tea in the Mess, discussing man-power and a knock-out blow to win the war as they went. Both of them, in secret recesses of their minds, simultaneously concealed not-to-be-uttered doubts of what would happen to themselves if this everlasting war should, incredibly, really end. But—and they likewise concealed their relief at the thought—it wasn't practical politics just yet. They ceased their discussion as they entered the room where the neat white table-cloth was laid. Both were old-time regular soldiers—and "shop" in the Mess was taboo.

The windows shook with distant gun-fire as they sat down.

G.H.Q.'s "Advanced" or Battle Headquarters were in the eighteenth-century Mairie of a fairly large and pleasant town whose cobbled streets were lined with shops that did a thriving trade and whose inhabitants had come to depend on the war as their principal source of revenue. Somewhere between "Advanced" G.H.Q. and the various Corps Headquarters, the Headquarters of the "Army" holding this particular sector completely filled all the available space in a yet larger and also cheerfully inhabited town. With its innumerable "Directorates" and Departments, the "Army" needed ample accommodation—it conducted a vast business with an army of uniformed clerks, feverishly busy in the matter of arranging for the alteration of railroad supply-trains to adjust with the Divisions constantly coming in and out of the line, ordering up vast quantities of ammunition and stores, superintending an infinite complexity of commissariat and road-transport, checking over colossal quantities of paper "returns," imposing its will on stiff-necked Corps staffs, and waging a fierce and ceaseless paper-warfare with G.H.Q. and the various bases for which the other war—with the enemy—merely provided an abstract justification. "Advanced" G.H.Q. did not concern itself with these routine matters. In a final hierarchical superiority, G.H.Q. proper attended to them—and filled two large towns, fifty miles back, with the uniformed population necessary for correct bureaucratic control of the millions of men of whom—somehow—only one out of every three could be spared for the actual fighting. That one-third renewed itself every day by drafts from home. "Advanced" G.H.Q. was a skeleton-force of picked staff officers which left its comfortable quasi-permanent home for the horrors of temporary billets when a new battle called for "close" supervision. Short sighted members of it had been known to exclaim "Oh, confound the war!" when they ordered their servants to pack.

One of those staff officers had been detailed as bear-leader to the eminent politician who had chosen to inflict himself on G.H.Q. at its busy time. His task, of course, was to give the eminent gentleman the illusion of seeing everything while at the same time preventing him from really seeing anything that really mattered. In company with his charge (privately and wittily designated as "Cuthbert") he descended from the G.H.Q.-flagged motor-car at the Mairie, and led the way upstairs to the room which was his office. He was tired and out of temper. The politician had insisted on "seeing something of the war," and he had taken him into the forward area, among the heavy artillery positions, to a

Splendid Failures

By Captain F. A. M. WEBSTER

ELEVEN MEN OF ENGLAND

THE moon was near her setting and the black hills of the North-West Frontier showed grim and spectral. Beneath their shadow stood a strong stone fortress. Before the walls eleven English soldiers were stretched upon the ground. They were dead, their bodies stripped and marred by many wounds. Not all their valour had served to capture the stronghold of the hill-men. Now the Afghan chief and his followers stood looking down upon the men they had slain.

Upon one wrist of each of their own dead the Afghans had bound already the green thread, which is the symbol of a fallen warrior's bravery, some bore also one red band to mark them as heroes.

SALUTE TO HEROES

"These Feringhees," said the chief, pointing to the dead Englishmen, "are doomed to the pit of Eblis and the eternal fire, for they were no true followers of the Prophet, and yet neither Mehrab Khan nor even the great lord Rustum were more brave than they. These white men came against us unstirred by anger, uneager for loot, nor even seeking renown. The path these followed was the path of duty. What matter if it has led them of death?"

An old hill-man of many wars and countless forays looked straight into the eyes of his chief.

"Mehrab Khan was a ruler who chose his own risks, and even Rustum bought his life at the price of a lie," he answered. "These men were as brave as the bravest. We dare not deny them the green thread to mark their valour."

The chieftain stroked his long black beard.

A GALLANT ACT

"The green thread?" he mused. "Nay, but I think these soldiers, though they be doomed to hell, have earned the blood-red cord of heroes. See that you bind it fast, so that Allah may know them and perhaps forgive them the fire for their valour's sake and for the honour we do them."

And later, when the English came to the hill, and found the body of the British sergeant and the bodies of his peerless ten bleaching in the sun and the wind, they knew that their dead comrades had done well in that lonely war, for had not the fair-minded Afghans bound the crimson thread that marks a hero, fast about both wrists of every man?

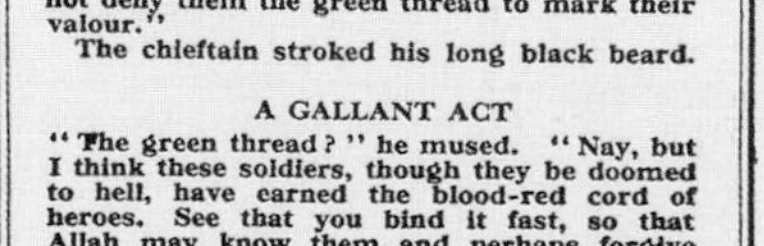

A BATTLEPIECE OLD STYLE *by* F. BRITTEN AUSTIN

hill from which he could see the smoke erupting all along the contested ridge. Coming back, they had been held up exasperatingly by endless columns of foot-slogging infantrymen marching through the rain—new Divisions coming up for next day's fight. He had with difficulty prevented the politician from making a speech to one battalion, halted in a village square for an intersecting stream of motor lorries. The politician had thought he might "cheer the lads up a bit." The staff officer had managed to conceal his horror, be duly tactful. Thank God, the trip was now over, the politician satisfactorily brimful of all the wonders he had seen. He invited him to a chair, filled a pipe for himself. In that confounded open car (he hadn't been able to get a limousine) he hadn't had a decent smoke all day. Rotten war!

The politician produced a cigar.

"It's been marvellous!" he said fervently. "I had no idea of the vast scale of everything.

future. Munitions. His brother was a munitions-manufacturer on an immense scale—was making an immense fortune. More than ever, next year. H'm! That boy of his brother's—in the infantry—he ought to have tried to see him—he wondered if the lad was in the battle whose dull persistent thudding rattled the window-panes. Two or three years! He'd try and get him out of the infantry—wangle him into a staff job. Would it be worth while speaking about him to this staff officer? No. Unsympathetic type. Better work it from the War Office end.

The weather outside seemed to be clearing a little. An evening light brightened the windows. From somewhere overhead came the loud drone of an aeroplane. It gave the politician an inward jerk of alarm—he had been in quite an unpleasant air raid as he came out of the theatre recently. He cocked an ear up to the sound.

"That's not an enemy, I suppose?" he asked. "Do they ever bomb you here? I take it you Headquarters are always one after another?"

The staff officer shrugged his shoulders.

"They have just tickled us up once or twice," he said, with a tolerant smile. "But, naturally, nothing very serious. It isn't done, you know."

The politician stared at him.

"Not done?"

The staff officer smiled again.

"Well, what about cleaning up a bit before dinner? I suggest a hot bath, personally. Want one after sitting in that chilly car all day. And —— " he glanced at his desk, piled with documents awaiting his signature, "—I've a devil of a lot of work to-night. Shan't get to bed till the small hours. If anyone ever tells you that we staff officers enjoy the war, you can tell them, sir—it's a first-class lie. There's not one of us wouldn't rather be with the troops."

A day or two later the politician was addressing a packed mass meeting in a munitions district. His audience was composed of working men and women who were earning more money than, in all their lives, they had ever dreamed possible. They were just then seriously considering the expediency of striking for yet higher wages. Hence the presence of the politician. His visit to the "front" had given him an additional importance. He spoke as a man who had been there and "knew"—the fact gave him, secretly, a very pleasurable feeling. A successful campaign now for the intensification of munition-output, the stalling-off of this threatened strike, would mean a place for him in the Cabinet at the next shuffling of the cards. He exerted all his eloquence, finished with a soul-stirring peroration—"On you—men and women—depends the destiny of nations. I ask you, the country

"That's right, along here. Bombers first; bombers and bayonet men."

And you really think we're getting the upper hand now?"

The staff officer just stopped himself from shrugging his shoulders.

"Looks like it," he said, diplomatically. "Of course, the army's got to be kept up to strength—the people at home must realize that. We're not at the end of it yet."

The politician puffed at his cigar. He was an amiable man, genuinely patriotic.

"How much longer do you think the war will last?"

The staff officer stared at his interlocutor. Not a question to be answered rashly! He took his pipe out of his mouth, looked at it, put it back again.

"Impossible to say, of course. It's one big machine up against another. Two or three years yet, perhaps, before we're through."

"Two or three—*years!*" The politician stared at him aghast. "You can't mean it. It's not possible." He was almost angry. "Think of the lives—at this rate, hundreds of thousands of lives—two or three years more will cost!"

The staff officer contemplated that toll of lives, unemotionally. These people seemed to think that war was a football match! Of course it would cost lives—but the country was still stiff with men not yet in the army. He must sustain the standpoint of G.H.Q.—good opportunity, in fact.

"Bound to have casualties in war, I'm afraid. We do our best to minimize them, of course. The fact is, it all depends on what the country gives us. We can't make bricks without straw. A really big effort, now, might bring the war to an end. We're planning it, in fact, for next year. But the country must give us men—and munitions—we shall need munitions on a bigger scale than ever next year."

The politician turned his mental gaze to that

"My dear sir—how d'you imagine we could carry on the war if we started knocking each other's Headquarters to bits? It's altogether too easy. They biff us—we biff them. Nothing to it. Better to fight like gentlemen—leave each other's Headquarters alone. Sort of unwritten law, you know—always has been. There'd be chaos, otherwise."

The politician tried a mental grapple with that problem. "Yes. Yes. I suppose so," he said, but his voice had a note of uncertainty to it.

They sat for a minute or two in silence, smoking. It was very quiet in this room. Only that rattle of the window-panes reminded the politician that a great battle was raging. He was, fantastically, sitting at the very heart of it, in the ultimate central ganglion of control. It gave him a feeling of awe. It was almost uncannily peaceful in this remoteness from the actual strife. He had suddenly a vision of that smoke-spouting ridge—of the monster guns pumping shells on to it. In that inferno men were dying—killing each other. It was difficult to realize it here. He wondered suddenly if this cool-mannered staff officer *did* realize it—wondered suddenly if *any* of the staffs pitting their brains against each other realized the translation to mud-and-blood horror of their intellectual syllogisms. Probably not. Natural protective screen of the human mind. They could only do their job by reducing it to abstract formulæ. Pleasant sense of power they must have—these millions of men moving at their will, killing one another. They didn't see anything of that. Agreeable life, theirs—ironically agreeable. Suppose the opposing Headquarters *did* bomb each other out of existence—so that they *couldn't* "carry on the war" . . .? What then? Absurd thoughts . . .!

The staff officer rose.

asks of you, magnificent though your patriotism has been, for yet one more effort—for one immense selfless effort worthy of the fathers and sisters and brothers of the lads who are fighting—one great final effort that shall finish the war!"

The grimy audience poured out into the street. One of those workmen summed up the general reaction to the orator's remarks. "Finish the war?—'E don't know what 'e's talkin' abaht!—This 'ere war can go on for ever for all that I care—or 'e cares either!—We shan't never 'ave such a time again—any of us. Come on Emma,—let's go to the movies."

Far away, in black night, on a ridge that was a morass underfoot, through an atmosphere that was poisoned, under vindictive murderous outbursts of shell-fire, soaked and weary infantrymen stumbled their difficult and dangerous ways to the line of water-filled shell-holes whence they would attack at the morrow's dawn. In a staff officer's room, twenty miles in rear of them, half a dozen uniformed press correspondents were writing despatches to a model thoughtfully supplied by higher authority. They were happy men, busy in a cloud of tobacco-smoke. One of them had just had a "brain-wave," copied by the rest with artistic variations—"The troops go forward with the joyous zest of men engaged in a great game—some units went into the last action dribbling a football. . . . It is only the skill and devotion of the Staff that makes scientific modern warfare possible on this vast scale. Even now, perhaps, the great public at home does not fully realize what war means. It has not come home to them as it does to us here——"

THE NEXT STORY. A BATTLEPIECE, NEW STYLE.

ROCKFIST ROGAN.
R.A.F

By Hal Wilton

SLIDING INTO HUNLAND

WOOF! Woof! Woof! Desperately Flight - Lieutenant Rockfist Rogan, ace flyer and fighter of the Freelance Squadron, pulled back on the control column as the dark drifting clouds below were cleft by scarlet tracer. Rapidly the six twin-engined British machines began to take evasive action as flak burst all round them.

Way down beneath, faintly visible through occasional breaks in the cloud, showed the dark outline of the Krieger chemical manufacturing installation. Madly the Nazi ack-ack batteries pounded into action.

Rockfist's eyes grew bleak as his Mosquito pitched and tossed through the air displacement of the exploding shells. The Krieger chemical factory had to be destroyed at all cost, but never had he experienced such a defensive barrage as this. Even the weather was against them.

A dark ominous shape loomed up on Rockfist's starboard wing and he kicked the rudder bar desperately.

Realisation swept over him like an icy douche; they were inside the balloon barrage with the flak increasing in intensity every moment.

For a moment Rockfist hesitated; finally he decided to depend on his own judgment.

"Break off and return to base!" The Freelance ace's terse order boomed out into the earphones of the flyers in all five other machines. It was impossible to carry out the operation under existing conditions.

Soon they were back in their quarters at the Freelance Squadron's 'drome.

"Am I browned off!" With this exclamation of disgust Curly Hooper, still clad in flying kit, flung himself down in an armchair. Six weary and utterly dejected pilots began to loosen their flying boots.

"No good getting that way about things, Curly," replied Rockfist evenly. "To destroy the Krieger factory under conditions like those was nothing short of impossible. It just can't be helped, lads, that's all."

"We know that, Rocky, old scout," burst out Archie Streatham anxiously. "The only thing is that if we don't do a certain job the blame falls on you as leader of the formation. That's what we don't like, Rocky."

barrage was about the last straw, though goodness knows how we can get over that."

"When will Blantyre be coming back?" asked Ted Hemmings, one of the other lads. "To-morrow, isn't it?"

"Correct first time," grinned Rockfist. "To-morrow evening to be exact. We've just got to have that perishing factory destroyed by then. I told him it would be a piece of cake. But the balloon barrage wasn't there then."

For the next half hour ways and means were discussed by which the task could be carried out.

"I don't know, Rocky," exploded Curly gloomily. "Apart from the possibility of someone baling out on to one of the wretched barrage balloons, sliding down the cable and blowing the joint up with a time bomb, there seems to be no solution at all. Maybe we'd better call the Chequers Squadron in to—— Hey! What's the matter with you, Rocky?"

With a wild whoop Rockfist had sprung out of his chair and was standing in the middle of the room with eyes glittering with excitement.

"Curly, you're a wonder; a blinking wizard, in fact. You've solved the whole problem, my lucky lad."

"What's the game?" gasped Curly in amazement. "You mean about our calling the Chequers boys in to help, I suppose?"

"No, you prize ass," chuckled Rockfist. "I mean your suggestion of someone baling out on to one of the balloons. That's exactly what I'm going to do, my cherub."

"You ass, you maniac—you, you lunatic!" burbled the horrified voice of Archie, whilst the voices of all the other flyers were raised in similar objections. Surely Rockfist must be joking.

"I was only trying to be funny, you twerp," gasped Curly. "You're pulling our legs, of course, Rocky?"

"Never more serious in my life," chuckled Rockfist merrily. "It's no good your crowd of mutts trying to

"Pack it up, lads. You'll have me crying in a minute."

Rockfist's face expanded into a broad, merry smile as he glanced at the anxious faces around him. Nevertheless, the marvellous team spirit in the squadron of which he was a member brought an instantaneous feeling of pride.

"As a matter of fact," said Rockfist more seriously, "the whole business wouldn't worry me at all except for the fact that Blantyre is away. It makes me feel that I've let old Groupy down. That balloon

put me off; the seed of Curly's idea has taken root."

Frantically the anxious lads tried to dissuade Rockfist from his seemingly suicide mission, but all to no avail. Despite the twinkle in their leader's eye, he was completely inflexible in purpose. When Rockfist once made up his mind nothing could stop him.

"Now pack up, you fellows, and let me work this thing out."

Flushed with excitement at the prospect of action, Rockfist pulled his chair up to the table. Slowly he named his requirements—a midget radio transmitter and some sticks of gelignite.

"O.K. then," continued Rockfist finally. "Everything is all fixed for the set-up. Curly will fly me over and the rest of you will hang on in readiness for my radio signal."

A short while later a lone Mosquito swept up from the Freelance Squadron advanced airfield and headed into the leaden skies. Visibility, if anything, had deteriorated.

Mechanically Rockfist watched the minutes tick by on his wrist-watch. With grim, solemn face, Curly Hooper sat silent at the controls, his eyes trying to pierce the menacing cloud formation.

"Boy, oh, boy!" exclaimed Rockfist suddenly. "This weather is just about what the doctor ordered for this type of job."

Carefully the Freelance ace rigged up the midget transmitter he was carrying, fixing the microphone part to his throat. This microphone was a specially constructed affair that operated by the vibration of the throat muscles, thus giving the person wearing it free use of his hands.

Mechanically Curly checked his position by dead reckoning. They had almost reached the objective. With a thunderous roar the Mosquito swung up into a steep climb, and the vague outlines of some of the barrage balloons were now apparent above the low-lying clouds.

"Drop her over on to one wing," yelled Rockfist excitedly. "I'm going to do my party-piece now. Cheer up, Curly, old sport, and don't forget to listen in for my radio message."

"Look here, Rocky, let me do this job," burst out Curly beseechingly.

He was too late. With a cheery wave Rockfist vanished into the yawning void and Curly set course for base.

The rush of cold air braced Rockfist's muscles with the effect of a tonic. Headfirst he hurtled downwards like a plummet, numb fingers feeling for the rip cord.

Crack! The white canopy billowed out immediately, a great mushroom growth against the dark, overcast sky. With a vicious jerk the rapid descent was abruptly halted.

Grasping the silken cords with both hands, Rockfist guided the swaying chute towards the silvery top of one of the huge balloons. Could he make it or was the stunt merely as reckless and futile as Curly apparently thought? Despite the breathtaking cold, small beads of perspiration gathered on his forehead.

ROCKFIST MUST HAVE FELT LIKE THE MAN IN THE MOON WHEN HE WENT RIDING ON A BARRAGE BALLOON

15

Desperately Rockfist tugged on one set of silk cords, pulling the chute over at an angle. His booted feet grazed something soft and resilient, something that swayed at the very touch. With a gasp of horror Rockfist saw the silvery surface slip away from beneath him. He had failed after all.

A wild sort of fury swept over the Freelance ace as he reached out frantically in a wild attempt to grasp one of the balloon support cords. It was all in vain. The great balloon drifted by only a few inches from his outstretched fingers.

At that moment Rockfist's slow descent came to a sudden conclusion.

It was two or three seconds before realisation dawned as to what had happened, and a slow smile spread over his features. The project was not doomed to failure after all. The parachute had fouled one of the balloon's fins. Rockfist hung suspended, swinging like a pendulum.

Gathering his knees up beneath him, Rockfist gradually increased the extent of the swing until his gauntleted hands were able to grasp one of the support cords. With a quick movement he punched the parachute release, allowing the harness to fall away free. Soon he was sliding down the oiled, steel cable that tethered the balloon.

Slow though the uncanny descent was, the friction of the metal hawser seared Rockfist's hands under his thick gauntlets. Powerful sinews tensed convulsively to slacken the speed.

Rockfist grinned triumphantly to himself as the cold wind swept over his perspiring features. He had made it, after all.

Seconds dragged by like hours as the nerve-racking descent continued; then, with startling unexpectedness, Rockfist's feet struck something solid. He had reached the controlling balloon winch at long last. Quickly he released his cramped hands and dropped nimbly to the misty ground.

Even as the Freelance ace reached the welcome security of firm ground a wave of apprehension pulsed through him.

There, watching every movement with immobile face, was the strangest, most gigantic Hun Rockfist had ever set eyes on. The descent had been spotted.

THE HUNT IS ON!

For a moment or so Rockfist could only stand and stare, so utter and complete was his surprise. The apparition was more like an animal than a man. A feeling of horror and repulsion swept over him.

All this time the great Hun gazed fixedly at Rockfist, watching his every movement with intensely baleful eyes.

Clad only in ragged trousers and a pair of field boots, the man towered some six feet four inches, displaying a huge, hairy torso which would not have looked out of place on a full-grown gorilla. Great arms hung limp from shoulders of terrific breadth, the tips of the fingers reaching below the knee.

The prolonged silence began to wear on Rockfist's nerves. What was the matter with the man? Why didn't he raise the alarm? Like a flash the answer drove home to him. The fellow was a deaf mute, a creature of little brain power, but colossal physical development. Slowly he inched forward.

The giant watched Rockfist's stealthy advance with the same fixed, glassy stare. Then the huge muscles tensed, and, with incredible speed, he sprang straight at the hard-eyed Freelance flyer like some great cat.

In a moment Rockfist's horror of the brute man vanished and his lips set in a thin, hard line.

Nimbly he avoided that deadly spring, at the same time hurtling out a straight left. But the Hun took the blow without even batting an eyelid. Rockfist was up against the toughest opponent of his whole career.

Again came that vicious rush, which Rockfist only just avoided, and again the Freelance champion's great fist smashed home with the noise of a drum-beat. Quietly the strange battle raged backwards and forwards over the crisp grass.

The giant was getting more wary now. Apparently the stunning force of Rockfist's blows had taken their toll, after all. At all costs the Freelance ace had to avoid the grip of those two terrible hands.

Crack! The whole world seemed to swim as the giant's wide-flung arm connected with the side of Rockfist's head, spinning him round on his heels. In a moment two great arms like steel hawsers wrapped themselves round Rockfist's waist in a vice-like grip. Slowly he was bent ruthlessly backwards.

A wave of sickness engulfed Rockfist as the terrible pressure increased. Desperately he brought an arm up behind the giant's back and smashed a bunched fist into the region of the kidneys. This was no time for Queensberry rules.

Immediately the cruel pressure was released and Rockfist staggered back dazedly. Shaking his head viciously in an effort to clear it, he rushed into the attack.

Thud, thud, thud! The great Hun stopped short in his tracks as Rockfist sailed into him with the ferocity of a tiger. Breath-taking, short-arm jabs exploded viciously against flesh and bone.

Never before had Rockfist fought with such savage desperation. He just had to win now; to withstand another bear hug like the one he had just experienced would be impossible.

Beads of perspiration poured down the Freelance flyer's face. Could he make it?

Wham! Rockfist's right fist smashed out and down in one terrific effort, his knuckles seeming to sink inches deep in the giant's solar plexus. Like a felled tree, the giant tottered, spun, and crashed to the ground. With a gasp of relief, Rockfist sank to his knees, every bit of strength played out in that last whirlwind encounter. Then, climbing to his feet, he checked over his radio transmitter, making sure it had not been damaged.

As he did so a sudden thought struck him—a thought that made a cold thrill run through his very marrow. He had been fighting with several sticks of gelignite fuses in his flying suit. One unfortunate blow on one of those, and—— Rockfist did not care to consider the rest.

He was ready at last; the midget transmitter was in perfect working order. Now for the next move.

Stepping over to the unconscious giant, Rockfist brought the butt of his revolver down with stunning force on to the great, bullet-shaped skull. Much as he hated having to do this, he would take no chance of the strange creature coming round at an inopportune moment.

The great chemical installation still lay wrapped in a thin blanket of ground mist.

Cautiously Rockfist made his way over the crisp grass to where the deep shadow of a huge retort house loomed up menacingly. Even as he did so, his keen eyes noted something that brought an excited smile to his lips. Drawn up against the cunningly camouflaged building stood a powerful-looking staff car. A means of escape was now presented for the time when the gelignite had been fused. Things were working out excellently.

As he made his way from the grass on to the tarmac car-tracks of the factory, so the enormity of the mission began to come home to Rockfist with ever-increasing force. At the time of thinking of the plan in the Freelance mess everything had seemed comparatively straightfor-ward. Now the main difficulty was beginning to present itself. Where was the best place for the explosives to be planted?

A sudden noise in the vicinity of Rockfist's elbow made the Freelance ace shrink back close to the concealing shadow of a wall. A thin, sickly glow of light penetrated the white mist as a door slowly opened. The sound of guttural voices resounded in Rockfist's ears.

"Take this over to the wax-solvent plant, Zimmer!" thundered a powerful, overbearing voice. "The next time I find you smoking near that place I'll have you shot, dummkopf! One single spark near the solvent would send the whole crowd of us sky-high!"

"Ja, Herr Direktor!" came a subdued reply, and the door shut with a slam.

Rockfist's mind raced like lightning as he listened carefully. Wax solvent meant special petroleum spirit of the most inflammable nature possible; just the place to plant a load of gelignite. Stealthily he followed in the wake of the retreating Zimmer, his ears straining to every sound.

The ghastly trek through the very middle of the great installation seemed like a horrible nightmare to the Freelance flyer. Even if he reached the solvent plant without a hitch, however, would he find his way back again to where the staff car stood parked?

Without warning Zimmer's soft footfalls came to an abrupt halt, and Rockfist heard the sound of leather scraping on metal rungs. Evidently the plant had been reached. Groping his way to the iron staircase, Rockfist made to ascend.

Crash! An empty petrol tin scudded away from beneath Rockfist's foot, and, with a sharp cry of surprise, the Freelance flyer fell sprawling to the ground. In a moment his inside seemed to freeze to ice.

"Himmel! Who is there?" The Nazi's voice rose in alarm from the top of the ladder. "Make no move! I have you covered!"

Rockfist's mind raced frantically, and in that one vital moment a desperate inspiration flashed to him.

"Zimmer, you fool!" he snapped icily in a remarkable imitation of the voice he had heard from the doorway a few minutes before. "It is I, the Herr Direktor. Give me a hand up this moment! I have tripped over a petrol can!"

"Ja, ja! Herr Direktor, I come now!"

Zimmer's voice fairly shook as he heard the bullying tones of his supposed chief. Quickly he ran down the stairway to where Rockfist was lying and bent hastily over him.

"Hilfe——"

The Nazi's short cry of surprise and fear was stopped short as a great hand fastened around his throat in a grip of iron.

Clop! Rockfist's free fist swept up in a vicious arc, connecting under the German's ear with appalling force. The man collapsed like a rag doll.

"Phew!"

With a short gasp of relief, Rockfist wiped dry a perspiring forehead; then in one wild burst of activity he shinned up the metal stairway. The strong smell of petroleum spirit hit him like a wall. He was on the outside of the wax-solvent plant at long last.

Feverishly Rockfist dragged the sticks of gelignite from out of his flying suit, touched off the fuses, and placed the deadly explosives inside one of the numerous air-vents that opened in the wall of the plant-house. The next moment he had slid down the iron-runged ladder and was sprinting like a madman back along the way he had come.

How he found his way back was one of those things he never really understood. With lungs almost at bursting-point, he raced past the welcome retort-house and out on to the grass near the balloon winch.

At that moment came disaster, and a wild feeling of despair swept over the Freelance flyer like a heavy cloud. There was no sign of the big staff car that he had relied upon to make good his escape from the terrific explosion to come. It had vanished completely.

Rockfist glanced around him hopelessly. He was trapped—helplessly trapped inside the doomed installation which at any moment might go sky-high. Even as this terrible thought ran through his mind, so came the final climax to his ill-luck.

With startling clarity the nerve-shattering whir of an electric bell pealed out incessantly from the gloom. Doors flew open everywhere and hoarse shouts resounded on all sides.

The alarm had been given; the hunt was on!

ONE-MAN BALLOON

Never before had Rockfist felt so utterly helpless and despairing. Someone must have found the unconscious Zimmer. The Freelance flyer's luck had run out at long last.

With a terrific effort Rockfist summoned his wits together. He must act, and act fast. His foot struck something half-concealed by the long grass, and, stooping down, he picked up a large pair of wire-cutters left by some careless mechanic. Even as he did so, a fresh train of thought raced across his mind, an idea so reckless and daring that even Rockfist himself was shaken.

In a moment the Freelance ace went into action. The staff car might have gone, but there was still one possible means of escape open to him. The wind was blowing strongly in the direction of the Allied positions.

Desperately Rockfist sprinted over to the balloon winch, from which was tethered the barrage balloon by which he had descended. He would come down by balloon, and he would go back by balloon. It was the only possible solution open to him.

As Rockfist reached the winch his quick eyes noted a change in the layout. Someone had partly brought the balloon down. Instead of a cable stretching some 3,000 feet into the blue, the blimp now reared only twenty feet above him. Desperately he went to work, spurred on by increasing sounds of panic from the direction of the installation.

With feverish fingers the Freelance ace snatched up a spare length of rope that lay near the winch and securely knotted it to the great steel cable in the form of a hanging loop. Rapidly he seated himself in this noose and, bending over, closed the jaws of the great wire-cutters on the section of cable immediately below him.

Powerful muscles bulged and strained as the snips bit deep into the hawser. Perspiration poured down Rockfist's face and the veins of his forehead stood out like whip-cord.

Crack! With a sharp, vicious report, the steel cable snapped and the released balloon soared upwards in a fierce rush.

So sudden was the rapid ascent that Rockfist almost tumbled from his precarious position, only averting disaster by a wild grab at the cable above him. From way down below the gloom was pierced by short stabs of crimson flame, accompanied by the sharp bark of small arms. The balloon's sudden breakaway had not passed unseen. Rockfist grinned widely. The Huns had drawn the obvious conclusion a little too late.

Woof! Even as Rockfist gazed down, so the whole earth seemed to leap up to reach him, whilst a great sheet of flame tongued upwards. The colossal explosion that followed almost burst the Freelance flyer's ear-drums. The gelignite was doing its deadly work with complete efficiency. The terrific blast knocked all the breath out of his body.

From then on the whole earth seemed to go mad as explosion after explosion cracked the doomed installation, turning the whole countryside into the grimmest firework display Rockfist had ever set eyes on.

Up, up, up raced the freed balloon like some monster silver bubble, soaring through the low cloud layers with ever-increasing momentum. Carefully Rockfist withdrew his feet from the support loop of cord and began to shin his way up the odd thirty feet of cable to the very bottom of the balloon itself. Within a matter of seconds he was hanging on to the protecting cord webbing, working his way to the top.

With a great gasp of relief, the Freelance ace gained the security of the top of the balloon and stretched out in welcome relaxation.

After a few minutes' rest Rockfist sat up on the top of the balloon and began to gaze interestedly around him. Visibility was improving rapidly, and from his elevated position he was able to see clearly the German positions through breaks in the cloud layer. Mechanically he switched on the midget radio transmitter and began to speak.

"R for Rocky calling C for Curly! R for Rocky calling C for Curly! Over to you! Over!"

Back came the instantaneous reply: "C for Curly calling R for Rocky! We are receiving you. Over to you! Over!"

A great wave of relief swept over Rockfist as he heard the welcome voice in his earphones. Rapidly he switched over the two-way contact and began to talk again, giving full details of all that had happened and his present precarious position.

"C for Curly calling R for Rocky! We are flying over to you. Keep talking, Rocky. We are taking bearings on you. Over!"

With a broad grin, Rockfist sat back on the top of the balloon and began to scan keenly the open heavens around him, all the while keeping up a humorous running commentary.

Despite the anxiety of his present position, he could not help but be struck by the novel and humorous side of the situation. The nerve-racking experiences he had just had were even now forgotten.

Minutes dragged slowly as the great balloon gently drifted towards the Allied positions. The only thing that was troubling Rockfist now was the rather intense cold. He shifted his seat cautiously and wished for the arrival of the Freelance flyers with increasing fervour.

Then a sudden soft, droning noise penetrated Rockfist's flying helmet. Turning round carefully, his keen eyes picked out several dots on the skyline—dots that increased in size with every second.

The wave of thankfulness that engulfed Rockfist dispersed immediately and a cold hand clutched at his middle. These were no Freelance machines that were approaching so rapidly—they were Hun kites, Focke-Wulf 190s.

For the first time the real danger of Rockfist's position came home to him with a rush. He was on top of a fragile couch of inflammable hydrogen, with enemy fighters bearing down for the kill! No parachute, no way of escape was open.

Rockfist's mouth set in a grim line and his eyes grew bleak. When would the Freelance Squadron arrive? In a metallic voice he informed his pals over the mike of the new danger that threatened.

Again it seemed to the Freelance ace that he was living in a horrible nightmare from which he would awake at any moment. With relentless purpose the Focke-Wulf 190s thundered forward towards their defenceless prey. Any second now they would be in firing range; incendiary bullets would tear remorselessly at the helpless balloon.

Rockfist sat back and prepared for the seemingly inevitable. At any rate, he had carried out his mission with success.

Rat-tat-tat! Sharply the silence of the skies was rudely shattered by the staccato chatter of death-dealing automatic weapons. Long lines of curling tracer whipped out across the grey expanse.

Even as he heard this ominous sound, so a dread feeling stole over the Freelance ace. This must be the finish of everything. He was doomed!

Several seconds elapsed, and still Rockfist was alive. Amazedly he lifted up his head and gazed around him. The sight that greeted his heavy eyes brought a broad smile to his lips, whilst a flood of relief almost stifled him. There, diving madly down on the Hun attacking force, were his pals of the Freelance Squadron, guns pounding madly.

In the excitement that followed Rockfist had great difficulty in restraining himself from leaping to his feet. Eyes glittering with daredevil enthusiasm, he spurred on the furious Freelance fighters by means of the transmitter:

"Go on, Archie, old top! Get under his tail! Give him the old one-two! Watch that blighter to starboard, Curly! Give Ted a hand; he's having difficulty!"

From then on Rockfist ignored all danger. Never before had he had such a perfect grandstand view of an air battle as this. A terrible game of hide-and-seek was being played out round the drifting balloon, the Huns trying to shoot it down and the Freelance flyers trying to prevent them. The object of the game paid little attention to all this; he was far too busy encouraging the players.

All this time the balloon drifted nearer and nearer to the Allied lines. The broad outline of Lake Angen was clearly visible.

Even as he made out the lake, so inspiration flashed through Rockfist's mind. Now was the time to get back to earth. Drawing his revolver from its holster he pumped three bullets into the silvery skin of the balloon beneath him, while the dog-fight increased in tempo with every second.

Hydrogen hissed out of the punctured balloon with a queer whistling sound, and the taut skin began to crumple and deflate. Slowly the balloon began to descend towards the lake—at first slowly, then with ever-increasing speed.

Twice a Focke-Wulf thundered by in an attempt to wipe out the lone flyer who had caused so much damage. Twice the attacker was skilfully intercepted by a roaring Freelance machine.

"So-long, fellows! I'm taking a header into the drink. Be seeing you!"

With a cheery farewell over the mike, Rockfist rolled to the edge of the almost-deflated balloon and dived off into the waters of the lake. Swiftly he struck out for the welcome shore, and soon he was back at the Freelance 'drome and reporting to his C.O.

"Well, Rogan, you've certainly pulled off a job to be proud of," Group-Captain Blantyre regarded his ace pilot with twinkling eyes. "What a title it would make for a song hit when you found the staff car gone! 'If I Only Had Wings' seems rather appropriate to me."

"Not half as appropriate as the one I have in mind, sir," replied Rockfist, chuckling.

"And what is it?" Blantyre demanded, with a smile.

"'Sailing Aloft on My Little Balloon'!" grinned Rockfist.

Next Friday Rockfist indulges in a leg-pulling contest that leads to big thrills.

Dan Will Give You All a Laugh—When He Goes and Joins the Raff!

DESPERATE DAN

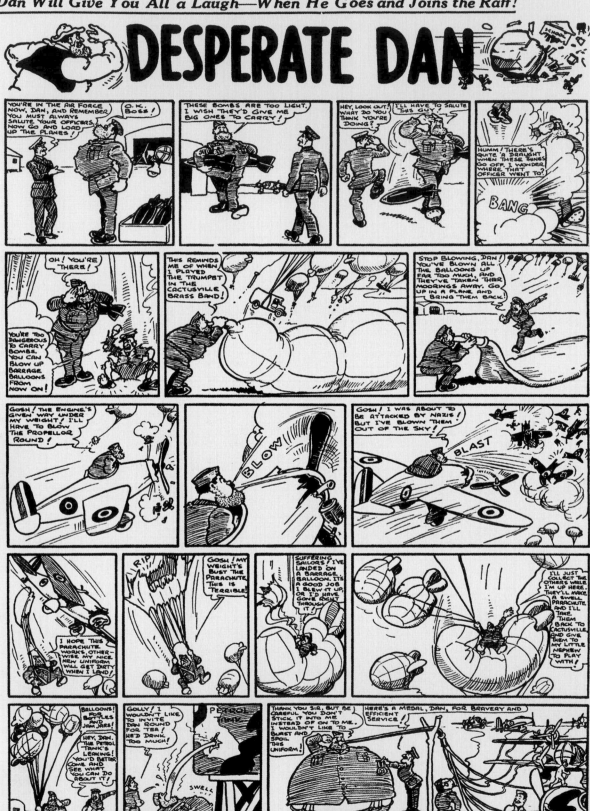

JU 87D –
ENEMY TANK–BUSTER

NO aeroplane ever inspired more terror than the JU 87D—the "Stuka." With the invasion of Poland, in 1939, the dive bomber played a major role. In the years before the War the Stuka had been planned and put into production especially for the purpose of dive bombing.

The principle of the dive bomber was very simple. You aimed your aeroplane at the target, and brought it down in a hair-raising power dive, gathering speed all the way until you reached a height of something under a thousand feet (this was all worked out in advance). Whereupon you released your bomb, which went screaming on downwards with the speed of an artillery shell, and you pulled your aircraft out of the dive and into a zooming climb.

When the dive bombers first made their appearance, it seemed that there was no answer to them. The scream of their attacking dive inspired fear and sometimes panic in people on the ground, and the bomb hurtled at its target with absolute sureness.

After the Polish invasion the German High Command placed great faith in the dive bomber, and Stukas continued to be produced in great quantities.

But the answer was found. A ground battery manned by determined gunners who were prepared to face up to the terror could bring the Stuka down during its dive, when it was most vulnerable, because it could not hold its attacking dive, and dodge, at one and the same time.

For the same reason, the pilot of a fighter aircraft could shoot down a Stuka by sitting on its tail during its attacking dive and giving it a burst of machine-gun fire. This the Stuka could not reply to effectively,

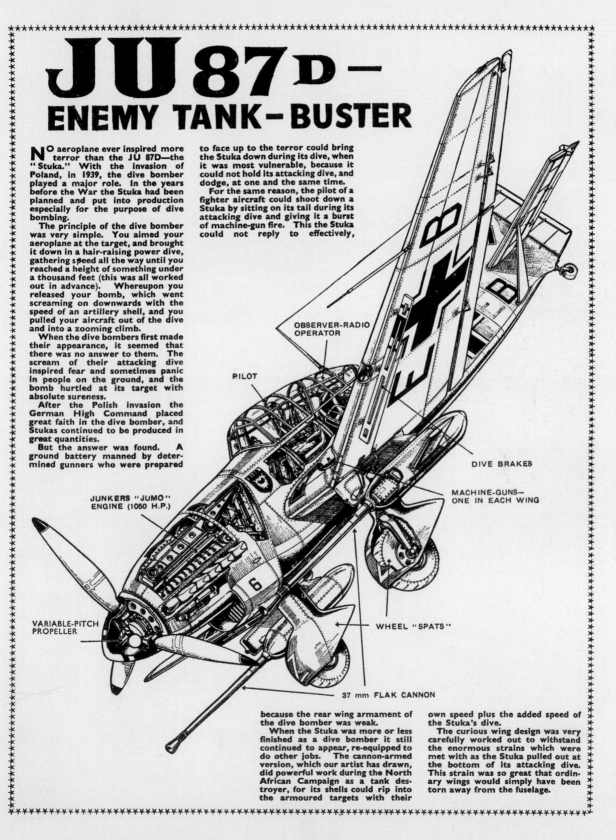

OBSERVER-RADIO OPERATOR

PILOT

DIVE BRAKES

MACHINE-GUNS— ONE IN EACH WING

JUNKERS "JUMO" ENGINE (1050 H.P.)

VARIABLE-PITCH PROPELLER

WHEEL "SPATS"

37 mm FLAK CANNON

because the rear wing armament of the dive bomber was weak.

When the Stuka was more or less finished as a dive bomber it still continued to appear, re-equipped to do other jobs. The cannon-armed version, which our artist has drawn, did powerful work during the North African Campaign as a tank destroyer, for its shells could rip into the armoured targets with their own speed plus the added speed of the Stuka's dive.

The curious wing design was very carefully worked out to withstand the enormous strains which were met with as the Stuka pulled out at the bottom of its attacking dive. This strain was so great that ordinary wings would simply have been torn away from the fuselage.

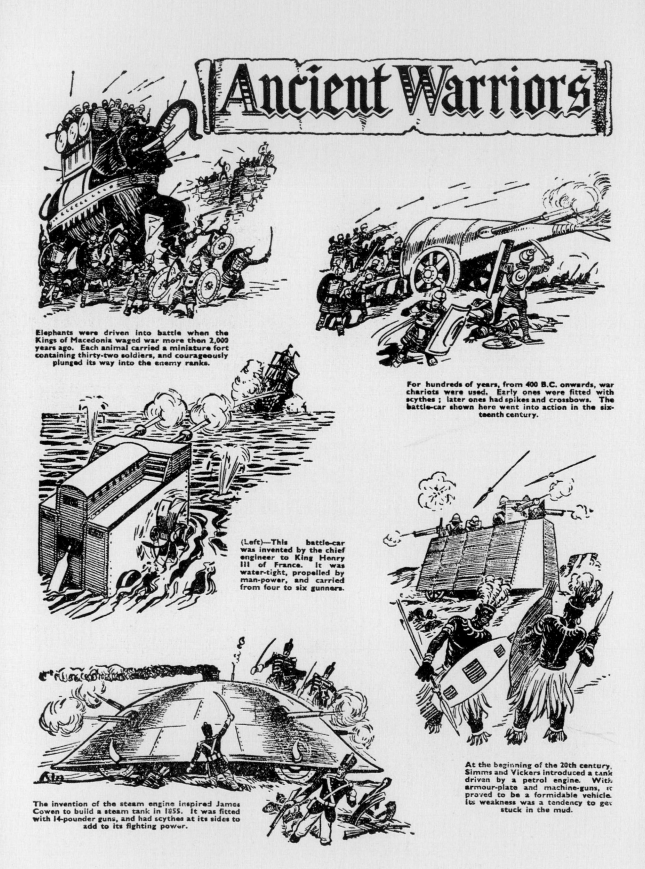

Ancient Warriors

Elephants were driven into battle when the Kings of Macedonia waged war more than 2,000 years ago. Each animal carried a miniature fort containing thirty-two soldiers, and courageously plunged its way into the enemy ranks.

For hundreds of years, from 400 B.C. onwards, war chariots were used. Early ones were fitted with scythes; later ones had spikes and crossbows. The battle-car shown here went into action in the sixteenth century.

(Left)—This battle-car was invented by the chief engineer to King Henry III of France. It was water-tight, propelled by man-power, and carried from four to six gunners.

The invention of the steam engine inspired James Cowen to build a steam tank in 1855. It was fitted with 14-pounder guns, and had scythes at its sides to add to its fighting power.

At the beginning of the 20th century, Simms and Vickers introduced a tank driven by a petrol engine. With armour-plate and machine-guns, it proved to be a formidable vehicle. Its weakness was a tendency to get stuck in the mud.

used Elephants as Tanks

This sixteenth-century battle-chariot was pushed by horses which had been given the protection of metal shields. The "tank" itself was made of steel and brass, and no fewer than eight guns could be brought to bear on the enemy. The horses were at the rear so that the tank acted as a shield for them.

Leonardo da Vinci hit on the idea of a tank fitted with twenty or so bellows "to terrify the enemy's horses." It also carried a squad of soldiers. Da Vinci emphasised that the machine was useful only for breaking up the ranks of the opposing forces. Hand-to-hand battles would follow.

Tanks with caterpillar wheels were introduced by the British during the first World War. They went crashing over the top of the German trenches, their guns inflicting terrific casualties. Unfortunately the early models travelled at little more than walking pace, and hundreds of them sank into the soft, muddy plains of France and Belgium, there to be battered by the enemy guns.

The Churchill tank of World War II was a speedy, 40-ton dreadnought which fought in hundreds of battles. Not only did it scatter the enemy in the deserts of North Africa, but it thundered through Italy and France, playing its part in driving the Germans from the countries which they had invaded.

Braddock's Beaufighter was stolen by two Germans—but now they bring it back!

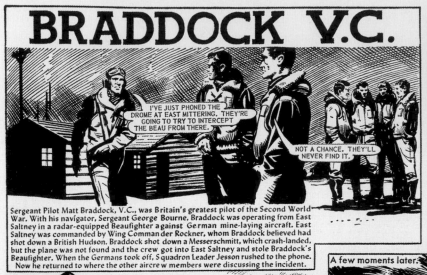

BRADDOCK V.C.

I'VE JUST PHONED THE DROME AT EAST MITTERING. THEY'RE GOING TO TRY TO INTERCEPT THE BEAU FROM THERE.

NOT A CHANCE. THEY'LL NEVER FIND IT.

DON'T WORRY, THE HUN WILL COME BACK. TELL THEM TO LIGHT THE FLARE PATH FOR HIM!

WHAT DO YOU MEAN, BRADDOCK?

Sergeant Pilot Matt Braddock, V.C., was Britain's greatest pilot of the Second World War. With his navigator, Sergeant George Bourne, Braddock was operating from East Saltney in a radar-equipped Beaufighter against German mine-laying aircraft. East Saltney was commanded by Wing Commander Rockner, whom Braddock believed had shot down a British Hudson. Braddock shot down a Messerschmitt, which crash-landed, but the plane was not found and the crew got into East Saltney and stole Braddock's Beaufighter. When the Germans took off, Squadron Leader Jesson rushed to the phone. Now he returned to where the other aircrew members were discussing the incident.

THE PILOT WILL GET A NASTY SHOCK WHEN HE SEES THE FUEL GAUGES REGISTERING NIL. THE TANKS ARE FULL, BUT HE WON'T KNOW IT. HE'LL HAVE TO COME BACK.

Because of the radar set in the Beaufighter, the lay-out of the electrical wiring and the switches was more complicated than usual. The electrically operated fuel guages would register nil until a special switch was pushed over—but the German pilot did not know this.

A few moments later.

YOU WERE RIGHT, BRADDOCK. THERE HE IS. I'LL GET THE FLARE PATH LIT UP.

I BET THEY WERE SCARED TO DEATH THEY WOULDN'T MAKE IT.

HE'S DOWN. HE'S CUT HIS ENGINES.

HEY, HE'S REVVED UP AGAIN. GET OUT OF THE WAY!

THE HUN HAS WRITTEN OFF THE PLANE! HE'S CRASHED IT INTO THE HANGAR!

" It's not the cricket season, mate!"

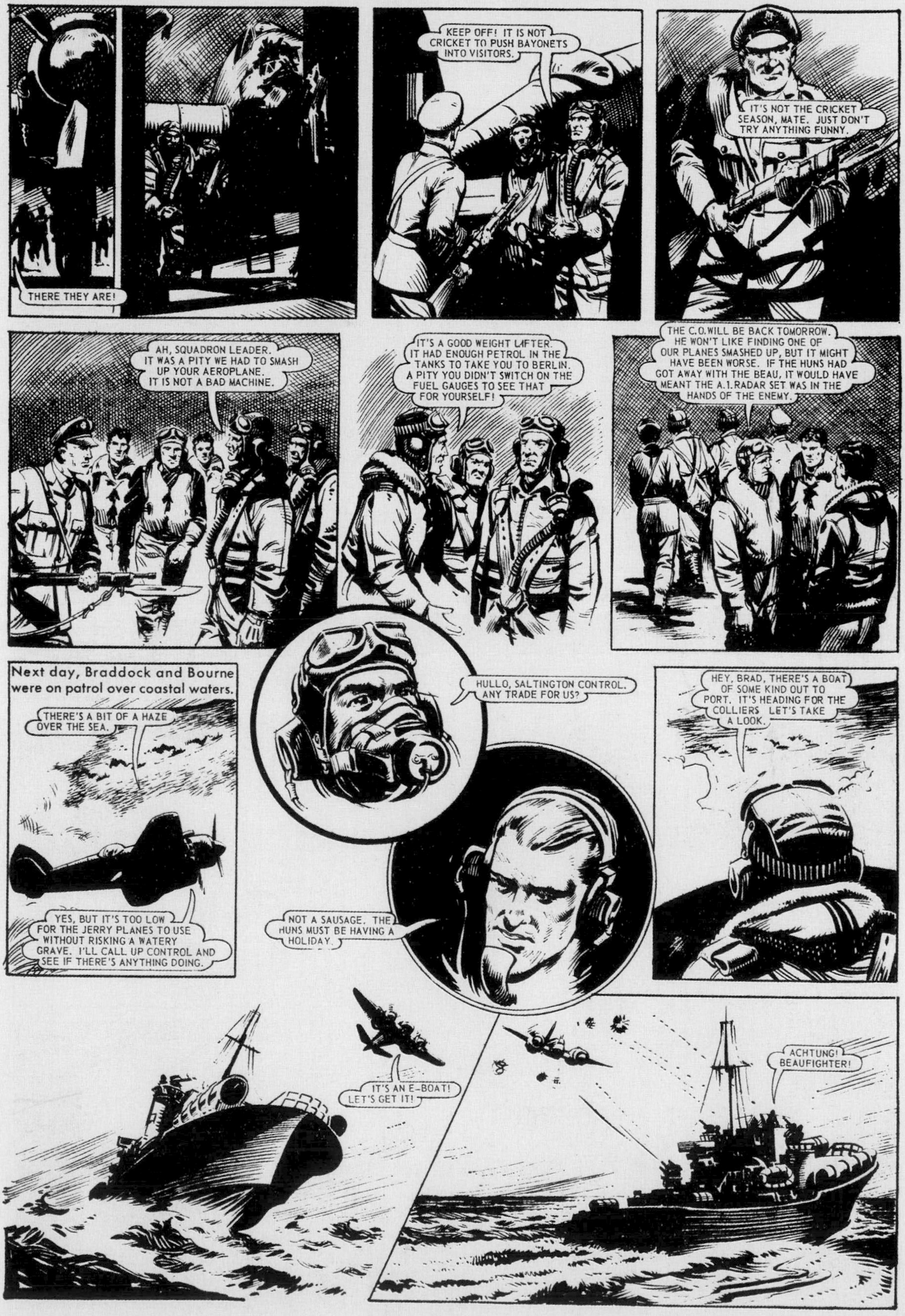
THERE THEY ARE!
KEEP OFF! IT IS NOT CRICKET TO PUSH BAYONETS INTO VISITORS.
IT'S NOT THE CRICKET SEASON, MATE. JUST DON'T TRY ANYTHING FUNNY.
AH, SQUADRON LEADER. IT WAS A PITY WE HAD TO SMASH UP YOUR AEROPLANE. IT IS NOT A BAD MACHINE.
IT'S A GOOD WEIGHT LIFTER. IT HAD ENOUGH PETROL IN THE TANKS TO TAKE YOU TO BERLIN. A PITY YOU DIDN'T SWITCH ON THE FUEL GAUGES TO SEE THAT FOR YOURSELF!
THE C.O. WILL BE BACK TOMORROW. HE WON'T LIKE FINDING ONE OF OUR PLANES SMASHED UP, BUT IT MIGHT HAVE BEEN WORSE. IF THE HUNS HAD GOT AWAY WITH THE BEAU, IT WOULD HAVE MEANT THE A.I. RADAR SET WAS IN THE HANDS OF THE ENEMY.
Next day, Braddock and Bourne were on patrol over coastal waters.
THERE'S A BIT OF A HAZE OVER THE SEA.
YES, BUT IT'S TOO LOW FOR THE JERRY PLANES TO USE WITHOUT RISKING A WATERY GRAVE. I'LL CALL UP CONTROL AND SEE IF THERE'S ANYTHING DOING.
HULLO, SALTINGTON CONTROL. ANY TRADE FOR US?
NOT A SAUSAGE. THE HUNS MUST BE HAVING A HOLIDAY.
HEY, BRAD, THERE'S A BOAT OF SOME KIND OUT TO PORT. IT'S HEADING FOR THE COLLIERS LET'S TAKE A LOOK.
IT'S AN E-BOAT! LET'S GET IT!
ACHTUNG! BEAUFIGHTER!

WE GOT IT!

IT'S SINKING! THE CREW ARE ABANDONING IT! GOOD SHOOTING, BRAD!

THERE IT GOES. I'LL CALL UP THE CONTROLLER AND TELL HIM WHAT'S HAPPENED. THEN THE NAVY CAN ROUND UP THE SURVIVORS IF THE COLLIERS DON'T.

HEY, GEORGE, THERE'S ANOTHER OF THE BLIGHTERS OVER THERE.

THEY'RE TAKING ADVANTAGE OF THE SURFACE HAZE TO MAKE DAYLIGHT HIT-AND-RUN RAIDS. UNLUCKY FOR THEM THE HAZE IS A BIT PATCHY.

THEY'VE SPOTTED US! THEY'RE LAYING A SMOKE-SCREEN! BUT THEY'RE JUST A BIT TOO LATE!

STAND BY FOR BLASTING!

I THINK WE GOT IT, TOO.

YOU'RE RIGHT. LOOK, THE CREW HAVE ABANDONED IT.

After reporting their successes, Braddock and Bourne completed their patrol without further incident then headed for East Saltney.

THERE'S AN AUSTER. IT'S PROBABLY STILL LOOKING FOR THAT MESSERCHMITT. THE JERRY PRISONERS WOULDN'T SAY WHERE THEY CAME DOWN.

I THINK THE HUN CAME DOWN A LITTLE TO THE EAST. LET'S LEND A HAND WITH THE SEARCH.

A few minutes later.

SOMETHING'S CUT A SWATHE IN THE REEDS DOWN THERE, GEORGE.

WE'VE FOUND IT, GEORGE. IT'S THE MESSERCHMITT! WE'LL MARK IT WITH A SMOKE FLARE FOR THE AUSTER.

HE'S SPOTTED IT. LET'S GET BACK TO BASE. I'M DYING FOR A CUP OF TEA.

Twenty minutes later they landed at East Saltney.

I JUST HEARD THAT YOU SANK TWO E-BOATS, AND I WAS TO MARK THEM ON THE BEAU. BUT IF I PUT A SWASTIKA FOR A JERRY PLANE, WHAT DO I PUT FOR AN E-BOAT?

WHAT ABOUT AN ANCHOR, JOE?

AIN'T THAT LOVELY, NOW?

JUST THE JOB. WELL WE'D BETTER GO AND REPORT ON OUR PATROL.

When they reached the intelligence room, they found Wing Commander Rockner waiting with the Intelligence Officer.

AH, BRADDOCK. I WANT A WORD WITH YOU ABOUT THE MESSERCHMITT YOU CLAIM TO HAVE SHOT DOWN.

I WANT TO SEE YOU, TOO—ALONE.

I HAVEN'T TIME TO LISTEN TO YOUR COMPLAINTS.

THEN YOU'D BETTER FIND TIME.

COME ON, BOURNE. WE'RE NOT NEEDED HERE.

WELL, BRADDOCK. WHAT DO YOU WANT?

TO CUT A LONG STORY SHORT, I WANT YOU GROUNDED!

The guns of L.C.T. 16 shoot down a Spitfire—then the Skipper recognises it as his brother's plane !

The FLOATING COFFIN

"Enemy planes on the port quarter!"

" Great shooting!"

JERRY ALMOST GOT US THIS TRIP. THAT SPITFIRE BUSINESS HAS FINISHED ME AS A GUNNER. I'LL NEVER HAVE THE CONFIDENCE AGAIN. ALL I'M GOOD FOR NOW IS HOLDING THE WHEEL!

Meanwhile.

WE'VE BEEN THINKING, SIR. COULDN'T YOU TAKE HER IN CLOSE TO THAT ISLAND? WE MIGHT BE ABLE TO RESCUE THE SPITFIRE PILOT.

FINDING HIM MIGHT RESTORE STRIPEY'S CONFIDENCE, SIR.

IT'S HARD TO REFUSE WHEN YOUR OWN BROTHER'S INVOLVED.

That evening.

ALL RIGHT. AS WE'RE ON OUR OWN, YOU CAN HAVE HALF AN HOUR. BUT TAKE CARE. I CAN'T RUN THIS SHIP WITHOUT YOU.

THESE GRENADES WILL COME IN HANDY.

WE WON'T TAKE ANY CHANCES, SIR.

The two ratings slipped quietly ashore then, not far from the beach.

THAT'S YOUR QUOTA OF EXERCISE FOR TODAY, ENGLANDER!

LOOK WHO IT IS, LOFTY! YOUNG CHRIS BARTON, HIMSELF!

I SEE HIM. WE'RE GOING TO HAVE TO BE PRETTY RUTHLESS WITH THESE JERRIES.

WHAT ON EARTH? BLOW ME DOWN, IT'S A COUPLE OF BODS FROM JOHNNIE'S SHIP!

NICE GOING, CHUM, BUT LET'S GET MOVING. THERE'S NO KNOWIN' HOW MANY JERRIES THERE ARE.

The cox'n shot off the lock and helped Chris out of the hut.

HIMMEL! THE PRISONER HAS ESCAPED!

HURRY IT UP, SIR. WE'RE WORKIN' ON BORROWED TIME!

I'D BETTER LET THAT PAIR HAVE ANOTHER PINEAPPLE.

COME ON, LADS. GET A MOVE ON.

LCT 16

WE'RE COMING, SKIPPER. PUT TO SEA.

WELCOME ABOARD, CHRIS. GLAD TO SEE YOU'RE STILL IN ONE PIECE.

THANKS FOR THE RESCUE JOB, JOHNNIE. BUT YOU WON'T BE SO PLEASED WHEN I TELL YOU THAT IT WAS MY PLANE THAT BOMBED YOU.

Chris Barton explained how his plane and two other British fighters had been forced down on the island by the Germans. The intact British fighters had been quickly converted to take small bombs, so that they could be used on sneak raids against the Allies. The German pilot who had bombed L.C.T. 16 had been boasting about his narrow escape.

After his brother's escape Johnny reasoned with Stripey.

SO YOU SEE, STRIPEY, YOU DIDN'T MAKE SUCH A TERRIBLE MISTAKE AFTER ALL. NOW I'M GOING TO RADIO BASE.

GOOD FOR YOU, MATE! THAT'S ANOTHER ENEMY KITE YOU CAN ADD TO YOUR SCORE.

SURE, SURE, I KNOW. I STARTED TO FEEL BETTER THE MOMENT THE SKIP'S BROTHER CAME ABOARD.

At dawn, Johnnie Barton expected the two Spitfires still in German hands to come for their revenge—and he wasn't disappointed!

GREAT SHOOTING!

THE BOMB'S GONE UP! YOU'VE CLOBBERED THE PAIR OF THEM!

LCT 16

THAT'LL TEACH THEM TO USE OUR KITES.

28

HELLMAN'S WAS A GROUND-BREAKING STORY IN THE CONTROVERSIAL COMIC, ACTION. THIS STORY WAS IN THE LAUNCH ISSUE, DATED 14TH FEBRUARY 1976

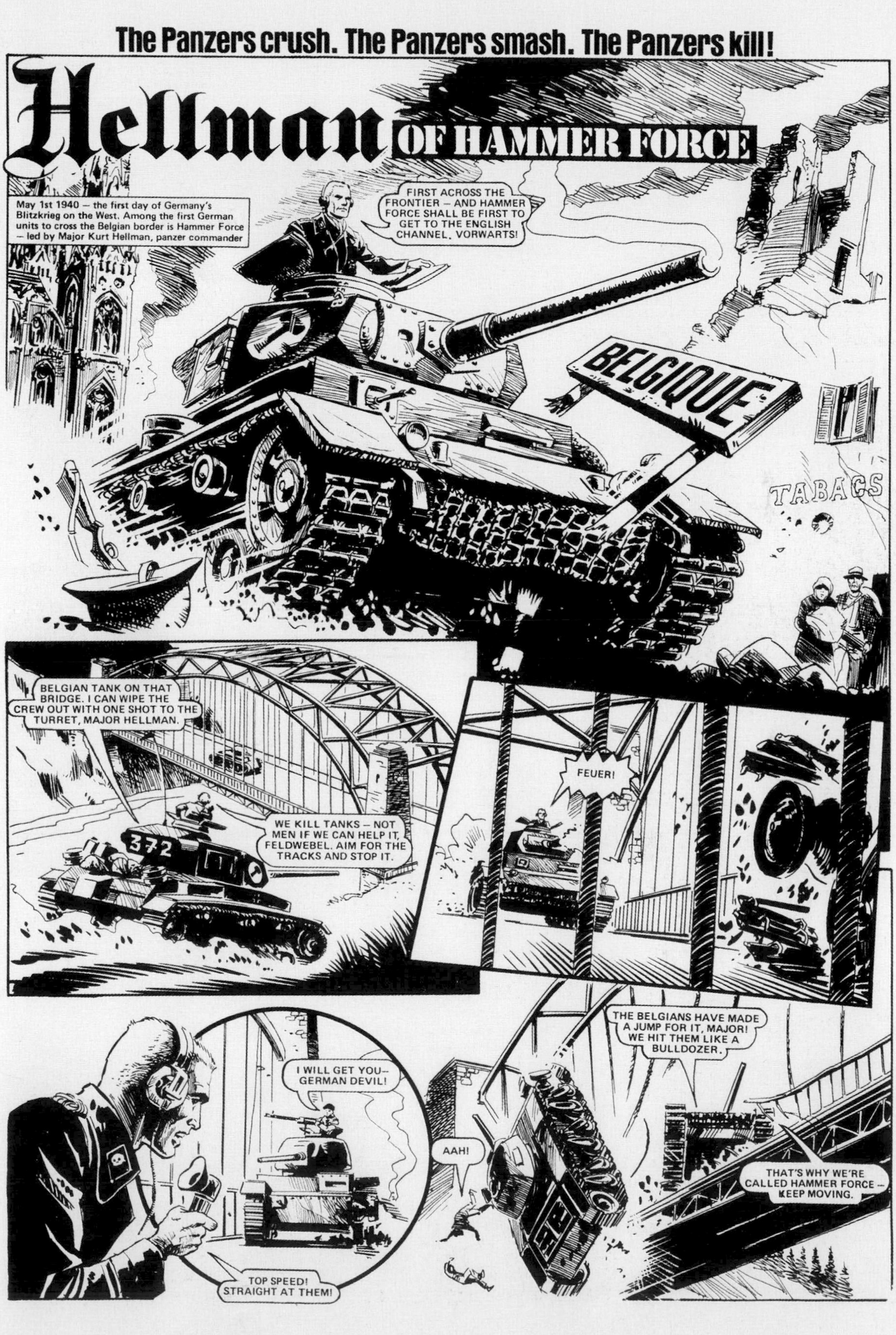

The Panzers crush. The Panzers smash. The Panzers kill!
Hellman OF HAMMER FORCE
May 1st 1940 – the first day of Germany's Blitzkrieg on the West. Among the first German units to cross the Belgian border is Hammer Force – led by Major Kurt Hellman, panzer commander
FIRST ACROSS THE FRONTIER – AND HAMMER FORCE SHALL BE FIRST TO GET TO THE ENGLISH CHANNEL. VORWARTS!
BELGIQUE
TABACS
BELGIAN TANK ON THAT BRIDGE. I CAN WIPE THE CREW OUT WITH ONE SHOT TO THE TURRET, MAJOR HELLMAN.
WE KILL TANKS – NOT MEN IF WE CAN HELP IT, FELDWEBEL. AIM FOR THE TRACKS AND STOP IT.
372
FEUER!
I WILL GET YOU– GERMAN DEVIL!
TOP SPEED! STRAIGHT AT THEM!
THE BELGIANS HAVE MADE A JUMP FOR IT, MAJOR! WE HIT THEM LIKE A BULLDOZER.
AAH!
THAT'S WHY WE'RE CALLED HAMMER FORCE – KEEP MOVING.

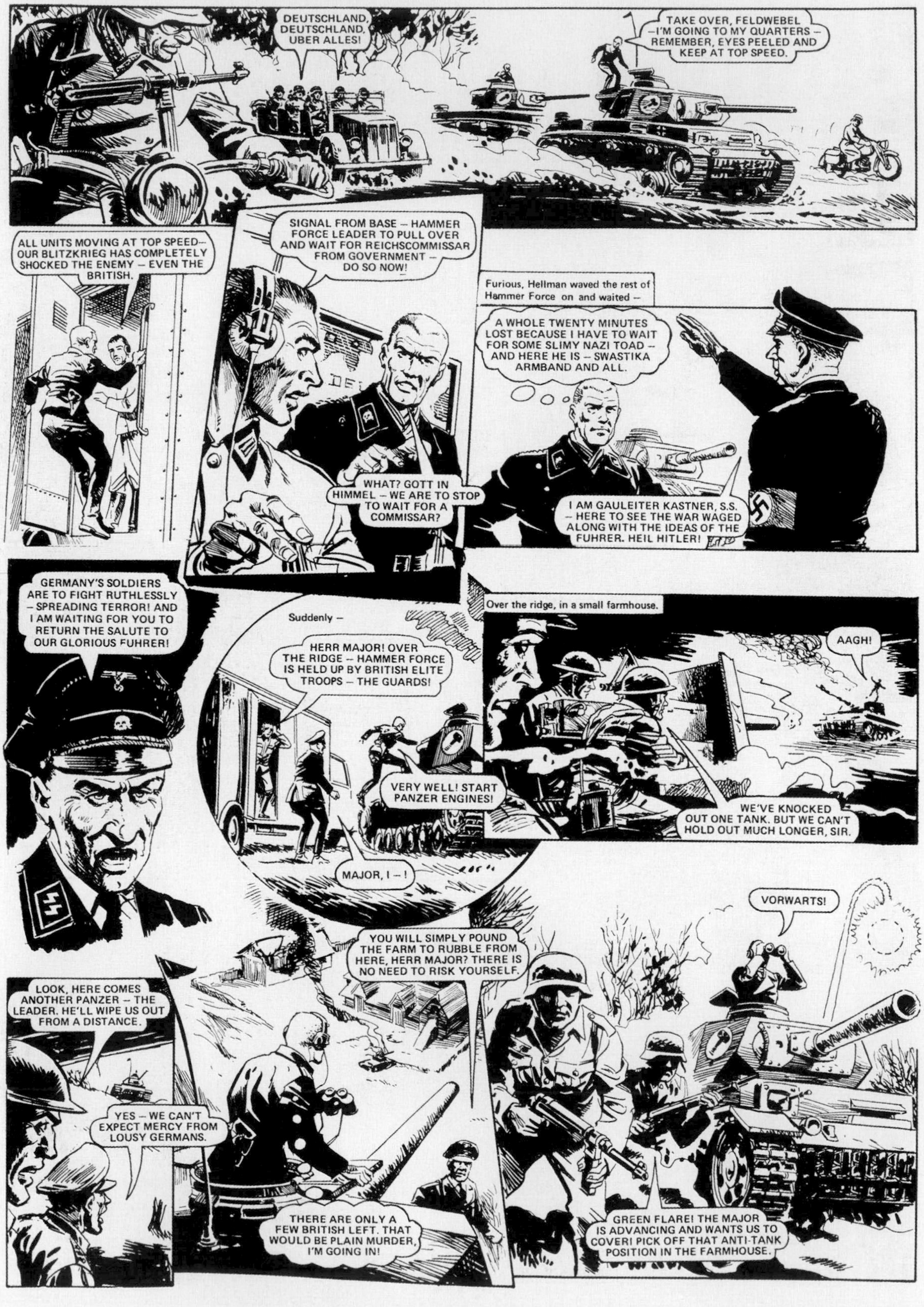
DEUTSCHLAND, DEUTSCHLAND, UBER ALLES!
TAKE OVER, FELDWEBEL —I'M GOING TO MY QUARTERS — REMEMBER, EYES PEELED AND KEEP AT TOP SPEED.
ALL UNITS MOVING AT TOP SPEED— OUR BLITZKRIEG HAS COMPLETELY SHOCKED THE ENEMY — EVEN THE BRITISH.
SIGNAL FROM BASE — HAMMER FORCE LEADER TO PULL OVER AND WAIT FOR REICHSCOMMISSAR FROM GOVERNMENT — DO SO NOW!
WHAT? GOTT IN HIMMEL — WE ARE TO STOP TO WAIT FOR A COMMISSAR?
Furious, Hellman waved the rest of Hammer Force on and waited —
A WHOLE TWENTY MINUTES LOST BECAUSE I HAVE TO WAIT FOR SOME SLIMY NAZI TOAD — AND HERE HE IS — SWASTIKA ARMBAND AND ALL.
I AM GAULEITER KASTNER, S.S. — HERE TO SEE THE WAR WAGED ALONG WITH THE IDEAS OF THE FUHRER. HEIL HITLER!
GERMANY'S SOLDIERS ARE TO FIGHT RUTHLESSLY — SPREADING TERROR! AND I AM WAITING FOR YOU TO RETURN THE SALUTE TO OUR GLORIOUS FUHRER!
Suddenly —
HERR MAJOR! OVER THE RIDGE — HAMMER FORCE IS HELD UP BY BRITISH ELITE TROOPS — THE GUARDS!
VERY WELL! START PANZER ENGINES!
MAJOR, I — !
Over the ridge, in a small farmhouse.
AAGH!
WE'VE KNOCKED OUT ONE TANK. BUT WE CAN'T HOLD OUT MUCH LONGER, SIR.
LOOK, HERE COMES ANOTHER PANZER — THE LEADER. HE'LL WIPE US OUT FROM A DISTANCE.
YES — WE CAN'T EXPECT MERCY FROM LOUSY GERMANS.
YOU WILL SIMPLY POUND THE FARM TO RUBBLE FROM HERE, HERR MAJOR? THERE IS NO NEED TO RISK YOURSELF.
THERE ARE ONLY A FEW BRITISH LEFT. THAT WOULD BE PLAIN MURDER, I'M GOING IN!
VORWARTS!
GREEN FLARE! THE MAJOR IS ADVANCING AND WANTS US TO COVER! PICK OFF THAT ANTI-TANK POSITION IN THE FARMHOUSE.

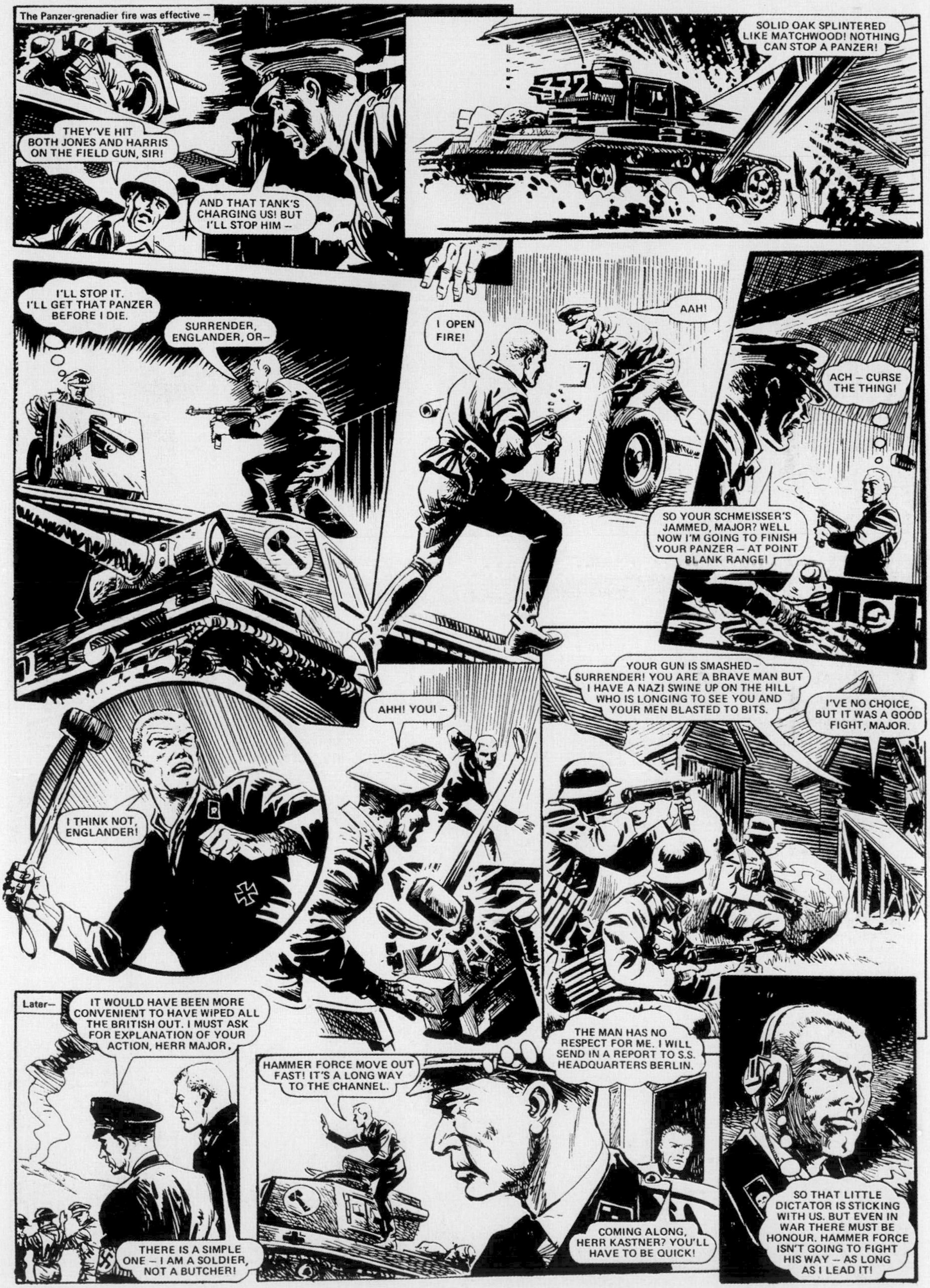

The Panzer-grenadier fire was effective –
THEY'VE HIT BOTH JONES AND HARRIS ON THE FIELD GUN, SIR!
AND THAT TANK'S CHARGING US! BUT I'LL STOP HIM –
SOLID OAK SPLINTERED LIKE MATCHWOOD! NOTHING CAN STOP A PANZER!
I'LL STOP IT. I'LL GET THAT PANZER BEFORE I DIE.
SURRENDER, ENGLANDER, OR–
I OPEN FIRE!
AAH!
ACH – CURSE THE THING!
SO YOUR SCHMEISSER'S JAMMED, MAJOR? WELL NOW I'M GOING TO FINISH YOUR PANZER – AT POINT BLANK RANGE!
I THINK NOT, ENGLANDER!
AHH! YOU! –
YOUR GUN IS SMASHED– SURRENDER! YOU ARE A BRAVE MAN BUT I HAVE A NAZI SWINE UP ON THE HILL WHO IS LONGING TO SEE YOU AND YOUR MEN BLASTED TO BITS.
I'VE NO CHOICE, BUT IT WAS A GOOD FIGHT, MAJOR.
Later–
IT WOULD HAVE BEEN MORE CONVENIENT TO HAVE WIPED ALL THE BRITISH OUT. I MUST ASK FOR EXPLANATION OF YOUR ACTION, HERR MAJOR.
THERE IS A SIMPLE ONE – I AM A SOLDIER, NOT A BUTCHER!
HAMMER FORCE MOVE OUT FAST! IT'S A LONG WAY TO THE CHANNEL.
THE MAN HAS NO RESPECT FOR ME. I WILL SEND IN A REPORT TO S.S. HEADQUARTERS BERLIN.
COMING ALONG, HERR KASTNER? YOU'LL HAVE TO BE QUICK!
SO THAT LITTLE DICTATOR IS STICKING WITH US. BUT EVEN IN WAR THERE MUST BE HONOUR. HAMMER FORCE ISN'T GOING TO FIGHT HIS WAY – AS LONG AS I LEAD IT!

STARTS TODAY!

HIGH SPEED ACTION IN THE MEDITERRANEAN WITH...

GOT HER!

AARGH!

Leutnant Paul von Leif commands Germany's top scoring E-boat, The Shark, in the Mediterranean. A few miles south of their base, they are engaged in battle with a British submarine.

THE SHARK

Those Jerries got us good! ABANDON SHIP!

SOMEBODY SOUND THE ALARM!

The E-boat picked up the survivors—

SEIZE THAT MAN! HE IS TRYING TO DESTROY SOMETHING!

Jawohl, Herr Kapitan!

T.S.1

STOP HIM! HE'S TRYING TO JUMP OVERBOARD!

WD. 23.6.79.

" *I GIVE THE ORDERS ON THIS SHIP!*"

Hmmm! Looks like some electric circuitry, and a map of the coast somewhere! I can't identify it but it must be important!

The Intelligence branch at base will soon sort it out, sir!

When they reached the base--

Those papers refer to a British radar post on the African coast. That Army captain was on his way back after fitting a new component. You are to embark an SS raiding party who will attack it tonight!

Yes, sir!

Later --

I hope you are more efficient than the smartness of your boat leads me to believe, Leutnant. It's like a garbage scow!

That's only since you S.S. men came on board. You will all have to remain on deck! There is no room below!

Before you go, I feel it is my duty to remind you Leutnant, that it is your job to land these men at the radar post and bring them back without delay.

Yes, sir! That's exactly what I'm going to do!

That evening—

Flashing light two points on port bow, sir! Looks like an aircraft dinghy.

Change course towards it, Muller.

What do you mean? We were told there are to be no delays! We cannot change course!

We can—and we will! I give the orders on board this ship! Now kindly return to your own part of the deck!

You will regret that, Leutnant!

T.S.2

So—

Get him below. Resume course and increase speed to maximum.

Thanks! I couldn't... have lasted... much longer!

WD. 23.6.79.

33

" WE'RE GOING IN FOR THE KILL!"

I'll see you court martialled for this! You deliberately disobeyed your own commanding officer's orders!

I used my own judgement. And I saved the life of a valuable fighting man.

As they approached the beach——

We are two minutes ahead of schedule, Herr Kapitan.

Good! Stand by to launch your boats, men!

Remember! At zero—four hundred hours, we shall come to within two hundred metres of the beach. Be ready! And good luck with the raid!

We SS men do not rely on luck! But I am surprised you have the courage to risk your neck that close to the beach!

QUICK, SIR! OVER HERE!

There's something on the starboard bow! Looks like an RN minesweeper!

You're right! Full speed! Right rudder! And—FIRE!

Why don't we use a torpedo, Herr Kapitan? She's an easy target.

Not yet, Trappe. I want to draw her further from the coast. If we sink her here the Tommies will home in like flies! We'll play it like fish! Half speed.

Meanwhile, on board the minesweeper——

She's slowed down, sir! We must have done some damage!

Good show! Full speed ahead! We're going in for the kill!

WD. 23.6.79.

" STAND BY ON THE GUNS! "

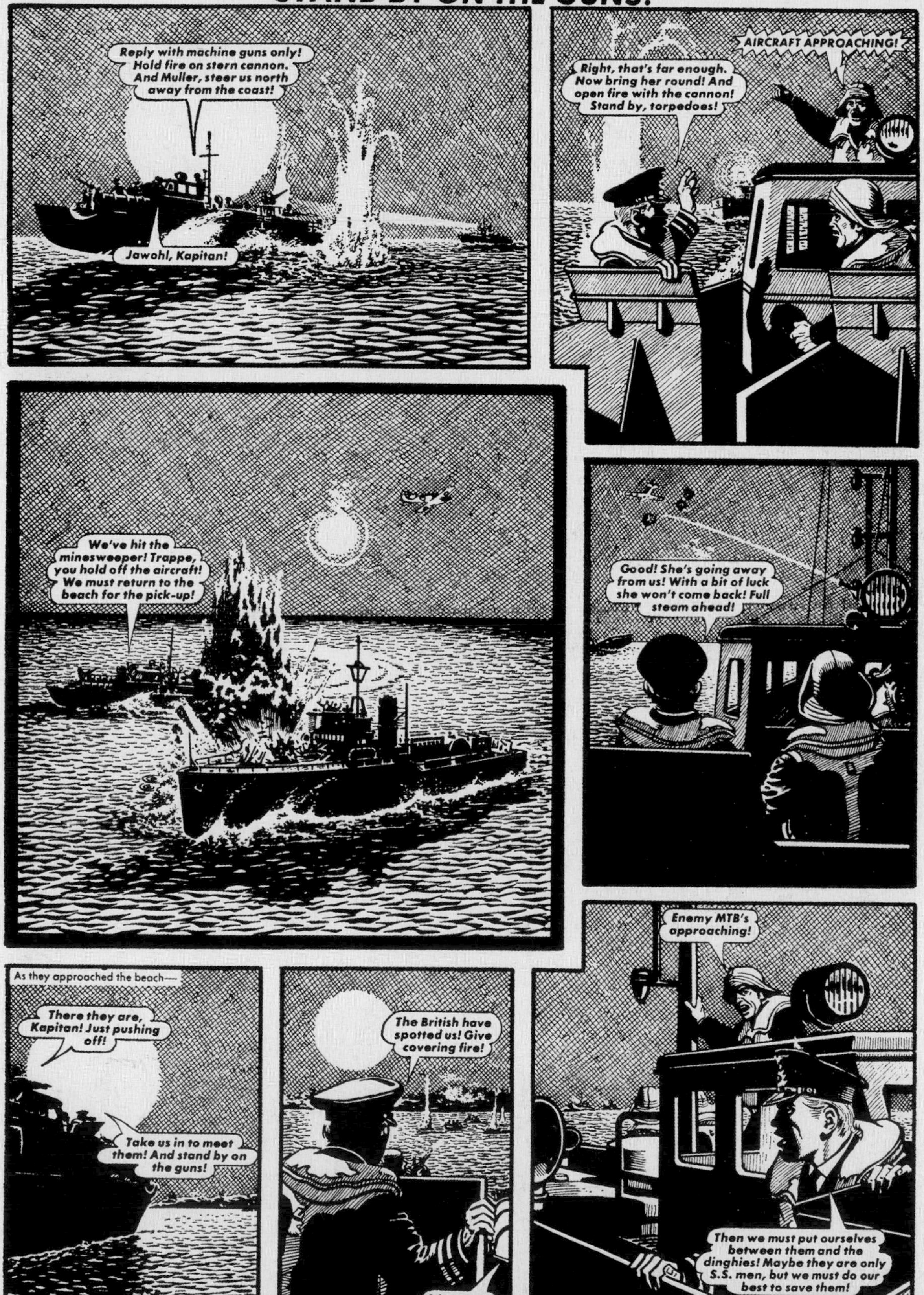

Reply with machine guns only! Hold fire on stern cannon. And Muller, steer us north away from the coast!
Jawohl, Kapitan!
AIRCRAFT APPROACHING!
Right, that's far enough. Now bring her round! And open fire with the cannon! Stand by, torpedoes!
We've hit the minesweeper! Trappe, you hold off the aircraft! We must return to the beach for the pick-up!
Good! She's going away from us! With a bit of luck she won't come back! Full steam ahead!
As they approached the beach—
There they are, Kapitan! Just pushing off!
Take us in to meet them! And stand by on the guns!
T.S.4
The British have spotted us! Give covering fire!
It's no use, sir! Look!
Enemy MTB's approaching!
Then we must put ourselves between them and the dinghies! Maybe they are only S.S. men, but we must do our best to save them!
WD. 23.6.79

Acknowledgements

Adam Riches, Tim Parker and Robert Frankland could not have created *When the Comics Went to War* without the support and assistance of a number of individuals. We acknowledge the assistance that we have received and express our thanks for their commitment to the book.

In no particular order we would like to thank:

Morris Heggie, Martin Lindsay, Bill McCloughlin and Roddie Watt
at D.C.Thomson and Co. Limited.
David Abbott at IPC Media Limited.
Melanie Leggett and Martin Morgan at Egmont UK Limited.
Bill Campbell and Peter MacKenzie at Mainstream Publishing
Alan Notton at www.comicsuk.co.uk
Graham Hambly
Keith Parker
David Gledhill
Donald Jessiman
Geoff at the Pelton Arms

And, of course, our families and friends who have accepted and understood our various mood swings during the creative process.

THRILLING SCHOOL AND WAR STORIES

THE HOTSPUR

Nº 471 — AUG 28TH 1943 — PRICE 2D

A MOSQUITO FIGHTER
PRANGS A NAZI ENGINE

AERIAL

NAVIGATION
LIGHTS

PILOT &
NAVIGATOR

METAL
AILERONS

4 20 M.M. CANNON
UNDER NOSE

CAMERA

4 ·303
MACHINE GUNS

2 MERLIN
XXI ENGINES